ONE WEEK IN APRIL

ONE WEEK IN APRIL

THE SCOTTISH RADICAL RISING OF 1820

MAGGIE CRAIG

BIRLINN

First published in 2020 by
Birlinn Limited
West Newington House
10 Newington Road
Edinburgh
EH9 1QS

www.birlinn.co.uk

ISBN 978 178027 632 8

British Library Cataloguing in Publication Data
A catalogue record for this book is available from the British Library

Papers used by Birlinn are from well-managed forests
and other responsible sources

Designed and typeset by Initial Typesetting Services, Edinburgh
Printed and bound by Clays Ltd, Elcograf S.p.A.

To the memory of
Thomas Muir, Andrew Hardie, John Baird and James Wilson,
who fought and died for democracy in Scotland
and
for my parents and all the men and women who came before me
and stand in spirit at my shoulder – weavers, colliers, domestic
servants, tenant farmers, seamstresses, railwaymen and women,
thinkers, story-tellers, poets and dreamers.

Contents

List of Illustrations   ix
Acknowledgements   xi

Foreword: One Week in April   xiii

Part I
The Roots of Scottish Radicalism

1   The Strike of the Calton Weavers   3
2   Thomas Muir of Huntershill and the Friends of the People   10
3   The People Are in Great Distress   21
4   Met in the Open Fields: The Thrushgrove Meeting   27
5   Lay the Axe to the Tree of Corruption   35
6   Pestilential Publications and Twopenny Trash   42
7   The *Spirit of the Union*   51
8   Keep Your Eye on Paisley   56
9   'We're All Radicals Here!'   61
10 Heroines and a Hero of Liberty: The Clayknowes and
        Dundee Meetings   65
11 Web of Deceit   70

Part II
One Week in April

12 Liberty or Death   83

13   'Stop the Work!' – The General Strike   94

14   That Fearful Night   99

15   'I Will Shoot All Glasgow to Please You!'   102

16   The March to Carron   109

17   The Battle of Bonnymuir   114

18   Tae Fecht for the Rights o' Auld Scotland   120

19   Radicals Arrested at Milngavie   129

20   'Remember Manchester!' – The Greenock Massacre   139

Part III
Aftermath

21   Levying War against the King   149

22   The Trial of James Wilson   159

23   'We Apprehend You on a Charge of High Treason!'   166

24   'Did Ye Ever See Sic a Crowd, Tammas?'   176

25   'I Die a Martyr to the Cause of Truth and Justice'   182

26   Banish'd Far Across the Sea   194

27   Reform Is Won?   202

28   The Scottish Radicals of 1820 Remembered   209

List of Men Executed, Transported and Imprisoned for
     Their Radical Activities   223

Author's Note   225

Select Bibliography   227

Notes   231

Index   247

List of Illustrations

Thomas Muir of Huntershill

Eliza Fletcher

James Turner of Thrushgrove

Janet Hamilton of Langloan

Granny Duncan

James Wilson

William Howat

John Fraser of Viewfield

Address to the Inhabitants of Great Britain & Ireland

The Radical Dyke

Pikes used by the radical army at Bonnymuir

The Radical Pend

Bonnymuir memorial

The coat and axe of the headsman of Wilson, Hardie and Baird

The plaque which marks the spot in Broad Street, Stirling, where Hardie and Baird were hanged and beheaded

The plaque in Condorrat which marks where John Baird lived

The memorial to James Wilson, Strathaven, with replica flag

The original Thrushgrove memorial

The Sighthill memorial in Springburn, Glasgow

The memorial in Greenock to those killed and wounded by the Port Glasgow militia

The Weaver's Cottage, Kilbarchan

Hardie and Baird: a broadside lament

Acknowledgements

I should like to thank the following people and institutions for the help they gave me with my research and in finding original documents, information and illustrations for this book: James Ward of the Devon Records Office; the National Archives at Kew, London; the National Army Museum; the National Library of Scotland, especially Reference Services and the Map Library at Causewayside, Edinburgh; the Mitchell Library, Glasgow, especially their Glasgow Life website; Michael McGinnes, Collections Manager at the Stirling Smith Art Gallery and Museum; the People's Palace, Glasgow; Carol Craig, Heritage Assistant at Renfrewshire Archives; Historic Environment Scotland, with special thanks to Beth Spence, Regional Collections Manager, and Amy Halliday; volunteers at the National Trust Scotland Weaver's Cottage at Kilbarchan; Eve Allan, Deputy Court Manager and Joyce Templeton, macer at the High Court of Justiciary in Glasgow; Marion McMillan of the 1820 Society; Falkirk Library; Bearsden Library; Bishopbriggs Library; Carol Murphy of Balfron Library and Pat Thomson of Balfron Heritage Society; Strathaven Choral Society; Professor Gordon Pentland of Edinburgh University; Niki Russell at Glasgow University Special Collections; Nicola McHendry, Heritage and Community Development Manager at Maryhill Burgh Halls Trust; Frances Rideout of Glasgow Museums; Laura Feliu Lloberas, Image Licensing at the National Galleries of Scotland; and Jamie Leonard of Royston Library, Glasgow.

Several websites have supplied me with enormously helpful information: Scotland's Places; Scotland's People; the British Newspaper Archive; the Scottish Archives Network and Historic Environment Scotland's SCRAN website; the Internet Archive; and

Google Books. My thanks go to all the archivists and volunteers who have worked so hard to make so much available online.

My thanks to Astrid Jaekel for her striking cover illustration and Jim Hutcheson for his jacket design, Helen Bleck for her incisive and meticulous editing, Andrew Simmons, Tom Johnstone, Lucy Mertekis and all at Birlinn who have helped produce the finished book.

My husband Will has been an extremely able research assistant and leg man, gamely climbing over seven-bar gates and walking up grassy hills carrying my camera and his own. He has also kept me fed, watered, supplied with clean clothes and frequent cups of tea, the life-giving fluid. Most importantly of all, he has steadied me when I've faltered and given me unstinting encouragement.

One Week in April

1 April 1820–8 April 1820

Two hundred years ago, Central Scotland and Ayrshire erupted into political protest. Over the course of one turbulent week in April 1820, thousands of weavers, spinners, colliers, artisans and labourers went on strike. Hundreds armed themselves with make-shift weapons, and mustered and drilled in and around their home villages. Scores marched out from their homes in the hope of bringing about political change, prepared to use force if necessary.

The demand was for reform of the corrupt Westminster parliament, universal suffrage, annually elected parliaments and the repeal of the hated Corn Laws. These kept the price of a loaf of bread artificially high, protecting the interests of landowners and grain merchants at the expense of the poor. The self-perpetuating and self-electing cronyism of Scotland's burgh and town councils was also in the protesters' sights.

They wanted a say and had none. The laws that governed their lives were made by the landed gentry and the aristocracy sitting at Westminster. At a local level, employers, mill owners, coal owners, merchants and the well-to-do made the decisions. The idea that ordinary working people were entitled to consider, discuss and vote on who should represent their interests was anathema to those who held the reins of power in Scotland and Britain.

Radicals were people who wanted radical change to this unequal system, believing root and branch reform was required. Political reform would bring about social reform too, effecting a desperately needed improvement in living and working conditions. Men, women and children worked punishingly long hours at home, in textile mills, down mines and on the land for very little reward. The economic slump which followed the end of the Napoleonic Wars in 1815 saw repeated wage cuts while rents and food prices rose. Thousands were struggling to feed their families and keep a roof over their heads. Thousands were leading bleak and desperate lives. Thousands were going hungry.

Throughout Britain, the grievances were the same, as was the yearning for change. The only legal way to try to bring this about was by sending petitions to the government and the prince regent in London, asking for something to be done to improve the situation of the working classes. In 1816, at a meeting in what were then green fields half-a-mile or so north of Glasgow Cathedral, 40,000 people gathered to agree the wording of one such petition and call for reform. At the time, it was the largest political meeting ever held in Britain.

Three years later, in Manchester in August 1819, 60,000 people came together at St Peter's Fields in what was intended to be another peaceful protest and call for political reform. A powerhouse of the Industrial Revolution, the city had grown rapidly. Yet it had no Member of Parliament to speak for it at Westminster.

As more and more people arrived at the vast open-air meeting, Manchester's magistrates were watching from a nearby first floor window. Panicked by the size of this enormous crowd of working people, they sent in the local yeomanry. The soldiers had been standing by, drinking while they were waiting. Made reckless by alcohol, they mounted their horses and rode into the crowd, slashing with their sabres. Foot soldiers fired into the throng. Fifteen people were killed, including two women and a child. Over 650 were wounded.[1]

With the Battle of Waterloo fresh in the memory, the massacre at St Peter's Fields was dubbed Peterloo. Radicals and reformers throughout Britain were outraged by this attack on unarmed civilians and many demonstrations were held in response. A month after Peterloo, 15,000 people gathered on Meikleriggs Moor at

Paisley to make their own peaceful protest against the 'slaughter at Manchester'.

The horror of Peterloo increased the frustration but also strengthened the resolve of Britain's radicals. In February 1820 came the Cato Street conspiracy, when plotters planned to assassinate the entire British Cabinet while they sat at dinner in London. The Cato Street conspirators wanted to establish a republican government on the model the French had adopted after their earth-shattering revolution of 1789.[2] Other radicals were much less extreme and deplored violence. Others again were beginning to think the only way forward might have to involve the use of force, or at least a show of strength.

There is strong evidence that a general strike and an armed uprising had been in the planning for some time before Scotland's Radical War of April 1820, and not only in Scotland. Radicals were in regular touch with one another, with particularly close links between groups in Scotland, the north of England and Nottingham.[3]

Unfortunately for them, government spies and informers had been infiltrating the ranks of the radicals. These shadowy figures had been active in Scotland in 1816 and 1817, when the big Glasgow meeting was held at Thrushgrove. In April 1820, under the direction of Home Secretary Lord Sidmouth, Lord Provost Monteith of Glasgow and Captains Mitchell and Brown of the Glasgow and Edinburgh police, the authorities and the local militia and yeomanry often seemed to be one step ahead.

That those who represented the political status quo were shaken by Scotland's radical rising of April 1820 is not in any doubt. Sixty thousand people had answered the call for a general strike. Shops in Glasgow were forced to close for lack of labour. A contemporary observer said the 'whole working class' of the city had joined the strike. Weavers who worked from their own homes, as many did, stood up and walked away from their looms. Picketing strikers closed all eleven textile mills in Johnstone in Renfrewshire. The picture was the same across much of Central Scotland and Ayrshire.

Drilling and rudimentary military training had been going on for some time at night in woods and moors near Paisley, Milngavie,

Kilsyth, Balfron, Coatbridge and other weaving and cotton spinning villages. There were plenty of demobbed and disaffected soldiers ready and willing to act as instructors.

In that first week of April 1820 these night manoeuvres and other activities became more overt. Thousands of pike-heads were fashioned in forges in Duntocher in Dunbartonshire, Camelon near Falkirk, Kilbarchan in Renfrewshire and elsewhere. Rough and ready though they were, these ancient weapons could potentially be used with brutal force. They were also the easiest and cheapest to make for people who could not afford firearms.

Workers began gathering together in the streets in Glasgow and in the villages. Those who opposed them spluttered in disbelief. The sight of so many working-class people in their corduroy trousers and short jackets not working and with time on their hands horrified them. It made them nervous too.

Anticipating a radical attack on the city, some of Glasgow's better-off citizens sent their wives and families to the presumed safety of Largs and the Clyde coast.[4] The local yeomanry, one of many volunteer militias around the country, was put on high alert. Commanded by Samuel Hunter, editor of the *Glasgow Herald*, they were known as the Glasgow Sharpshooters. Military reinforcements from the regular army were swiftly called in to ensure the defence of the city.

None of this stopped one group of Scottish radicals from arming themselves with those home-made pikes and marching out of Glasgow with the intention of taking control of the Carron Ironworks near Falkirk. They hoped to seize cannons there. They were led by two weavers, Andrew Hardie from Glasgow and John Baird from Condorrat at Cumbernauld. Both men had also been soldiers. Andrew Hardie served for five years in the Berwickshire militia. John Baird had been in the regular army, his regiment the 95th Rifles. He had fought in Argentina and been part of the Duke of Wellington's army in Spain.

The two young veterans and the troop they led never made it to Carron, encountering the Stirlingshire Yeomanry and soldiers from the 10th Hussars on a grassy hill above the Forth and Clyde canal near Camelon and Falkirk. The skirmish which followed has become known as the Battle of Bonnymuir. The little radical army fought fiercely with their pikes and a few commandeered guns but they were soon defeated, arrested and imprisoned in Stirling Castle.

In Strathaven in Lanarkshire, James Wilson was a long-standing supporter of political reform. A well-respected man in his late fifties, he too was a weaver. Wilson and his fellow radicals spent an evening at his house fastening pike-heads to wooden shafts, long branches cut from trees. They marched out of Strathaven heading north, carrying a flag which read 'Scotland Free, or Scotland a Desart' [sic].[5]

The Strathaven Pioneers, as they called themselves, thought they were going to rendezvous with a large French army they had been told was waiting to meet them on the Cathkin Braes, to the south of Glasgow near Rutherglen. There was no such army. Government agents not only spied and informed, they spread false information too.

The militia, yeomanry and police moved in quickly to quell the uprising, arresting hundreds of men. Almost a hundred were indicted on a charge of high treason, an offence punishable by death. Gaols in Glasgow and Paisley were soon overflowing with radical prisoners. With no room left in Paisley, five prisoners were sent to Greenock, escorted there by the Port Glasgow Volunteers, another local militia.

They found a hostile crowd waiting for them at Greenock. That crowd managed to free the prisoners, but at a terrible cost. When the part-time soldiers opened fire, eight people were killed, including a man in his sixties and a boy of eight. Many more were injured. The tragedy caused huge distress in Greenock. Official inquiries into the incident exonerated the men of the militia.[6]

Over the summer of 1820, radicals were put on trial in courts in Stirling, Glasgow, Dumbarton, Paisley and Ayr. Ninety-eight men were accused of high treason. Fifty-two went to ground and never appeared before any of the specially convened courts. In all, forty-two men were tried. Twenty-four were found guilty of high treason, two not guilty and the rest acquitted.[7]

The trials were conducted under English law, a circumstance to which many people in Scotland took great exception. Four men were sentenced to death. In one case the sentence was commuted to transportation to the penal colony of Botany Bay in Australia. Nineteen other men and boys were also transported there.

Three men were hanged and then beheaded. Their bloody heads were held up afterwards by the executioner, who pronounced the words, 'Here is the head of a traitor!' All this was done in public, *pour encourager les autres*. Or as the prime minister, Viscount Castlereagh, put it, the executions of these men who had killed nobody were necessary to teach 'a lesson from the scaffold'.

A mere twelve years later, the Great Reform Act of 1832 laid the first paving stones on the long road which eventually led to democracy.

The Scottish Radical War was a sensational event at the time, reported in newspapers far and wide throughout the British Isles. Some have kept the memory of it alive. Those who care about it care passionately, and there is growing interest in the subject.

Yet mention it to most Scots today and a blank stare is still usually the result. The Scottish Radicals of 1820 stand in the shadows of a badly lit corner of the storehouse where we keep our history. Two hundred years on, it is time for them to step forward into the light.

To put them into the context of their times, we have to start a little farther back. They themselves took inspiration from two events in particular and the people who took part in those. They were the strike of the Calton Weavers in 1787 and the Friends of the People agitation of the 1790s.

PART I
The Roots of Scottish Radicalism

CHAPTER I

The Strike of the Calton Weavers

July–September 1787

On a wet summer's day in Glasgow, the Calton Burial Ground in the city's east end looks somewhat forlorn. The intensely green grass needs mowing and rain drips off the leaves of a few big, mature trees. The paths are a bit unkempt. A man walking his dog tells me he has to watch where his pet puts his paws. He doesn't want him to step on a discarded needle. Coming in here and leaving behind the reassuring splash of car tyres rolling through puddles out on Abercromby Street can seem like a bad idea.

Yet the place is hugely evocative, full of atmosphere and the ghosts of the past. About ten years ago, an impressive amount of work was done to tidy up the graveyard and show off its historical importance. The initiative was led by local people. Set into the pavement outside, carved slabs tell the history of the burial ground and of the Calton. Through the striking modern metal gates, with cut-out letters reading *Calton Burial Ground*, there are more plaques on the paths and against the far wall. The story is well told.

This green space was originally called the Weavers' Burial Ground, the plot of land bought in 1787 by the Incorporation of Weavers of Calton and Blackfaulds. Abercromby Street was then known as South Witch Loan. Some of the earliest burials here were of weavers shot dead by soldiers during what is considered to be the first real industrial dispute in Scotland, the strike of the Calton Weavers. At the time it was against the law for workers to come

together in what were then called 'illegal combinations', the fore-
runners of trade unions.

* * *

When politicians get a rough ride from an audience whose members throw questions and critical comments at them, we say they
are being heckled. The word comes from part of the spinning and
weaving process. The heckle was a tool, two rough combs which
smoothed out the fibres of flax and hemp before these were first
spun and then woven. The worker who wielded the heckle was
called a heckler. That this word acquired the meaning it has for us
nowadays is an indication of how involved weavers and spinners
were in radical politics.

Weavers were known throughout Scotland and Britain for their
intelligence and thirst for knowledge, and also for their refusal to
accept the status quo. They did not believe only the ruling classes
had the right to govern and make life-and-death decisions about
the working classes. Nor were they scared of making their feelings
known at public meetings and demonstrations.

In the good years, when earnings were high, weavers often
chose to limit their working hours to allow themselves more leisure. Many used this time to read, write and discuss with others.
This self-education inevitably led to them asking questions about
how the world was run, who held the reins of power, and why that
should be. Generally, this did not endear them to the people who
gave them their work.

The motto of the burgh of Calton, then separate from the city
of Glasgow and with its own provost and town council, was 'By
Industry We Prosper'. Doing so became more difficult when manufacturers announced they were going to pay 25 per cent less for the
weaving of muslin. So called because it was believed to have origin-
ated in Mosul in modern-day Iraq, this type of cotton could come
in different weights, from sheer and delicate through to the stronger
and more tightly woven calico. Glasgow was well-known for the
production of this cloth, especially the high-quality printed variety
popular in the fashions of the time.[1] Weavers worked at handlooms

in their own homes but were dependent for that work on the manufacturers who employed them. The pay cut being demanded was the second in less than a year, and the Calton Weavers decided enough was enough. In June 1787 they went on strike.

Seven thousand Calton Weavers gathered at a meeting on Glasgow Green, determined not to accept lower pay. Although they issued a declaration after the meeting saying they would not use violence to persuade non-striking weavers to join them, there was some intimidation and destruction. Webs being woven on the looms of non-strikers, and material taken from some warehouses, were burned on bonfires in the street. These protests extended into what could then be called the adjacent village of the Gorbals and, a little further to the west, Anderston. Long since swallowed up by Glasgow, Anderston too was a village of handloom weavers. One non-striker was forced to 'ride the stang', a way of meting out rough justice by ritually humiliating someone who had transgressed in some way. It was used all around Scotland at this time. The stang was a narrow plank of wood which the unfortunate victim was forced to straddle before being carried painfully around.

There was of course no strike pay, no social security, not much form of assistance unless given in the grudging form of parish relief. Yet many of the strikers dug their heels in, staying out over the summer.

On Monday, 3 September, a group of strikers gathered at the Drygate Bridge, about a mile north-west of the Calton. The Drygate Brig, as they would have called it, carried the road over the Molendinar Burn – the heart of Glasgow, where the city's patron saint, Mungo, had established his church more than 1,200 years earlier.

In 1787, Glasgow was still centred around the curving line of the High Street, which linked Glasgow Cathedral down to the Saltmarket and the River Clyde. Founded in 1451, Glasgow University, known as the Old College, sat on the High Street a minute or two's walk up from Glasgow Cross. Behind its buildings was the College Garden and an observatory. Its extensive further policies were called College Lands and ran pretty close to the Calton, lying a little to the north of the weavers' village.

Although industry was developing rapidly and Glasgow was beginning to expand north, south, east and west, there were still lots of open green spaces like College Lands. The city's name is supposed to come from the Gaelic *Glaschu*, meaning 'the dear green place'. The Calton Weavers assembling at the Drygate Brig would have got there by walking along paths around fields, as John McArthur's 1778 *Plan of the City of Glasgow* shows.[2] The original name for Abercromby Street, South Witch Loan, also makes that clear. A loan was a lane or narrow cart track out in the country.

The striking weavers planned to march up the Drygate to Glasgow Cathedral, making themselves visible and continuing to make their point. Throughout the turmoil of the radical years, people set great store by walking in good order, like soldiers on parade. The aim was to demonstrate they were a disciplined and rational group, not a mob.

Glasgow's Lord Provost and magistrates came to the Drygate Brig to order them to disperse. One of the strike leaders, James Grainger, tried using logic to defuse the situation, demanding to know how the weavers could be expected to cope with a much lower income when the cost of rents, food and everything else was rising. He does not seem to have got an answer to this eminently reasonable question. Growing increasingly angry and frustrated, some of the striking weavers did act like a mob, throwing stones at the officials. The Lord Provost called in the military.

Colonel Kellet commanded the 39th Regiment of Foot, an infantry regiment within the British army. They had been stationed at Fort George in Inverness until May 1787. When the soldiers opened fire, later claiming it was self-defence, three weavers were killed on the spot: John Page, Alexander Millar and James Ainsley. Others were wounded and four or possibly five more died later of their injuries. The Lord Provost and the magistrates issued a statement:

> ... although they deeply regret the disagreeable
> necessity to which they were reduced, and are exceed-
> ingly sorry for the unfortunate individuals who have
> suffered on this occasion; yet, as they are informed,

that the operative weavers are still continuing the before-mentioned lawless and unwarrantable practices, the Magistrates and Sheriff, think it their duty, to give this public intimation, that they are determined to continue their utmost exertions to suppress these daring combinations, by every legal means within their power, whatever the consequences may be to the unfortunate individuals who suffer by their exertions.[3]

The city fathers went on to ban any large gatherings in the streets, particularly during the evening or night. Anyone who disobeyed would be 'punished with utmost rigour of the law'. Giving us a glimpse of the way society was structured at the time, 'parents and masters are hereby strictly required to keep their children, servants, and apprentices within their quarters, in the evenings, and in the night time, as they shall answer at their highest peril'.

Even after the deaths at the Drygate Brig, the authorities were clearly still afraid of the combined power of the weavers. The next day the Lord Provost called in more soldiers but the dispute was effectively over. Perhaps the strikers lost heart after the shootings, or perhaps hunger and necessity forced them back to work and acceptance of the lower rates of pay.

The soldiers were honoured and rewarded for their work. At the end of September, Colonel Kellet of the 39th and Major Powlet of the 56th Regiments of Foot were made freemen of Glasgow. An 'elegant dinner' for them and other officers was held in the Tontine Hotel, which stood at Glasgow Cross. Officers and men were thanked for 'their good conduct and behaviour during their residence in town, for their services in assisting to quell the late riots and insurrections, and, for their alacrity, chearfulness [sic], and good order, with which those services were performed'. There was a gift for all the private soldiers garrisoned in Glasgow too, a new pair of 'good shoes and stockings' each.[4] For the strikers and the families of those who had died or been wounded, these expressions of Glasgow's gratitude must have been a bitter pill to swallow.

Several of the strike leaders were arrested but only one was brought to trial. A year later, on 22 July 1788, at the High Court in Edinburgh, James Grainger was found guilty of forming one of those illegal combinations. He was sentenced to be whipped through the town by the common hangman. He was then banished from Scotland, forbidden to return for seven years. He was a man of thirty-eight at the time, married with six children. Whether his wife and family joined him in his exile is not recorded.[5]

In 1825, five years after the Radical Rising of 1820, a memorial stone was laid over the grave of the three men who died at the Drygate Brig. The names of the other weavers who died or were involved in the strike were also carved in stone, including that of James Grainger. In fact, he lived to fight another day, taking part in a subsequent weavers' strike in 1812, and dying at the age of seventy-five.

Although badly weathered now, the original nineteenth-century memorial stones are still in the burial ground, fixed against the wall to the right inside the modern southern gates. In 1931 and 1957, the weavers' memorial was re-dedicated. The plaques placed in the graveyard more recently contain the lyrics of an old folk song: 'Oh, I am a Weaver, a Calton Weaver', also known as 'Nancy Whisky'.

In 1987, on the bicentenary of the Calton Weavers' Strike, the artist Ken Currie was commissioned to paint six panels commemorating the history of Glasgow's working people. They can be seen in the People's Palace museum on Glasgow Green. The second panel depicts the Radical Rising of 1820, the first the strike of 1787.

In the Calton Burial Ground there is a modern stone which bears these words:

THEY,
THOUGH DEAD,
STILL LIVETH. EMULATE THEM.
WE'LL NEVER SWERVE,
WE'LL STEADFAST BE
WE'LL HAVE OUR RIGHTS
WE WILL BE FREE

THEY ARE UNWORTHY OF FREEDOM,
WHO EXPECT IT FROM HANDS,
OTHER THAN THEIR OWN.

Wresting that freedom from the hands unwilling to surrender the reins of power was never going to be an easy task. The road to win workers' rights and basic democracy was to be long, muddy and rough. Yet there were many who found the courage to walk – in good order – along it.

CHAPTER 2

Thomas Muir of Huntershill and the Friends of the People

1792–1794

Less than two years after the Calton Weavers' Strike came the French Revolution of 1789. With its rallying cry of *Liberté, Egalité, Fraternité* and its sweeping away of the aristocracy, it convulsed France, sent shock waves across Europe and galvanised Scotland's radicals into action.

As Kenneth J. Logue wrote in *Popular Disturbances in Scotland, 1780–1815*, for working people in Scotland 'the French Revolution was a revelation. There existed in Scotland a deep-rooted egalitarianism and, with the example of France before them, many Scots saw that this could be translated into political democracy'.[1]

Another example before them was the American Revolution of 1776, with its declaration that all men are created equal and the insistence they would have no taxation without representation. Although it has to be said they did mean men, and white men at that. Be that as it may, the idea was a revolutionary one in a society based, until then, in both Europe and European-settled America on a strict hierarchy and rigid class system.

Thomas Paine, an Englishman who had emigrated to America, promoted these startling new ideas in his writings. His words had a huge influence on people who wanted reform, encouraging them to call for annual, fairly elected parliaments and universal suffrage. *Rights of Man* also advocated family allowances, free education for all and old-age pensions. It sold 200,000 copies throughout Britain. Banning the pamphlet only made it more popular.

Reformers in Scotland and Britain adopted two potent symbols from America and France. One was the liberty tree, the original of which grew on Boston Common. Early pro-democracy protests under its branches inspired the planting of more liberty trees in France during the Revolution, and in Scotland in the 1790s.

One was planted in Dundee in 1793. There are colourful stories as to how it happened. Inspired by the French Revolution, a group of Dundonians planted an ash sapling at the town cross. They decorated it with ribbons, oranges, rolls and biscuits.[2] Then they lit a bonfire and set off fireworks. The Tory Lord Provost of Dundee and his magistrates were not amused.

There are two versions of what happened next. In one, Provost Riddoch arrives at the tree and the bonfire, bows to the tree, walks three times around it, and firmly calls out 'liberty and equality forever'. Then he goes home. In the other version, the provost is dragged out his bed by the revolutionary mob, forced to the tree wearing only his nightgown and made to dance around it.

Both stories end the same way. The following morning, while everyone's sleeping off their revolutionary fervour, the provost has the tree dug up 'and threw it in jail, thus achieving history as the only civic head in the world to have jailed a tree'.[3] If that part of the story's not true, it ought to be. The tree was replanted and flourished for many years.

The other favoured symbol was the Phrygian cap, a soft conical bonnet with the top bent over that dated back to the ancient world. During the French Revolution, it came to signify liberty. The revolutionary headgear was often carried aloft on a tall pole during political demonstrations in Scotland.

Scotland has many cherished symbols of her own, of course. Major John Cartwright was a veteran English campaigner for reform who travelled throughout Britain in pursuit of support for this goal. He made a connection between the liberty tree and cap and the Scottish thistle while on a campaigning visit north of the border. 'In the garden of Mr. Carnegie, of Louer [Lour], near Forfar, I this morning saw a true national thistle twelve feet high. As the

English motto to this armorial ensign signifies in English "No one injures me unpunished", I conclude this is the tree, and the Scotch bonnet the cap, of Liberty.'[4]

* * *

One of many reformers inspired by the ideas of Thomas Paine and the ideals of the French Revolution was Thomas Muir of Huntershill in Bishopbriggs. In 1792 he was twenty-seven years old and a lawyer to trade. Despite his relative youth, he was also an elder of Cadder Kirk near Kirkintilloch, a deeply religious young man as well as a political firebrand. In the autumn of 1792, a year after the first part of Paine's *Rights of Man* was published, he organised a meeting to promote the radical cause and discuss what might be done to improve the situation of working people. In 1792 this was even more difficult than usual. That year's harvest had failed and there was famine in many parts of Scotland.

The meeting Muir organised was held on 30 October 1792 at the Star Hotel in Glasgow.[5] The hotel was on Ingram Street, on the corner of present-day Glassford Street. Not so very long before, Ingram Street had been Back Cow Loan, what is now Queen Street being Cow Loan. Cows being driven to pasture up at Cowcaddens ambled along both these routes. The names are again a reminder of how interconnected the urban and the rural were in Scotland at this time. By the 1790s, however, the city was fast developing into the planned grid of streets we know today, although until well into the nineteenth century the middle of what is now George Square remained a swamp where eels slithered and puddocks hopped.[6]

Muir urged people to come together and get organised. He himself worked tirelessly to help set up Scottish branches of the Friends of the People, which first started in London. The organisation was founded in 1792 and aimed to bring about peaceful reform of parliament, the parliamentary system and an extension of the right to vote, though not anywhere as far as universal adult male suffrage. It was quite an exclusive group, made up of gentlemen who were either Whig Members of Parliament or Whig supporters. The Whigs later developed into the Liberal Party. The Friends of the People advocated reform, not revolution, and were quick to disassociate themselves from the French Revolution and the writings of Thomas Paine.

In other parts of England, and in Scotland, branches of the Friends of the People with a much wider membership were formed. More than a hundred years later, the then Labour MP Tom Johnston (he was subsequently to become Secretary of State for Scotland and the prime mover behind the establishment of the hydro-electric schemes of the 1930s), wrote that Muir 'toured the weaving districts and addressed the mobs at Kirkintilloch, Kilmarnock, Paisley, Lennoxtown, and innumerable other places ...'[7] Groups were established in Glasgow, Edinburgh, Paisley and many smaller places. Textile workers were once again to the fore. Branches mushroomed in communities dominated by spinners, weavers and bleachers such as Milton of Campsie, Kilbarchan in Renfrewshire and Strathaven in Lanarkshire.

The Scottish and some of the English branches of the Friends of the People were more democratic in organisation and cheaper to join than the original group. Nor did they restrict their membership to the gentry, members of the professions and the burgeoning middle class. Many in that group were also in favour of reform, often irked by the deference demanded by the gentry and aristocracy. It got in the way of business, for one thing, and their growing sense of self. They were understandably much less keen on the increasing violence of the French Revolution. This scared many, who were fearful the same thing might happen in Britain. Thomas Muir declared himself to be no republican and to be against violence. He did advocate universal adult male suffrage.

Driven by his ideals, and clearly a man of enormous mental and physical energy, Muir organised the first 'Edinburgh Convention' of reform societies. This was held over three days in the middle of December 1792.[8] Eighty different groups sent 150 delegates. The venue was Lawrie's Dancing School in James Court, off the Lawnmarket at the upper end of the High Street – a dancing school had a ballroom big enough to accommodate them all.

At the end of the meeting, all the delegates stood up, raised their right hands and swore to 'live free or die'.[9] One of those delegates

was James Wilson, a Strathaven weaver who was to play a pivotal role in the Radical Rising of 1820. At the time of the first
Edinburgh Convention in 1792, Wilson was in his early thirties.

The statement the delegates produced sounds pretty moderate
to modern ears, calling for 'an equal representation of the People
in Parliament and a frequent opportunity to exercise their right
of election'. The delegates planned to advance their agenda by
the peaceful and entirely legal method of sending a petition to the
Westminster parliament in London. However, this moderate call
shook the implacable enemies of reform to the core. The response
was repressive.

As ever, radicals, reformers and anyone who threatened the
political status quo were being watched. In the autumn of 1792,
between the founding of the many Scottish branches of the Friends
of the People and the holding of the first Edinburgh Convention,
one government informant wrote that: '... the success of the
French Democrats has had a most mischievous Effect here ... it
has led them to think of founding societies into which the lower
Class of People are invited to enter – and however insignificant
these leaders may be in themselves, when backed with the Mob
they become formidable'.[10]

The description here of 'French Democrats' is not in any way
complimentary. Democracy was a dirty word. The very idea that
the people might have a say in how they were governed was
unthinkable to the opponents of the radicals. The excesses of the
French Revolution and the wholesale guillotining of so many aristocrats were also in the minds of many, making them deaf to more
reasonable calls for reform. Although the Edinburgh Convention
of 1792 made clear its peaceful intent, scare stories were rife.

Eliza Fletcher was the young wife of Archibald Fletcher, a lawyer
who later defended several of the would-be reformers in court. The
Fletchers lived in Edinburgh, first in Hill Street and then Queen
Street, when the New Town really was new. Husband and wife
were both passionate supporters of political reform. Those who
were opposed to reformers alleged that Eliza guillotined hens in
her back garden 'in order to be expert when "French principles"
and practice [...] should prevail in our land'.[11]

We might wonder how she persuaded the feathered creatures to meekly accept their fate without slicing off a couple of
her own fingertips in the process. Sadly for lovers of tall tales,
the allegation turns out to be a foul calumny. Eliza's daughter later wrote that when the story reached her father's ears, he
was 'amazed and amused'.[12] Like many people, the Fletchers
wanted reform, not revolution. Friends of Thomas Muir though
they were, Archibald Fletcher turned down an invitation to join
the Friends of the People. To Fletcher, the movement's aims were
too radical.

Yet revolution and rebellion were clearly in the air. Three
Edinburgh printers, another profession known for its radicalism,
were found guilty of drinking a toast to 'George the Third and last,
and damnation to all crowned heads'. Messrs Morton, Anderson
and Craig were sentenced to nine months' hard labour.[13]

Robert Burns got into trouble when he was rumoured to have
made a similar toast: 'Here's the last verse of the last chapter of the
last Book of Kings.'[14] He went a lot farther than this, arranging
and paying for two cannons from the Carron ironworks to be sent
to the revolutionaries in France. As an exciseman and government
employee with, as he said himself, 'a wife and little ones' dependent
on him, he was warned to watch what he said.

As we know from his poems and letters, the warning does
not seem to have had a great effect. As well as 'Scots Wha Hae'
and 'Parcel o' Rogues', he also penned 'The Rights of Woman'.
Admittedly it owes as much to male gallantry as anything else but
these are fine words all the same:

> While Europe's eye is fix'd on mighty things,
> The fate of Empires and the fall of Kings;
> While quacks of State must each produce his plan,
> And even children lisp the Rights of Man;
> Amid this mighty fuss just let me mention,
> The Rights of Woman merit some attention.

In 1792 Mary Wollstonecraft published *A Vindication of the
Rights of Woman*, perhaps the earliest written expression of

the feminist point of view. In 1818 her daughter Mary Shelley gave the world the story of Frankenstein.

Thomas Muir described the House of Commons as 'a vile junta of aristocrats', making the mistake of putting those words in a political pamphlet. Letters meant for him were delivered in error to a different Mr Muir, who handed them over to the authorities. They too were judged to contain seditious statements. He was arrested on a charge of sedition and of circulating the banned works of Thomas Paine. Sedition was defined as encouraging others to rebel against established authority, whether by physical actions, writing or the making of speeches. Released on bail, Muir travelled to France in a vain attempt to persuade the revolutionaries there not to execute their king and queen. He knew this would damn the cause of reform in other countries.

He was granted a French passport and planned to head for America. He sailed first from France to Belfast. From there he took the enormous risk of making what was meant to be a secret visit to Scotland to say his farewells to family and friends. Arriving by ship from Belfast at Portpatrick in Galloway, he was recognised by a customs officer, arrested at nearby Stranraer and taken to prison in Edinburgh.[15]

He was charged in the indictment on several counts. He had 'created disaffection' by giving seditious speeches at meetings of reformers. Two were specifically mentioned: Kirkintilloch in November 1790, followed by another the same month at Milton of Campsie. He had encouraged people to buy 'seditious and inflammatory writing or pamphlets', particularly 'The Works of Thomas Paine, Esq'. He had circulated these writings and pamphlets in Kirkintilloch, Milton of Campsie and Lennoxtown. He had attended the 1792 Edinburgh convention of the Friends of the People. He had read out a seditious address from the United Irishmen.

Muir conducted his own defence at the High Court of Justiciary in Edinburgh in August 1793. It met in a room within what is now the Court of Session in Parliament Square. In the three-hour speech he made from the dock, he set out his belief in democracy with dazzling clarity.

What then has been my crime? Not the lending to a relation a copy of Mr Paine's works, but for having dared to be, according to the measure of my feeble abilities, a strenuous and active advocate for an equal representation of the People, in the House of the People; for having dared to attempt to accomplish a measure, by legal means, which was to diminish the weight of their taxes, and to put an end to the profusion of their blood.

As for me, I am careless and indifferent to my fate. I can look danger, and I can look death in the face, for I am shielded by the consciousness of my own rectitude. I may be condemned to languish in the recesses of a dungeon. I may be doomed to ascend the scaffold. Nothing can deprive me of the recollection of the past; nothing can destroy my inward peace of mind, arising from the remembrance of having discharged my duty.[16]

His eloquence did him no good. The chief judge was Robert MacQueen, the notorious Judge Braxfield. He too made his views on democracy crystal clear. Only the gentry, the aristocracy and other landowners had the right to be represented. He didn't have a high opinion of the French, either.

And what kind of folks were they? I never liked the French all the days of my life, and now I hate them . . . Multitudes of ignorant weavers . . . Mr Muir might have known that no such attention could be paid to such a rabble. What right had they to representation? I could have told them that Parliament would never listen to their petition. How could they think of it? A Government is like a corporation and in this country it is made up of the landed interest which alone has the right to be represented.[17]

Muir was found guilty and sentenced to be transported to

Botany Bay in Australia for a period of fourteen years. The penal colony had been set up five years before, when the 'First Fleet' of eleven convict ships reached what was to become Sydney. He was soon followed by fellow radicals Thomas Fyshe Palmer, William Skirving, Maurice Margarot and Joseph Gerrald, who had also been tried for sedition. The harshness of the sentences outraged many and inspired several poets to put pen to paper, including Robert Burns.

Burns wrote 'Scots Wha Hae' in 1793. The story it tells is of the Scottish victory over the English army at the Battle of Bannockburn in 1314. However, it is believed it was inspired by the case of Thomas Muir and the other transported radicals. A year later English poet Robert Southey wrote to a friend remarking 'Muir's mother is actually dying of a broken heart'. He included a manuscript version of a poem he had written in honour of the transported men, 'To the Exiled Patriots':

> Martyrs of Freedom – ye who firmly good
> Stept forth the champions in her glorious cause
> Ye who against Corruption nobly stood
> For Justice Liberty & equal laws—
>
> Ye who have urged the cause of man so well
> From when Corruptions torrent swept along—
> Ye who so firmly stood . . . so nobly fell
> Accept one grateful Briton's grateful song.[18]

There are several more verses, including a reference to 'Freedom struggling with Oppression's chain'. Perhaps Southey was unconsciously echoing Burns' reference in 'Scots Wha Hae' to 'oppression's woe and chains'. The final verse of Southey's poem claims the example of the radicals will 'fire each soul . . . in each freeborn breast for ever'. It ends like this:

> Ages unborn shall glory in your shame
> And curse the ignoble spirit of the time—

And teach their lisping infants to exclaim
'He who allows Oppression, shares the crime.'

Or to paraphrase the words often attributed to Edmund Burke, all that is required for evil to triumph is for good men to do nothing. And as Thomas Muir said: 'The time will come, when men must stand or fall by their actions; when all human pageantry shall cease; when the hearts of all shall be laid open.'

Thomas Muir was allowed visitors while he was held in prison in Edinburgh after his trial. His parents were indeed distraught. Australia was thousands of miles away and they were in their late fifties. The chances of their ever seeing him again were slim. Their farewell gift to their son was a small Bible he could keep in his pocket. They inscribed it 'To Thomas Muir from his afflicted parents'.[19]

They handed the Bible to him at Leith in November 1793, after which they stood and watched as he was rowed out to the *Royal George*, on which he sailed to Woolwich, to travel onwards from there to Australia. As the tender pulled away from the quay at Leith, Muir looked back at his parents and pointed to the sky. He was trying to console them with the thought they would meet again in heaven. Cold comfort, but a spar of hope for all three of them to cling to.[20]

Muir spent two years in Australia. His social status and not being a common criminal allowed him a large measure of freedom. This gave him the chance to escape on an American ship which called in at Sydney in February 1796. He crossed the Pacific and eventually made landfall at Monterey in what was then Spanish California. Another shorter sea voyage was followed by an overland trek to Mexico City and Vera Cruz and on to Havana in Cuba.[21]

He planned to go from there to Philadelphia but was prevented from doing so, and put on board a Spanish ship heading for Spain. She was intercepted by a small squadron of British frigates. In the subsequent naval skirmish Muir lost an eye and suffered a shattered cheekbone. He made it to Cadiz in Spain. After some months, the French government interceded in the shape of their foreign minister, Talleyrand. Muir was allowed to travel north. He never fully recovered from his injuries, dying at Chantilly in France in 1799 at the age of thirty-four. His parents did not long outlive him. His father James died two years later, aged sixty-seven. His mother Margaret died two years later again, in 1803 at the age of sixty-five.

Cross North Bridge in Edinburgh from the Old Town to the New and look in the direction of the Firth of Forth. The view is dominated by a tall obelisk soaring up into the sky from the lower slopes of Calton Hill. The Political Martyrs' Monument was erected there in 1844 in a campaign driven by Scots doctor and MP Joseph Hume. The cost was raised by public subscription, what we might nowadays call crowdfunding. Hume also promoted the raising of a second memorial to the Scottish Radical Martyrs of the 1790s in Nunhead Cemetery in London.

Both monuments commemorate Thomas Muir and his four fellow radicals who were also tried for sedition. The words the father of Scottish democracy spoke at his trial are carved into the plinth. 'I have devoted myself to the cause of the People. It is a good Cause — It shall ultimately triumph — It shall ultimately prevail.'

CHAPTER 3

The People Are in Great Distress

1815 onwards

The unrest of the 1790s did not go away during the long years of
the Napoleonic Wars. It resurfaced in the Glasgow weavers' strike
of 1812, and periodically before and after. One of the main aims of
the 1812 industrial dispute was the setting of a minimum wage. As
during the Calton Weavers' Strike of 1787, the strike spread and
the mood grew bitter.

In November 1812, the Sheriff of Renfrewshire issued a proclamation accusing 'certain evil-disposed persons' of trying to
intimidate other weavers into joining the strike. It was alleged
these flying pickets were also stopping and threatening carters who
had been hired to move the raw materials to be woven elsewhere.
The proclamation warned that such activities were 'illegal, of a
Criminal Nature, and highly punishable'.[1] The strike lasted for
nine weeks but ended in failure. Although the strikers took their
case for a minimum wage to the law courts and had that agreed,
the manufacturers refused to implement the decision.

Three years later, the economic depression which followed the
end of the war was deepened by the flooding into the labour market of some 400,000 soldiers and sailors, discharged by a less than
grateful nation.[2] Some who had been badly wounded were granted
a small pension. Most came home with nothing. Many soldiers
who had been weavers before they took the king's shilling and
joined Wellington's army could not find work.

More people seeking employment also meant wages for those in work could be cut. According to Paisley radical John Parkhill, after the end of the war weavers abruptly found themselves earning half of what they had earned before. If they complained, they would swiftly find themselves with no income at all. There were plenty of other men queuing up to take their badly paid place.

As John Parkhill also observed, people were dispirited by the human cost of the war, the deaths of those soldiers who never came home. Mothers had lost sons, young women had lost the men they might have married. In a poignant foreshadowing of what was to happen a hundred years later, after the First World War, he wrote that many women of this generation remained single all their lives, not by their own choice.[3]

Repeated wage cuts and the difficulty in finding work meant many weavers and their families were in a pitiful state. One of them was Alexander Rodger, who lived and worked at the Drygate toll in Glasgow, right by the Drygate Brig in the shadow of Glasgow Cathedral. This had been the flashpoint during the strike of 1787, where the weavers had been shot and killed.

Known to everyone as Sandy, Rodger was a radical and also a poet, as so many weavers were. It was said that every third weaver in Paisley composed verses in his head while working at his loom, jotting them down from time to time in notebooks perched on their looms, or committing them to paper later. There's a theory that in using their hands and feet to work their looms, they were attuned to the rhythm of words as well as the weaving of cloth. In 1819, Sandy Rodger wrote a poem called 'The Twa Weavers', featuring a poetic dialogue between Tammas and Robin:

When War and Taxation has fleec'd us right sair,
And made us, like scaur-craws, a' ragged an' bare,
Twa poor weaver bodies ae day chanc'd to meet,
Wi' scarcely a shoe on their stockingless feet:
Their lank ribs were seen through their cleeding to shine,
And their beards might hae pass'd for a hermit's langsyne.[4]

When Tammas asks Robin if he's still living where he always

did, Robin replies angrily that he doesn't *live* anywhere, he *starves*. Despite getting up at three o'clock in the morning and working all day long, he's earning a pittance. He's not alone either. Thousands 'now pine in starvation, and sigh in despair' and Robin knows where the blame lies.

There's Prime Minister Pitt, who entered into 'that lang, bloody *war*'. There are the bankers, who've substituted paper money for 'good yellow *coin*, that clinket sae sweetly in days o' langsyne'. He'd like to cram their bank notes down their throats. People clearly didn't trust paper money. There are the politicians and apathetic folk who allow them to get away with their corruption and laziness.

> And see – we submit, like a parcel o' slaves,
> To be tax'd and oppress'd by a junto o' knaves,
> Wha buy themselves seats in our HOUSE, *up the gate*,
> There laugh at our sufferings, and ca' that debate,
> Whilst at our expense, their ain pouches they line;
> Lord send them a Cromwell! Like Cromwell langsyne.

The opulent lifestyle of the prince regent, who succeeded to the throne as George IV on the death of his father in January 1820, caused outrage. He lived in idleness and luxury while hundreds of thousands of his subjects lived in damp and cramped houses without enough food to eat. Conditions in the mills and factories were brutal.

In Scotland there was one honourable exception to the exploitative practices of the employers. In 1768, working initially with inventor and entrepreneur Richard Arkwright, David Dale of Glasgow established a cotton spinning mill near Lanark harnessing the motive power of the Falls of Clyde, and built decent houses for his workers to live in. Education was provided for the children who lived and worked there. By 1796, Dale was employing sixteen teachers to instruct over 500 children in reading, writing and arithmetic.

Even at New Lanark, with its utopian ideals, children as young as ten worked a twelve-hour day and then spent two hours in the factory school. By the standards of the time, they were much better off than child workers elsewhere. They were well fed and slept in clean dormitories where fresh air and lots of light were much prized. Dale's daughter Caroline married Welshman Robert Owen. When he took over ownership and management of New Lanark, he built on his father-in-law's work. Music and dance were introduced into the educational curriculum. New Lanark was a working mill until 1968. Occupying a picturesque site on the banks of the Clyde, it is now a World Heritage Site.

While some in the early nineteenth century began to see New Lanark as a model community, many of Owen's fellow mill owners saw his ideas as dangerously radical and resisted all attempts to improve working conditions in their own mills and works.

In 1819 the Factory Act was passed, but it applied only to cotton mills. It allowed children to be employed from the age of nine and restricted the working hours of those under sixteen, but only to those punishing twelve hours. Impossible to imagine modern Scottish boys and girls working so long and so hard from such a young age. The mills were noisy, hot and unsafe and there was no defence if the people in charge of the young workers were unkind or cruel. Behind his back, workers at one mill in Paisley with a tyrant of a boss described the place as the 'Temple of Terror'.[5]

As Enid Gauldie points out in *Spinning and Weaving in Scotland*, there were no restrictions on the hours adults worked. Children might come home to a cold and empty house and have to wait several hours for their parents to get back. Those parents had little choice about their children working. Families needed every penny they could earn.

Gauldie writes: 'There are terribly affecting tales of men who could not themselves find work carrying their tiny children on their backs to the mills, the children dragged sleeping from their beds to work twelve and fourteen hours on end.'[6]

Before 1799, conditions in the coal fields were even worse. Until that year, Scotland's coal miners and their families had the legal status of serfs. Basically they were paid slaves, bound to the place where they were born and to the coal owner. If they ran away and were caught before they had succeeded in staying away for a year and a day, they were treated like soldiers who had deserted. They were flogged and sent back down the pit.[7]

Reading through letters and documents of the time, it is not uncommon to find a warning of radical activity in different areas followed by sympathy for the state of the working population. Writing to a William Kerr at the General Post Office in Glasgow on Monday, 3 April 1820, an unnamed correspondent offers his opinion. 'I think there is every reason now to apprehend some disturbance and it is melancholy to think that many will have been drawn to it from want and despair – for the people are in great distress . . .'[8]

In Ayrshire, Alexander Boswell of Auchinleck was a captain in the local militia. He was the son of James Boswell, friend and travelling companion of Dr Johnson on his journey through the Highlands and Islands of Scotland. Alexander Boswell was violently opposed to the reform movement, boasting that he would 'ride in Radical blood up to his bridle reins'.[9] He is also credited with being the author, or at least the collector and refiner, of the exquisitely poignant song of farewell to life and friends, 'The Parting Glass'. People are infinitely complex.

On 27 December 1819, Alexander Boswell sent a letter to Lord Sidmouth, the Home Secretary. He was sounding a warning and he was pretty sure his information was accurate: ' . . . respecting the most infested quarters of this County where there are a number of radically bad men who work upon the wounded minds of the destitute and forlorn. In this neighbourhood and in other places the Gentlemen of the County have provided labour for a considerable number of the Weavers out of employment'.[10]

Alexander Boswell too had provided employment but he wasn't sure there was much gratitude for this. 'I cannot avoid mentioning with disgust the worst feature that has reached me, the establishment of Schools to instil into the minds of Youth the doctrines of the Radical Reformers.'[11]

So any sympathy for the plight of working people did not allow for the possibility that they might choose to better themselves through education. Or that the holding down of the people who did most of the labour by working them into exhaustion while not paying them enough to feed, clothe and properly house their families was morally wrong.

Some better-off folk did try to help the unemployed and underpaid in their areas by collecting and redistributing clothes and providing meals. Most did not. Compassion was often in short supply, even from those who might have been expected to offer it.

Balfron in Stirlingshire has a long history. Until about 1790 it was a small place, a hamlet or clachan. The building of a cotton mill and a planned village to house the workers saw a population explosion. In only a year, the number of inhabitants jumped from around 50 to 900.[12]

That was fine in the boom years but in the post-war slump 300 of Balfron's weavers found themselves unemployed. One family had days when they had nothing to eat but cabbages, presumably grown on their own small plot. The weavers drew up a petition and presented it to the local minister, asking him to approach the Balfron heritors on their behalf. These were local people who owned land, occupied positions of authority or were of a higher social status. The minister told them 'he had no power to do this and that in any case if they [the weavers] were now in want it was as a result of their own improvidence'.[13]

With so many people struggling to survive and receiving little or no help to relieve their distress, it was inevitable that frustration was going to explode into anger and some form of direct action. Yet for several years, people continued to use peaceful and constitutional methods of trying to effect change, as at Thrushgrove in Glasgow in October 1816.

CHAPTER 4

Met in the Open Fields:
The Thrushgrove Meeting

Tuesday, 29 October 1816

In the attempt to achieve fair wages and better living and working conditions, reformers throughout Britain sent numerous petitions to the prince regent in London. Scotland alone sent seventy-nine separate ones to ask for the repeal of the Corn Laws.[1] Other politely worded missives asked for a reform of parliament and intervention to help the struggling working classes and the unemployed.

The resolutions of one of many such Scottish petitions were decided on at a huge mass meeting held in Glasgow on Tuesday, 29 October 1816. The organisers of the gathering were an eminently respectable group of local businessmen, manufacturers and shopkeepers. Despite this, the Lord Provost and the Glasgow magistrates did everything they could to try to stop the gathering from taking place.

Its organisers had initially wanted to hold the meeting on Glasgow Green, time-honoured place of protest. James Black was Glasgow's Lord Provost between 1816 and 1818. He said no. If the meeting took place there without permission, he would bring in the army and 'dragoon' the protesters to break it up.[2] A company of the 42nd Regiment, the Black Watch, would be standing by. At the first sign of any trouble they would move in, forcing the crowd to scatter in panic, and very possibly inflicting injuries in the process.

The would-be reformers tried for the Trades House in Glassford

Street. Permission to hold the meeting there was also refused. Their third choice was a tavern in Maxwell Street, off Argyle Street. The Eagle Inn was also a coaching inn, with large stables and a stable yard. Landlord Daniel Caldwell agreed to allow the meeting to take place there, until he too was threatened with dire consequences: if such a meeting took place at the Eagle Inn, Caldwell would be guilty of enabling sedition, for which he might end up in gaol.[3]

At this point James Turner stepped in. He was a tobacconist with a shop in the High Street near the Old College, the original site of Glasgow University. Turner and his business prospered, allowing him to move to larger premises down the road at Glasgow Cross and also to buy the small estate of Thrushgrove, a mile or so up the road. He lived there with his wife Jean. Since the ground it occupied was at that time outside the Glasgow city boundary and also private property, the Lord Provost had no power to stop a meeting there from going ahead.

The mansion house of Thrushgrove and the green fields around it have long since disappeared. It vanished under the development of the railway, industrial development and tenement housing. Those houses have now disappeared too, replaced by high- and low-rise modern housing, although the original lie of the land, the slope behind Mr Turner's house, can still be seen. Thrushgrove lay to the right of modern-day Springburn Road, a little south of Sighthill Cemetery on the opposite side of that road and close to the modern Royston public library. The land once occupied by the estate is bounded by Royston Road to the south and Charles Street and the recently closed St Rollox engineering works to the north. Now known as Royston, older residents of the district continue to call it by its previous name of the Garngad.

The fuss over the other venues had been wonderful free advertising. The gathering at Thrushgrove became the biggest political meeting yet seen, not only in Scotland but throughout Britain, attended by men and women carrying 'banners demanding political reform, large brooms to sweep away corruption and caps of liberty to symbolise the call for freedom'.[4] As many as 40,000 people made their way up past Glasgow Cathedral and the Royal Infirmary. That magnificent building had opened its doors in 1794 and by the time of the Thrushgrove meeting had expanded to be able to offer beds to 200 patients.

The meeting in James Turner's fields was a sensational event, reported in newspapers throughout the British Isles. The vast majority of the press was hostile to the reform movement. Yet all the papers agreed on the huge number of people in attendance and on how enthusiastic the crowd was. 'The Resolutions were received with the warmest applause, and passed without a dissenting voice. The speakers were frequently interrupted by loud cheering from the immense multitude, waving of hats, and every other method of expressing their exultation.'[5]

On Monday, 5 November, just short of a week later, the London-based *Morning Chronicle* offered its readers a detailed report of the proceedings.[6] Benjamin Gray, a shoemaker in Nelson Street, gave the first speech. He painted a grim picture of life in the post-war slump:

> It is now universally admitted that almost all classes in this country are labouring under an overwhelming load of indescribable calamity. Differences of opinion there may be as to the cause, but there can be none as to the existence of the evil. In every corner of this once flourishing country, one hideous picture of misery presents itself. Commerce, and Manufactures, and Agriculture, all groan beneath impending ruin. Bankruptcy crowds upon bankruptcy.

Gray went on to lament the number of shops which had closed and the many other businesses where employers had reluctantly had to tell their workers they could no longer afford to keep them on. This was a calamity for the 'industrious working poor', many of whom were going hungry. Some had been forced to sell what few treasures they owned, what he called their 'keepsakes'. 'Homeless and heartbroken', some had gone on the tramp to beg for their bread because they couldn't find work.

Gray blamed the government ministers in London for doing nothing to alleviate the situation. He heaped scorn on their defence that the current difficulties were temporary, the result of 'a sudden transition from a state of war to a state of peace'. The country had been at peace now for eighteen months and the distress was only becoming worse.

He criticised the recent conflict, considering 'the wars against the French people to have been carried on for no other object than the restoration of whatever was detestable, bigoted, and despotic to the discarded Monarchies of Europe'. He called too for a complete reform of the way Britain was governed. 'The people must have their legal share in the government of the country – they must have Representatives of their own choosing. [. . .] – nothing short of a radical Reform can save them.'

This was a call for fundamental and groundbreaking change but not for revolution. It was agreed that Glasgow should submit a petition to the prince regent, asking for a return of the rights the people were entitled to expect. Yes, Prince George was surrounded by men who sought only to advance their own careers and feather their own nests and who had no sympathy for the distress of so much of the population.

Despite this, Gray advised, the reformers had to persevere. 'Let us be true to ourselves, and we are certain to succeed. [. . .] Our complaints will one day be heard.' Addressing what must have seemed like an impossibly unfair balance of power, he gave the example of Martin Luther. This 'obscure monk' had brought about the Protestant Reformation. Scotland's John Knox had built on that, using as his weapons 'bold discussion, and a resolute diffusion of knowledge [. . .] To doubt, therefore, the efficacy of union and discussion, is unworthy of an enlightened or a constant mind.' Keep the faith and we'll get there in the end.

The speeches were long and the day was a cold one. Yet people stood for four hours, listening attentively to what was being said. The sheer size of the crowd made that difficult for those furthest away from the hustings. Some walked up onto higher ground behind Thrushgrove so they could at least see what was going on. It must have been an impressive and moving sight, a sea of people gathered together to call for reform and groundbreaking change. They must have known they were part of history, that something was shifting and changing beneath their feet.

Meanwhile, Lord Provost Black and Glasgow's magistrates were gritting their teeth and hoping everything would stay the same. The soldiers of the 42nd Regiment were standing by at Eglinton Toll, south of the River Clyde. A signal had been agreed. If there was any trouble at Thrushgrove, a flag would be raised above the gaol.[7] There were two prisons in Glasgow, one in Duke Street, off the High Street, and one just north of the Clyde, part of the High Court of Justiciary. It is unclear over which one the warning flag was to be raised. Maybe both of them.

If they saw the flag being run up the flagpole, the dragoons were to canter up the High Street and Castle Street and on to the meeting to scatter the crowd. The plan did not entirely settle the nerves of the Lord Provost and the magistrates. Many in this Highland regiment had relatives in Glasgow and might well have been reluctant to mete out violence to forcibly disperse people who could be members of their extended families.

The huge crowd remained resolutely non-violent, if noisy, cheering and waving their hats in approval of what they were hearing. Somehow votes were taken approving the resolutions to be put to the prince regent. Was there a forest of hands, or thousands of full-throated shouts of 'Aye!' rising up into the cold October air? One communal roar of approval was heard a mile away.

John McArthur, an ironmonger in Argyle Street, spoke after Benjamin Gray. He praised Scotland and the Scots, evoking John Knox and other Scottish heroes.

> We are assembled to lay a state of our national grievances at the foot of our Prince. I trust this will be a glorious day for this great city. That it will be evinced to the world, that the soundness of intellect, the superior intelligence, regularity of conduct, and steadiness of principle for which the people of Scotland always were famed, are still alive amongst us. Let us not forget that the glorious Patriot William Wallace, bled and conquered on this very ground. The descendants of Wallace, Bruce, Buchanan, Knox, Belhaven and Fletcher still inhabit our dear native country.[8]

The spirit and example of William Wallace were often evoked by Scottish radicals. Uttering that sacred name at Thrushgrove was also making a local connection. Tradition has it that before he died a hideous death in London on the orders of Edward I, the Hammer of the Scots, Wallace was betrayed and seized at Robroyston, three miles east of Mr Turner's fields.

Buchanan was George Buchanan (1506–82), historian, scholar, royal tutor and early Protestant reformer. Lord Belhaven and Andrew Fletcher of Saltoun sat in the Scottish parliament before the Union with England. Due to his determined opposition to the Union of the Parliaments of 1707, Andrew Fletcher too was known as 'The Patriot'.

More of Scotland's religious heroes were invoked by John Russell, a Glasgow manufacturer. He quoted the Covenanters, comparing their conventicles and worshipping out in the country to the meeting at Thrushgrove. 'You are this day met in the open fields, and not far from the tombs of the Martyrs, who in former times lost their lives for the cause of civil and religious liberty.'

This was another local connection. During what became known as the 'Killing Times' of the seventeenth century, when the Covenanters had to fight (and were punished) for the right to worship God in the way they believed He wanted them to, Glasgow's place of execution was the Howgait, just north of Townhead. Until comparatively recently, three Covenanting martyrs who were executed there were remembered by the Martyrs' Church. The building which was the Martyrs' School is still there. The speakers knew their Scottish history and knew their audience did too.

This being Glasgow, there was humour and a few wisecracks. John Russell made one in a tirade against all the taxes being imposed to help pay for the recent war. 'We are grievously harassed and borne down with the salt tax, and the leather tax, the soap tax and the candle tax, the man-servant tax, the cart tax, the horse tax and the dog tax, and with such a tremendous list of other taxes, that the very name of them is like to break our hearts and frighten us to death.'

It was that mention of the dog tax which got him a laugh. Dog licences had first been introduced in the late 1790s. Lists of some of those who stumped up for one can be found online, or the Scotland's Places website.

Speakers like John Russell clearly saw no contradiction in evoking Scotland's heroes while at the same time addressing the crowds as Britons. Cursing the war, he paid tribute to 'British blood and British valour'. In the next breath, he separated Scotland from 'the neighbouring nations', and shared some lines from 'your patriotic countryman Thomson'. They contrast the poor widow and her orphan children living in 'starving solitude' with 'luxury, in palaces, straining her low thought to form unreal wants'.

James Thomson was yet another weaver-poet but of an earlier generation, living from 1700 to 1748. He also wrote the words for 'Rule Britannia'. The relationship between Scotland, England and Britain has long been a complex one.

The petition drawn up at Thrushgrove was delivered to London by hand. The man who took it there was Major John Cartwright, the English reformer who had long been a dedicated advocate of political reform. Supporting a moderate approach, he encouraged the creation and signing of as many petitions as possible. He travelled extensively through the Midlands, north of England and Scotland to try to bring this about. He always aimed to bring together middle-class and working-class reformers.

In Scotland he travelled to Edinburgh, Glasgow, Stirling, Kircaldy, Cupar, Dundee, Forfar, Arbroath, Montrose and Aberdeen. He may also have visited Robert Owen at New Lanark. In a letter to his wife he praised the beauty of the nearby Falls of Clyde, 'equally attractive to the painter, the poet, and the philosopher'.[9]

A week before Christmas 1816, Major Cartwright presented the Thrushgrove petitions and others from towns around Glasgow and further afield to Home Secretary Viscount Sidmouth. James Turner was annoyed that the petition was not given to the prince regent personally. Like many, he believed the people had a right to present their concerns directly to the Crown. With the benefit of hindsight, it seems odd that so many reformers clung on to the hope that feckless Prince George would actually do something to alleviate the suffering of his people. He did nothing. All the petitions were ignored.

The government in London responded to Thrushgrove and other large meetings which followed it throughout Britain over the next couple of years by passing what became known as the Six Acts. This legislation aimed to stifle political protest, not least in the form of, and in the wake of, mass meetings such as at Thrushgrove in 1816 and Manchester in 1819, when an even larger group of people gathered to call for reform. It's estimated that there were 60,000 people at the meeting which became infamously known as Peterloo after the local yeomanry charged into the crowd, sabres slashing and guns blazing. The Six Acts included a ban on meetings at which more than fifty people were present and outlawed training and drilling unless it was being carried out by the regular army or local militias.

After the Six Acts came into force at the end of 1819, a few months after Peterloo, anyone who continued with such activities was breaking the law. The penalty was transportation to Australia. All the repressive legislation achieved was to harden attitudes on both sides, pushing many reformers towards the view that physical force might be necessary to bring about change.

When the Thrushgrove meeting broke up on that October afternoon in 1816, the crowd was asked to leave in an orderly fashion. They took half an hour to file through the open gate which led out of the field, waiting patiently for their turn to move. Those who were there were proud that no damage was done, not a creature injured, not a sixpence stolen, not a fence-post broken, no debris or mess left on the grass. The pro-reform *Liverpool Mercury* was not the only British newspaper which gave this good behaviour its nod of approval. 'Not the slightest injury was done to any article upon the ground: even the boxwood borders of the inclosure were left uninjured: no accident of any kind occurred: and the whole was conducted with an order and decorum which strikingly proved how groundless have been the prejudices against popular meetings in this part of the country.'[10]

The reformers had shown themselves to be responsible people. Although some were growing impatient, others continued doggedly to call peacefully for political change.

CHAPTER 5

Lay the Axe to the Tree of Corruption

1816–1819

The meeting at Thrushgrove had given people hope. The way ahead was clear. Gather lots of signatures on as many petitions to the prince regent as they could muster and hope this would bring about reform and the desperately needed improvements in living and working conditions which would flow from it. During the struggle to abolish the slave trade in the British Empire, petitions had made a great impact. Why should they not have the same effect here?

More meetings were held. Between 5,000 and 6,000 people attended one at Dean Park in Kilmarnock on Saturday, 7 December 1816.[1] It was a bitterly cold day, with repeated showers of hailstones and flurries of snow. The wintry weather didn't put anyone off. Several speakers addressed the crowd, calling for change.

Mr Alexander Maclaren, described as 'a talented tradesman', gave a brief but impassioned speech on how the country was suffering. He blamed 'the narrow-minded policy of her rulers'. James Johnston was equally convinced a huge extension of the right to vote was required. He made his point by referring to Ayrshire in particular. Kilmarnock's population stood at just short of 13,000 but only one person had the right to vote in parliamentary elections.

> This county is supposed to contain nearly 170,000 inhabitants, and of this number only 156 have any right to vote for a member to serve in Parliament;

and even these do not vote freely; for it is notorious
that two powerful individuals have ruled the elections in this county for the last forty years. Thus you
see that in Ayrshire, there is a population of 169,844,
who have no right to vote, not are any more represented in Parliament, than the cattle on the hills.[2]

According to Peter Mackenzie, a prolific journalist and chronicler of the radicals of this period, the MP for Edinburgh at this time
was chosen by a mere thirty-three men who were eligible to vote.

Next up at Kilmarnock was Archibald Craig. He spoke about
the economic damage the war had done and the soaring national
debt. He demonstrated the size of this by 'by one or two ingeni-
ous calculations'. Then John Kennedy spoke. At the time of the
Kilmarnock meeting he was a man in his late twenties. He had
been born into a weaving family but 'disliking the loom' he had
enlisted, joining the Royal Ayrshire Militia as a lad of nineteen.

Kennedy spent eight years as a soldier. He did not enjoy them,
relieved beyond measure when he was demobbed in 1815. What
he most disliked about the army was the frequent floggings
meted out to soldiers. He spoke with great passion at Dean Park
about how degrading such punishments were. He also had some
stark statistics.

Scotland at this time had around two million inhabitants, yet
only 2,700 of them had the right to vote, which meant, almost
incredibly, that more than 99 per cent of the population could not
vote. Kennedy pointed out that the disenfranchised were all tax-
payers. This was either through the hated income tax introduced to
help meet the cost of the Napoleonic Wars or by having to pay the
taxes levied on all manner of goods and commodities. As he put it,
the vast majority of Scotland's voters had 'no more right of voting
than if they were an importation of slaves from Africa'.[3]

Two speeches were read from people unable to make the
meeting. John Burtt's concentrated on the misery so many were
experiencing. Mr White – his first name is not given – emphasised
the unfairness of low wages and high prices. His views were the
most radical of all the speakers. He stated that 'nature had formed

all men in the same mould, had gifted them with kindred minds – and that the *few* had no right to hold over the *many* an unlimited authority'. That last phrase might just strike a modern resonance.

John Kennedy, who had become a schoolmaster after leaving the army, closed the meeting by asking the people attending to always behave well, think for themselves and support the cause of liberty.

All the speeches were printed in a pamphlet. Four hundred copies were 'thrown off'. John Baird of Kilmarnock published and sold them, getting himself into very hot water. He and one of the speakers at Dean Park, Alexander Maclaren, were arrested at the end of February of the following year and charged with sedition. They were tried at the High Court in Edinburgh in March 1817. Found guilty, they were imprisoned in the Canongate Tolbooth of Edinburgh for six months and thereafter released on bail. Their friends believed imprisonment damaged both men's health. Neither lived to a ripe old age.[4]

It wasn't long before disillusionment set in over what might be achieved by the sending of petitions to the prince regent. The suspicion was growing that he never did look at them. People kept trying this only legal and constitutional way of making their protest all the same. As elsewhere in Britain, there were several mass meetings in Kilmarnock over the course of 1819.

James Paterson was a Kilmarnock journalist and author. He contributed most of the succinct biographies which accompanied John Kay's *A Series of Original Portraits and Character Etchings*. This is a collection of etchings of Edinburgh characters of the 1790s, including Thomas Muir and the political martyrs of the 1790s. Fifty years after the events of the radical times, Paterson looked back to a midsummer meeting, when thousands of men 'and women too' marched into the town, 'with banners flying, bagpipes playing and drums beating'. The bass drum was being hit 'with herculean power, by a brawny carpet weaver, who had once done the same duty in defiance of the French'.[5]

There were masses of brightly coloured flags and banners, with various slogans on them. *Radical Reform in Kilmarnock. Lay the axe to the tree of corruption. No Lords, no Bishops. Down with Places and Pensions.* A baker carried an oversized loaf, or a model of one, on a pole, a reference to the hated Corn Laws. A cap of liberty was carried by a 'masculine, good-looking amazon, whose husband took an active part in the proceedings of the day, and afterwards became a bailie of the burgh'.[6]

Since we're told she was good-looking, we might wonder if she was also described as masculine because she was tall and well-built. Or was it because she was playing such an active role in the proceedings? Not that Scotswomen have ever been slouches at standing up for what they believe in. They were often present at pro-reform meetings.

It was a glorious, warm day. James Paterson could see glory in people's expressions and demeanour too. 'The morning was one of the finest in midsummer, and on came the long rushing line, with the steady, stately "tramp of the Kilmarnock men" the banner-men waving their defiant flags, as if they had been so many weaver's beams, and every face flushed and bright with the consciousness of playing a part in the great political game, which would forever immortalise their name.'[7]

The marchers had come from twenty miles around and the four routes by which they approached Kilmarnock had them converging at the Cross. Although they briefly got stuck there in a human traffic jam, the mood was buoyant. 'No one could doubt that a spirit had been awakened, which, repressed and discomfited as it might be, must ultimately prevail.' Sorting themselves out, they marched off to the Gas Brae. They were singing 'Scots Wha Hae' as they went.

Although many were armed, ready to defend themselves if attacked by the hussars stationed in the town, there was no violence. Whether to cause mischief or through jangled nerves, someone yelled out that the soldiers were coming. It was a false alarm. The crowd dispersed safely and in good order.

There was another march a month or so later, on Saturday, 18 September. This time 7,000 people marched into Kilmarnock, although there weren't many flags. There had been trouble over those at a huge meeting held on Meikleriggs Moor at Paisley just the week before. However, at Kilmarnock 'the men of Galston and Newmilns indicated their love of country by carrying large Scotch thistles',[8] a coda to Major Cartwright's comment about the thistle being the Scottish version of the liberty tree. Universal suffrage was again the demand, although nobody was holding out much hope of their voices being heard. Despite this, they agreed to send another petition.

One month later, on Saturday, 23 October 1819, there was a meeting at Rutherglen. Now part of Greater Glasgow, it was then still an independent burgh. It was a crisp, sunny morning, with a touch of frost in the air.[9] The crowd built over the course of the morning. Bands from what was then simply Kilbride, Glasgow's Townhead, Calton, Bridgeton, the Gorbals, Tradeston, Anderston, Pollokshaws and Cambuslang were in attendance.

The crowd fell back as the marching bands arrived, making a corridor for them to walk through to the hustings. They played the 'Dead March' from Handel's oratorio *Saul* as they moved forward. It's a piece of music to stir the blood, slow and solemn. In 1799 it had been played at George Washington's funeral in America. Given the admiration pro-reform campaigners felt for the United States, this may be why it became popular at radical gatherings. It is generally played on flutes, trumpets or cornets, and small side drums, all easy instruments for working-class musicians to be able to afford. Watching and listening out in the fresh air, the people at Rutherglen must have been enthralled and inspired.

There were lots of colourful and vivid flags and banners. One depicted a mother and baby being slashed at by a sabre-wielding hussar at the Peterloo Massacre in Manchester two months before. Another showed hands joined together, with the motto 'Arise Britons and assert your rights'. On the reverse were the words 'We shall be free. Remember Manchester'. Another again showed 'tyranny falling under the arm of an ancient Caledonian'.[10] One bore the message, 'Taxation, without representation, is injustice'. On its other side the rose of England, the thistle of Scotland and the harp of Ireland were intertwined. Other legends included 'Annual Parliaments', 'Universal Suffrage', 'Liberty or Despotism', 'Rights of Man'.

The bands played 'God Save the King' followed by 'Scots Wha Hae' and 'Rule Britannia'. This choice of music may surprise twenty-first-century Scots but nineteenth-century Scots were at a different stage on the long journey of Scottish history. The line in 'Rule Britannia' affirming that 'Britons never shall be slaves' struck a powerful chord.

The cap of liberty was placed on the head of Mr Paterson, chairman of the meeting, and the speeches began. The usual request for good behaviour was made. The resolutions passed began with a ringing statement of belief. 'That all Governments are founded in, and exist only by the consent of the people, the basis being the equal security and protection of the whole', and are 'wholly for the mutual benefit, strength and happiness of the whole community'.[11]

War was deplored, as was 'with the deepest horror and indignation [. . .] the outrages and tyrannical transactions at Manchester' where blood had been 'so barbarously shed'. Even worse than the bloodshed was the clear intention of killing off all 'that now remains of British Freedom'.

At none of the numerous Scottish meetings calling for political reform were any resolutions passed demanding the reinstatement of the Scottish parliament in Edinburgh. The enemy was the corrupt Westminster government. It had to be reformed before anything else.

One month later, on Saturday, 20 November 1819, there was another Kilmarnock meeting. Even more people came to this, an estimated 14,000 to 16,000. This time flags were carried, including an old Covenanting banner said to have been flown at the Battle of Drumclog. There was music here too, 'drums, clarionets, and bagpipes'. The clarionet was an early form of clarinet.

Archibald Craig, who had spoken at the Dean Park meeting in 1816, was crowned with the cap of liberty. There were eight or nine speakers altogether and they all put the radical point of view. At none of these meetings was there any support or call for violence, what reformers then and later referred to as physical force, to achieve their political aims. However, in Kilmarnock and elsewhere, some were beginning to think moral force was getting them nowhere. Reasoned argument, huge demonstrations and petitions were not working.

In Derbyshire in England in 1817, this frustration boiled over. Betrayed by William Oliver, a government undercover agent still active in 1819–20, the Pentrich Rising was short-lived. The story is beautifully told by Sue Wilkes in her meticulously researched book, *Regency Spies*. Led by Jeremiah Brandreth, known as Jerry, a framework knitter, the rising was fuelled by poor living and working conditions. Existing grievances came to a head when a number of workers in the area were sacked for having attended meetings of the pro-reform Hampden Club.

Plotted at the White Horse pub in the village of Pentrich, the plan was to march on the Butterley Ironworks in nearby Ripley, where George Goodwin was the works manager. He very quickly had thirteen pikes made and waited with a group of some locals and special constables at the nearby Red Lion pub, ready to resist the radicals, who were now about a hundred strong.

On their way to Ripley, they called at a house demanding weapons. The householder was a Mrs Hepworth and she refused to let them in. A shot was fired through a window, hitting and killing Mrs Hepworth's servant Robert Walters. Jeremiah Brandreth is believed to have fired the fatal shot.

As they drew nearer to Ripley, marching through the darkness of a very wet night, Goodwin retreated to the Ironworks and barricaded himself and his co-defenders into the works office. Brandreth demanded Goodwin's surrender. The works manager refused, came out of the office and told Brandreth and his band to go home, warning them they would be hanged if they didn't. He's said to have pushed them, trying to get them to turn around and leave the Ironworks. The rebels decided to march on through the rain to Nottingham, where around another hundred men had gathered. They were intercepted by a company of dragoons before they could get there. Discarding their weapons, they scattered.[12]

Government spies such as William Oliver having been active, many of the Pentrich rebels could be easily identified. Almost fifty men were found and arrested over the next week. Three were executed – hanged and then beheaded – in front of Friar Gate Gaol in Derby. They were Jeremiah Brandreth, Isaac Ludlam and William Turner. Fourteen men were transported to Australia.[13] It was a foretaste of things to come.

CHAPTER 6

Pestilential Publications and Twopenny Trash

1819–1820

Despite their restricted leisure time, and the never-ending and exhausting struggle to make ends meet, many working-class people carved out the time to educate themselves and their children. They knew life was unfair and the world was ill divided. Reading and discussing what they read and the possibilities there might be for change continued to give them hope. It led some to the conclusion that direct action and physical force were needed.

Over the autumn and winter of 1819–20 many local 'unions' were formed. These clubs were not unions in the modern sense of trade unions, but reading and discussion groups. Union societies started among the English radicals and quickly spread to Scotland. Their growth was led by Yorkshire radical Joseph Brayshaw, who toured Scotland in 1819 spreading the word and the radical message.[1] He came from Yeadon, near Leeds, and also travelled extensively in the north of England.

Brayshaw did not have much faith in petitions to the prince regent, but nor was he in favour of physical force. He promoted an idealistic agenda. Working people should aim for high moral standards. They should refrain from alcohol, tobacco and tea. This would deprive the government of the taxes on these items but would also demonstrate that reformers were respectable people and not drunkards, as was too often alleged by their opponents.

James Turner of Thrushgrove wanted to call the union societies Wallace or Fletcher clubs but Brayshaw advised against it.[2] Perhaps this was for reasons of solidarity, sending a message that Scottish and English reformers were united in their aims. Brayshaw also advised against secrecy when it came to the union societies. They should meet openly, like an evening class where you would go to acquire knowledge and thus improve your understanding of the world around you. There could surely be no objection to that. This proved to be the triumph of optimism over experience.

Some Scottish union societies which left behind a record of their activities did very quickly become political groups. It might be a reasonable assumption that a large proportion of them did. The union societies certainly formed the nucleus of local radical committees, which sent delegates to monthly meetings of a secret radical committee in Glasgow.[3] More openly, many bands grew out of union societies. All the musicians at the Rutherglen meeting were union society members.[4]

Union societies were kept small, with no more than twenty members, encouraging the formation of more groups. In Paisley, many met at their place of work at the end of the day. In other parts of Renfrewshire, public spaces were hired for the meetings of union societies.[5] In Strathaven in Lanarkshire, a group of around twenty of the town's weavers came together in the house of James Wilson. A lifelong advocate of political and societal reform, he had been a delegate to the 1792 Edinburgh Convention.

A working-class intellectual, Wilson was a man of many talents. As a hosier weaving the ubiquitous knee-length stockings of the time, he had developed a method of using the purl stitch of knitting on the frame at which he worked. This allowed for a quicker and more efficient method of producing the goods and earned him the nickname of Purlie or Perlie Wilson. He also mended clocks and guns, and bred pointer dogs.[6] He was a convivial man and a loving husband, father and grandfather, although he and his wife Helen had known great sorrow. Of their six children, only one daughter survived to adulthood.

He could be cheerfully sarcastic, was probably agnostic when it came to religion and like so many weavers, loved to write poetry.

His verses were described as comical and political, although unfortunately none of them have survived. He was elected 'class leader' of the Strathaven union. Sharing the cost of the publications, one of the members would read out articles from radical journals and newspapers such as the *Black Dwarf* and the *Manchester Observer*. A discussion then followed. On at least one occasion they had a speaker. Joseph Brayshaw, the Yorkshire reformer, addressed them, staying over at the Wilsons' house.[7]

In Kilmarnock, a group of ten men met in the home of William Semple, who was a cobbler. Willie lived with his wife in one small room on the first floor of a building in Wellington Street. They were a devoted couple who loved to go out for a walk together on Sundays. He was 'tall, muscular and wiry'. She was shorter. Although they dressed in their Sunday best for their weekly walks, one observer thought they both routinely looked as if they had been 'dipped in saffron, possibly arising as much from the want of ablution as from any positive tint of skin'.[8]

The reading club at the Semples' house met each Monday, Wednesday and Friday. They read the *Black Dwarf* and the *Glasgow Chronicle*. Starting life as the *Sentinel*, the *Chronicle* was set up by some Glasgow reformers. They were frustrated by the way other newspapers in the city did not cover stories connected with political reform. The *Glasgow Herald* was one of the main culprits here. The *Glasgow Chronicle* was a newspaper which stood solidly behind reform, although for some radicals its position later become too mild.

James Paterson, who gave us the information on the Kilmarnock union in his *Autobiographical Reminiscences*, painted a vivid word picture of the scene.

> There sat Willie, who might be styled the speaker of the house, with spectacles on nose, and an ample Kilmarnock red cowl on his head, busy, over the oil lamp which burned before him, with his awl and hammer; he whose duty it was for the night to read aloud to his fellows, had the use of a candle, contributed from the general fund. The audience were

intense listeners, and generally all remark was suspended until the news of the day had been exhausted. Then the more important topics were taken up and discussed.[9]

Willie seems to have kept working by the light of the oil lamp while he listened, with his wife sitting beside him helping with the process. A Kilmarnock cowl could be of blue, black or red and in two or three different styles. Some were hoods, others flat bonnets with a toorie or pompom in the middle, what we might also call a tam o' shanter. We go back here to Major Cartwright's comment about 'a Scotch bonnet' being Scotland's cap of liberty. Traditional headgear for working men, a Kilmarnock cowl or bunnet was often worn indoors by people like weavers and shoemakers.[10]

There was a range of opinions in this Kilmarnock club. One former soldier detested the Duke of Wellington. He had personal reasons, having been flogged and dishonourably discharged from the army. He didn't believe his undescribed 'misdemeanour' had justified such a draconian punishment.

A lot of people felt the Iron Duke had 'behaved with heartless sternness towards his army', whom he had notoriously referred to as the scum of the earth. Dislike of Wellington grew in the years following the Napoleonic Wars, when many injured veterans had their pensions reduced for some minor infringement of the rules. James Paterson of Kilmarnock, in his *Autobiographical Reminisicences*, said this was often done 'because of some trifling informality or inaccuracy'.[11] He commented drily that the substantial financial rewards given to the duke were always safeguarded.

More generally, all members of the club which met at the Semples' house were in favour of reform. They all agreed 'there should be no king, no lords, no gentry, no taxes!' Some wanted to go even farther, as far indeed as the seizure of all property, followed by its distribution among all ranks of society. Paterson quoted the words of a 'Kilmarnock rhymer' to illustrate the genesis of this demand.

I carena for mysel' a fig,
My head an' han's can work it;
But when I see a toom meal-pock, [an empty bag of oatmeal]
An' duddie weans ill sarkit, [ragged children in tattered clothes]
I'm like to think there's something wrang—
A something ill providit;
In plain braid Scotch, I'm fain to say—
This warl' is ill dividit.[12]

There are several more verses elaborating on the theme of the world being ill divided. The poem laments how some people own whole counties while others have no land at all they can call their own. Then there's the contempt with which the rich look down their noses at the people they consider to be their social inferiors. Such people 'measure worth by length o' purse', while the poor are forced to beg for their bread. The working classes at this time were often referred to as the sooty rabble.[13] Radicals were disparagingly known as Rads, Black Nebs or ragamuffins. During the Chartist agitations of the 1840s, when again the demand was for universal suffrage, secret ballots and parliamentary reform, the phrase 'the great unwashed' was coined.

Perhaps the recurring last line of each verse of the poem by the unnamed Kilmarnock poet, 'this warl' is ill dividit', inspired a later songwriter, Mary Brooksbank of Dundee. In the early twentieth century she took a traditional chorus, added verses inspired by her own and her workmates' experiences and wrote the 'Jute Mill Song'.

O dear me, the world's ill divided,
Them that works the hardest are the least provided . . .
Shiftin', piecin', spinnin' — warp, weft and twine,
They fairly mak ye work for your ten and nine.

Arguments for the equal division of property were not popular with all members of the Kilmarnock union society. In a bit of a dig at more extreme radical views, James Paterson quoted Geordie Tamson, who objected strongly to the prospect of the kailyard or vegetable patch he'd inherited from his father and countless previous generations of the Tamson family being confiscated. Such an act would be 'downright robbery'.[14] Or, as might be said: 'I agree with the principle until it actually affects me.' On the other hand, given the family in Balfron who sometimes only had cabbages to eat, owning a kailyard could help a family survive during hard times.

A contemporary newspaper report written after another big reform meeting in Glasgow mentions reading rooms. These seem to have existed alongside the union societies. Over six weeks in October and November 1819, six were set up in Paisley, two in Greenock and one in Johnstone. The Paisley reading room had around eighty-six members and the one in Johnstone 120. Everyone contributed a halfpenny and the accumulated money was used to buy the reading material.[15]

In November 1819 Captain Brown of the police force went with two officers to search reading rooms in Paisley. They were asked if they had a warrant. Yes, came the answer but we don't have to show it to you. A deputation from Paisley's reading rooms later called on Brown, requesting to see the warrant. Again he refused to show it but there was a small victory here. The authorities held the power but working-class people were beginning to find the confidence to challenge that.

* * *

The opponents of reform were infuriated that the people they also routinely described as the lower orders were reading radical and revolutionary newspapers and news-sheets. On 1 August 1820, four months after Scotland's Radical War, William Connell of Walworth Common in London's Southwark wrote a sickeningly sycophantic letter to Home Secretary Viscount Sidmouth.

> Among the many excellent measures of the Administration of which Your Lordship is so great an ornament, none more deserves the gratitude of every true friend to his Country, than that to suppress those cheap pestilential publications which

inundated the Kingdom, destroying by their pestiferous influence on the lower orders every just principle
of Religion and Morality . . .[16]

Trouble was, Connell went on, there were still daily, evening and
weekly papers of the 'rankest' sort being read in 'what are called
Coffee Rooms'. These dens of iniquity were springing up everywhere in London and, he understands, 'in all the Manufacturing
Towns in the Kingdom'. This was having a 'baneful' effect on the
lower orders.

Coffee houses had been popular throughout Britain for at least
150 years before Mr Connell wrote his irate missive, mainly as
meeting places for businessmen, merchants and master tradesmen.
Perhaps he thought a coffee *room* was a few steps down the ladder
socially, although James Paterson in Kilmarnock also used the term
coffee room, stating they were only for the elite. Greenock also had
at least one coffee room where its shipyard owners, ships' captains
and other businessmen met.

Clearly doing his rising blood pressure no good whatsoever, Mr
Connell refers to the aforesaid lower orders 'drinking their cheap
substitute for coffee' while at the same time they 'imbibe those
Principles which render them discontented with, and disaffected
to, the Government of their Country'. So in his view, the turmoil of
1819–20 was caused by the working classes having the temerity to
drink coffee – even if it was only some substitute made from chic-
ory – reading radical publications and daring to offer and exchange
views on how the country should be run.

Janet Hamilton, working-class author and poet, who lived
with her husband and children in the village of Langloan, now
part of Coatbridge, also disapproved of radical publications. She
described the *Black Dwarf* as 'a small, mean-looking sheet, overflowing with scurrilous epithets and venomous invectives against
the Government, and utterly subversive of all lawful authority and
social order, and interlarded with scepticism and blasphemy, clearly
indicating that both the writers and readers of this and similar pro-
ductions were as inimical to the Word and Government of God as
they were to the Government of Britain'.[17]

The Black Dwarf ran from 1817 to 1824, printed and published in Fleet Street in London. Its editor was Thomas Wooler, a radical journalist. The paper was financially supported by Major Cartwright, who had fostered the growth of union societies. Wooler was more than happy for people to share the paper. Even with an initial price of two pence, later rising to four, poor people couldn't afford it. The reading and discussion unions and clubs could buy one copy between them, as Wooler stated in his edition of Wednesday, 5 January 1820. 'A single copy may be read by a hundred and retain all its value.' At its peak, the paper had a circulation of 12,000. On the basis of its popularity with union societies, the readership must have been much higher.

Its masthead offered a statement of intent: 'Satire's my weapon . . .' Wooler offered damning analysis too. It must have been extremely interesting for Scottish readers of the *Black Dwarf* to read his criticism of David Owen of New Lanark. 'It is very amusing to hear Mr Owen talk of re-moralizing the poor. [. . .] Talk of the poor being demoralized! It is their would-be masters that create all the evils that afflict the poor, and all the depravity that pretended philanthropists pretend to regret.'[18]

Wooler believed workers should be paid a fair wage and not have so much of it clawed back in the shape of taxes on all manner of goods. The rich should be taxed instead. Likening the workers to industrious bees robbed of their honey, he wrote: 'Do not take from them what they can earn, to supply the wants of those who will earn nothing.'

The *Manchester Observer* ran from 1818 to 1821, operating out of premises in the city described by *The Times* as Sedition Corner.[19] The Thunderer included Manchester's radical paper among its 'pestilent publications'. In keeping with its name, the masthead of the *Manchester Observer* included a drawing of the all-seeing eye. We're watching you. In July 1819 it warned MPs in the House of Commons that the choice was radical reform or revolution. 'One or other must shortly ensue.'[20]

The newspaper was always in a precarious situation. It was too radical to attract enough advertising to cover its costs and its journalists were repeatedly sued for libel and sometimes sent to prison for it. The *Manchester Observer* was heavily involved in inviting Henry Hunt to speak at the huge reform meeting which became infamous as Peterloo. The paper folded in 1821. It recommended and handed the baton over to the newly established *Manchester Guardian*, now simply the *Guardian*.

Looking down its patrician nose, *The Times* criticised the poor for 'squandering' their meagre funds on radical and rebellious newspapers and journals. Many of the poor went right on reading their 'twopenny trash' and their pestiferous and pestilential publications. For a brief period, a shorter-lived Scottish radical newspaper was also read in Strathaven and at other union societies: the *Spirit of the Union*.

CHAPTER 7

The *Spirit of the Union*

October 1819–January 1820

The *Spirit of the Union* was a weekly newspaper published in Glasgow on Saturdays at the end of 1819 and the beginning of 1820. Its editor was Gilbert McLeod, who was in his late twenties at the time. He and his wife, Catherine Ross (Scotswomen were routinely and legally referred to by their maiden names even after marriage), had two young children, a son and a daughter. McLeod didn't have a high opinion of the newspaper par excellence of Glasgow's establishment. In a damning description, he summed up *Glasgow Herald* editor Samuel Hunter, chief officer of the loyalist Glasgow Sharpshooters '. . . as dishonest a scribbler as ever stained paper'.[1]

The articles published in the *Spirit of the Union* were equally forthright, the point of view of radical reformers strongly put. In the first edition, published on Saturday, 30 October 1819, McLeod lambasted the comfortably-off for not caring about the poor.[2] The *Glasgow Herald* editor was very overweight, and it seems likely McLeod had Samuel Hunter in his sights when he described a man 'who has just had a remarkably good dinner, and cannot conceive how you who are starving can complain of being hungry'. Could such a man and his like have any idea what it was like 'to go to sleep without having tasted breakfast, dinner, or supper, and without blankets to cover him, they having been carried off by the tax-gatherer, to defray the duty upon window-lights, or some other God knows what sort of a duty . . .'?[3]

He took a side-swipe at harsh punishments and the *Glasgow Chronicle*, alleging one of its contributors had complained scaffolds were too low. They needed to be built higher so the onlookers could see more of the 'hempen-science of compressing windpipes'.[4]

McLeod never missed his targets and hit the wall. He was too angry to be anything other than savagely honest. In the same editorial he described the 'House of Corruption, vulgarly called the House of Commons', as being a 'farcical mummery', a place where it was openly admitted wealthy men could buy themselves a seat. Here mushrooms sprang up on 'the dunghill of corruption . . .'

His fury over the deaths and injuries at Peterloo was white-hot in its intensity. Compounding his anger and sorrow was the fact that the 'perpetrators of the murderous atrocities committed at Manchester' had been thanked for what they had done. In the second edition of what he called 'our little weekly sheet',[5] he returned to Manchester. A complaint had been laid against two of the yeomanry 'for maliciously cutting and maiming, on the 16th of August, in St. Peter's area'. The case was heard at Warrington.

While witnesses brought from Manchester were waiting at an inn, a 'posse of constables' swarmed into the tavern, swearing at them and making fun of their wounds. Gilbert McLeod was particularly outraged by what happened to seventy-one-year-old Alice Kearsley. She had been cut twice by a sabre wielded by one of the yeomanry soldiers by the name of Meagher. One blow almost sliced off her ear, the other caught her neck and shoulders. 'Damned' is not spelled out in full in the following passage because it was a much stronger word then than it is now.

> But the most brutal part of the conduct of these royal rioters was to Alice Kearsley, who, instead of meeting that compassion which her age, her wounds, and her poverty were peculiarly calculated to excite, experienced the most rancorous abuse; Caldwell, the constable, telling her, in a taunting tone, 'What, you have been wounded, have you?' and thrusting his hand under her bonnet, added, 'they have only cut off your ear, I see; I wish they had cut your head off

you d----d old devil, and then you could not have come here to trouble us'. Nay, more; this Caldwell gave the poor woman a thrust with his umbrella, and also a severe blow upon the hand. An assemblage of people served to protect the witnesses, and to disperse those assailants.[6]

For reformers in Scotland and throughout Britain, Peterloo was an open wound in the psychological sense too. In the sixth edition of the *Spirit of the Union*,[7] McLeod wrote a long leading article on it. He argued passionately against the charge made by the apologists for the Manchester massacre, that the pro-reform crowds had been carrying flags, quoting a debate in the House of Commons at which Sir Francis Burdett said, ' . . . flags are carried at every election which takes place at Westminster; where, then, is the illegality?'[8] Reading the Riot Act – if anyone had been able to hear it at Manchester – was supposed to be followed by allowing people time to disperse. It was outrageous that people had been 'wantonly sabred, trodden down and shot'.

McLeod went on to describe the passing of the repressive Six Acts.

> Thus laws are about to be passed without the consent of the people, for they are not represented, which will, in a great measure, change the nature of the British Constitution. The selling of seats in Parliament, which was boldly avowed by the criminal himself, was scarcely so bad as this – it passed unpunished; and although, by the contemplated measures, Ministers prove themselves traitors to the people, yet there is not a man in Parliament who has had the spirit to impeach them![9]

McLeod struck a spark of hope all the same. Change was coming. Soon the country would be run 'upon the broad basis of universal justice'.[10] In a sarcastic open letter to Glasgow Lord Provost Monteith, who was in office from 1818 to 1820, and

Samuel Hunter, editor of the *Glasgow Herald*, he poked fun at the establishment's fear of the radicals.[11] Maybe police constables would have to sleep on hammocks in the town hall (which was what he called the city chambers), so as to always be on the alert.

Whether the radical reformers wanted universal suffrage to include women is not clear. The resolutions passed at the various meetings seldom qualify the demand for the right to vote. Continuing to mock the establishment's fear, McLeod wrote that of course these dangerous radicals didn't want to extend the franchise 'to all paying direct taxes, except madmen and females (thanks to the court buffoon for that hint)'.[12] Which might make feminist hackles rise were it not for that comment about the court buffoon. This would seem to refer to the prince regent. Perhaps the younger George had expressed incredulity at the idea that everyone except madmen and women might be allowed to vote and McLeod was mocking him for this.

McLeod went for Lord Provost Monteith with wounding words, italics and three exclamation marks. He had seen 'a whining letter' from the provost to Home Secretary Sidmouth in which the provost expressed alarm at what was going on in Glasgow, declaring *'he would rather see Glasgow burned to ashes than that the cause of Radical Reform should prosper!!!'*[13] There must have been a mole burrowing away among the provost's clerical staff who copied and leaked the letter to McLeod.

McLeod called on the talents of weaver-poet Sandy Rodger to leaven the bread, taking him onto the staff. His verses appeared on the back page of the paper under the heading, in Gothic script, of 'Original Poetry'. One of Sandy's satirical ditties was 'The Muckin' o' Geordie's Byre'. Ostensibly about a lazy farmer, with a byre and a farm in dire need of a good muck out and clean up, in reality it was poking fun at George III and his son, the prince regent. The 'poor body' in the following lines is the king. His deteriorating mental health was why his son served in his stead.

> At last the poor body grew silly,
> Or rather, gaed wrang in the head,
> So they made his auld son – a queer billie –

Half factor, half laird in his stead;
But he grew sae drunken and crazy,
He dosed [*sic*] for hale days by the fire,
Or boozed wi' some fat-hippit hizzey,
An' ne'er wair'd a thocht on the Byre.[14]

Glasgow's radical newspaper lasted for eleven weeks before the print shop in Glasgow's Trongate where it was produced was raided and Gilbert McLeod arrested on a charge of sedition. That was the end of the *Spirit of the Union*. Tried and found guilty, its editor was sentenced to be transported to Australia for a period of five years. Although he was granted a pardon before the five years had passed, he decided to stay on in Sydney. His wife and children were allowed to join him a year after he got there.

He died tragically young, at the age of only thirty-seven. A few precious copies of the *Spirit of the Union* survive, held at the Mitchell Library and Glasgow University Special Collections, so his words and his passion for radical reform live on. The pen is mightier than the sword.

CHAPTER 8

Keep Your Eye on Paisley

Saturday, 11 September 1819

The city of Paisley celebrates its textile heritage in the names of its streets. Near the beautiful twelfth-century abbey lie Gauze Street, Silk Street, Cotton Street and Incle Street, an incle being a type of small handloom. In its nineteenth-century heyday as a centre for the production of textiles, Paisley was famous for the spinning of thread and the weaving of shawls. Inspired by originals from Kashmir, brought or sent home as presents from Britons in India, these gave their name to the Paisley pattern, the classic curved tear-drop design in jewel-bright colours.

Paisley was also famous for its radical politics and its intellectual weavers and poets. The most famous of these weaver-poets was Robert Tannahill, whose statue stands in the Abbey Close, in front of Paisley town hall. The well-loved folksong, 'The Wild Mountain Thyme/Will ye Go Lassie, Go' was based on Tannahill's poem, 'The Braes o' Balquhidder'. Sadly, prone to depression, he took his own life by drowning in 1810. The house where he was born and lived his too-short life is still there in Queen Street in Paisley.

Not far from Tannahill's statue stands one of his friends and another of Paisley's famous sons. Alexander Wilson too was a weaver and poet. He wrote poems inspired by romantic love and the beauties of nature. He also penned satirical verse highlighting the unfairness of the treatment the weavers were getting from the men who gave them the work. Several of his targets accused him of libel. He was arrested and forced to publicly burn some of his writings.[1] Short of money and prospects, he emigrated to America where he became known as the father of American ornithology.[2] He is said to have inspired John James Audubon, who went on to write the iconic and gorgeously illustrated *Birds of America*. A copy of it is one of the greatest treasures of the Mitchell Library in Glasgow.

Like their radical brothers and sisters in nearby Glasgow and elsewhere, Paisley's radicals kept in contact with those in England who shared their views, especially just over the Scottish/English border at Carlisle, and farther south at Nottingham and Manchester, where the most infamous public meeting of this period of unrest and turbulent politics took place.

It began as a huge but determinedly peaceful demonstration. It was held on the Sabbath, and many of the tens of thousands who walked to St Peter's Fields that day wore their Sunday best. As ever, the aim was to emphasise the respectability of the radicals. They were calling for peaceful reform, not bloody revolution as had been unleashed in France almost thirty years before.[3]

Via their flags and banners, and by a speech from Henry Hunt, nicknamed Orator Hunt, they set out their demands: universal suffrage; civil and religious liberty; annual parliaments elected by secret ballot. People were cheerful, enjoying a rare day out, straining to hear what was being said. Until the nervous local magistrates panicked at the sheer number of people and ordered the militia to charge the crowd, resulting in fifteen deaths and over 650 injuries. People throughout Britain were shocked to the core by such violence being meted out to unarmed civilians. It wasn't only radicals and reformers who felt that shock.

One of the biggest responses against the violence at Peterloo came at a meeting near Paisley a month after the Manchester massacre. Upwards of 15,000 people gathered at Meikleriggs Moor, then just outside the town.[4] The authorities issued dire warnings to anyone thinking of attending. Particular attention would be paid to anyone carrying radical flags, which 'were imbued with a special significance'.[5]

The flags of the Peterloo protesters had been a special target for the militia. 'Have at their flags!'[6] It was as if the soldiers were going after an enemy standard as a trophy. Flags and banners were also dangerous, hugely influential in communicating a message, as they did at many pro-democracy meetings in Scotland.

The activities of Scotland's radicals were well reported in several newspapers of the time, both north and south of the border. The *Westmorland Advertiser and Kendal Chronicle* wrote up the disturbances at Paisley in their edition of Saturday, 25 September 1819, a fortnight after the event. As was common at the time, much if not all of the front page was devoted to adverts.

William Green was offering *A Description of the Lakes & Mountains in Cumberland, Westmorland & Lancashire*, in two volumes, with sketches. The cost was one guinea for the two books with a map and twelve prints. If you wanted a map and twenty-four prints, 'on a superior Paper', the cost was two guineas.

A mansion house called Armistead two miles from Settle, in a 'genteel' neighbourhood, was to be sold by auction. It came with nearly 400 acres and 'an excellent pew' in the local church. Gentlemen with families might like to know the house was very close to the 'ancient Grammar School of Giggleswick, which is now in high repute, under able educators'.

The newspaper masthead describes it as 'A Commercial, Agricultural, Literary, & Political Journal'. Of the five columns on the front page, the two dealing with the latest news are devoted to what had happened at Paisley on Saturday, 11 September 1819, and an associated disturbance in Glasgow. They acknowledge that the report had first appeared in the *Glasgow Chronicle*.[7]

Although the magistrates of Paisley had banned the carrying of flags, there were plenty to be seen at Meikleriggs. The words they bore varied. 'Justice, Liberty. Magna Charta [sic], Liberty, Civil and Religious. Annual Parliaments. Abhor the inhuman butchery at Manchester.' The platform party were dressed in mourning, in honour of those who had been killed at Peterloo, and their flags were edged in black.[8]

Before the speeches began there was music from a marching band. 'The band from Neilston came into the field playing "Scots wha hae wi' Wallace bled," and other national airs.' Then the speeches began. (The 'preses' was the chairman of a meeting.) 'Mr

Taylor was chosen preses, and began the business of the meeting by enjoining attention and good order. He then stated that the reformers had no wish for disturbance and revolution; they merely wished an end put to all unnecessary places, pensions and sinecures, and a proper share in the legislature of their country.'

Taylor went on to refer to 'the inhuman butchery' at Manchester, as did all the other speakers who followed him at Meikleriggs Moor. They didn't hold back, speaking of Manchester's magistrates, 'who gorge their bloated carcases on the blood of the artisan'. Another speaker observed that 'the British sword had been drawn upon starving men and fainting women; [. . .] and will you allow your brethren to be murdered without raising your voice against the infernal deed? No! sooner shall the lake wash Benlomond [*sic*] from its eternal site, than the sons of Caledonia shall be silent.'

Before the meeting closed, a collection was made for the injured and suffering of Manchester. A little of the money went astray. 'Some light-fingered gentry honoured the meeting with their presence.' There was a bit of a panic when someone yelled out, 'Hussars!' People were jumpy, fearful what had happened at Manchester could happen elsewhere, but it was a false alarm. Order was restored and everyone left Meikleriggs Moor.

The Neilston band and many others made it home without being molested. Or did they? A couple of months later, Gilbert McLeod asked via the columns of the *Spirit of the Union* if anyone could confirm or deny that members of the band had been arrested for playing 'Scots Wha Hae'. Those heading in the other direction, back through Paisley to get to their homes in Glasgow, definitely didn't get away easily. When they reached Paisley High Street they found special constables lining both sides of the road.

Near the cross, one of those constables grabbed one of the flags being carried by the radicals. Fighting broke out, stones were thrown and windows were broken. Shortly after 10 p.m., the Riot Act was read and the cavalry sent for from Glasgow. They cantered in about one o'clock in the morning. 'When they arrived, the people gave them a hearty cheer, and immediately dispersed.'[9] Presumably those were ironic cheers.

The trouble was not yet over, breaking out sporadically over the next few days. On Sunday evening the Riot Act was read three times before nine o'clock.

> Our Sovereign Lord the King chargeth and com-
> mandeth all persons, being assembled, immediately
> to disperse themselves, and peaceably depart to their
> habitations, or to their lawful business, upon the
> pains contained in the Act made in the first year of
> King George the First, for preventing tumults and
> riotous assemblies. God save the King.[10]

The trouble spilled over into Glasgow on the Monday night, with lamps broken and shops broken into and looted. The *Glasgow Herald* reported that 'John Cochrane, spirit dealer, had his house completely emptied of rum'.[11]

The advice to 'keep your eye on Paisley' is attributed to Benjamin Disraeli, who was twice Tory prime minister later in the nineteenth century. It is taken to mean that Paisley is a place where things happen. You never know what the Paisley buddies are going to do next.

The trouble which followed the meeting at Meikleriggs Moor died away, but not for long.

CHAPTER 9

'We're All Radicals Here!'

Autumn 1819–Spring 1820

Another phrase associated with Paisley is the response which a weaver in Maxwellton in the Renfrewshire town is said to have given to constables looking for radicals. 'You'd better take all of us. We're all radicals here!'[1] One of those Paisley radicals was John Parkhill. In the memoir he published forty years after the events of 1819–20, he described his involvement. Looking back on his younger self with gentle mockery, he wrote about the wild enthusiasm of other young men.

The first political meeting Parkhill ever attended was the huge but peaceful one at Thrushgrove in 1816. After that he began attending regular meetings in Paisley. There was a lot of discussion and plenty of what he called speechifying. As time wore on, Parkhill observed that many younger radicals were beginning to grow impatient with all this talk. What was needed was action. Their eagerness for a fight was clear, even if they had not yet fully realised what the bloody reality of that might be.

> Training after nightfall became quite common, and officers, if not appointed, were talked of. Pikes, guns, and pistols were getting in readiness, and, over and above drill, large public meetings added to the general agitation, whilst the fatal meeting at Manchester on the 18th of August, 1819, was a culminating plan in the insurrectionary movement.[2]

In the autumn and winter of 1819–20, drilling and training were happening all over, in Milngavie, Balfron, Kilsyth and other places. Janet Hamilton of Langloan, wrote about it. In her mid-twenties at the time, she was already the mother of five children. She was only thirteen when she married her shoemaker husband John in 1808. This was perfectly legal at the time. Scots Law followed Roman law, allowing girls to marry from the age of twelve, boys from the age of fourteen. However, such marriages were increasingly rare, and the bride's youth shocked many people. She and her husband had a long marriage and ten children: three daughters and seven sons. She outlived three of her children.[3]

Janet had no formal education but she learned to read before she was five years old and never stopped. 'When about eight, I found to my great joy, on the loom of an intellectual weaver, a copy of Milton's *Paradise Lost* and a volume of Allan Ramsay's *Poems*. I carried them off in triumph to the kitchen, returning day after day to devour the contents.'[4] Her father was a member of the village library, and so she was able to read widely. The books she read opened up the world to her. She loved the poems of Robert Fergusson and Robert Burns and she read her Bible too. Her mother disapproved of her daughter reading poetry and novels and would sometimes threaten to burn such books. Janet developed a technique to stay her mother's hand: 'a good fit of crying'.[5]

Janet was not a supporter of the radicals. She allowed that the working class of which she was a proud member was suffering great distress. She admitted the government was 'not very wise and good' but she was horrified by what she understood the radical programme to be. No taxes, property to be seized and equally divided, religion to be reformed, and all this to be achieved by force of arms, including a radical army marching on London. As she put it, this army would grow larger, 'in snow-ball fashion, gathering as they went along'. She didn't think much of the local Coatbridge and Airdrie radicals, or their marching and drilling. Nor did she pull her punches when describing them:

> And a sorry sight it was to see bands of these would-be insurgents, with their lean, pale faces,

unwashed, unshaved and uncombed, thinly clad, and out at knees and elbows, with reckless and defiant looks, come trampling along to the sound of a couple of fifes, these frequently being their only musical accompaniments; and many 'a banner with a strange device' was borne aloft by them in their disorderly marches through our village to their usual place of meeting, a little to the eastward.[6]

At the front of the column someone would carry the cap of liberty on a pole or willow branches fastened together. This symbolised unity and strength. One flag bore the legend 'Liberty or Death', another read 'Bread or Blood, and no Taxes'.[7]

In Paisley, Parkhill recorded that many of the young men involved in drilling thought it was great fun. Some 'spoke of blood and wounds like old campaigners'.[8] Quite a lot of them were actually young campaigners, having served in the army during the Napoleonic Wars.

James Parkhill recounted that a meeting was held in Nottingham, to which John Neil of Paisley went as a delegate from the Scottish radicals. He was a weaver who lived and worked in the town's Maxwellton Street, where the disembodied voice had taunted the constables by shouting out that they were all radicals. Neil came home with the message that Scotland's radicals were not to rise until they had word that 200,000 English radicals had taken to the field. This might seem like a huge number, but radicals were active in many places throughout the British Isles, and had been for some time.

There is evidence that a rising was being planned in 1817. A letter exists from this period detailing how many men could be expected to come from large English cities like Birmingham. The numbers easily add up to 200,000.[9] This proposed rising came to fruition only in Derbyshire, in the Pentrich Rising in November 1817.[10] In April 1820, preparations were made and communicated to the rank and file by the leaders of the Scottish radicals. Some of what they said had the opposite effect to what was intended. Enthusiasm for the fight was tempered by fear of the possible consequences.

Our leaders were very industrious, and ever and anon
were telling us of officers they had secured; that sur-
geons and a medical staff were also in a state of great
forwardness, and that even women were employed to
prepare dressings for the hospitals. These last things
were not altogether very palatable to many of us.
They indicated blood and gunshot wounds, and [. . .]
it appeared we were approaching a stern reality, and
that a cataract of horrid carnage was in sight . . .[11]

Despite the fear, a date was fixed for a general strike and rising.
This was to start on the first Sunday of December 1819. It didn't
happen, probably because the Scottish radicals were waiting for
their English counterparts to act, while the English were waiting
for the Scots to take the lead. What did happen, on 1 November
1819, was yet another big march and meeting at Clayknowes in
Glasgow.

CHAPTER 10

Heroines and a Hero of Liberty:
The Clayknowes and Dundee Meetings

1 November and 10 November 1819

At the Clayknowes meeting, held off Glasgow's Gallowgate at the beginning of November 1819, the uselessness of sending petitions to the prince regent was overtly stated in one of the resolutions accepted by acclamation from an 'immense crowd'.[1] Gilbert McLeod of the *Spirit of the Union* reckoned 30,000 people were there.[2] A large proportion came from union societies in Glasgow and the surrounding towns and villages.

> Most gladly would this meeting have presented their humble petitions at the feet of His Royal Highness soliciting his intervention on their behalf ... but from the neglect and even contempt with which their former petitions ... have been treated ... they prefer the only alternative that remains, an appeal to the people. Let us turn our attention wholly towards the attainment of universal suffrage, annual parliaments and election by ballot for only these can be ours and our Country's salvation.[3]

Even so, the meeting did start with the band playing 'God Save the King', during which many people respectfully removed their hats.[4] Not many republicans here, then. Or maybe it was advisable to play that anthem, which had also been played at the Rutherglen meeting.

These mass meetings were never exclusively male gatherings. The *Glasgow Herald* was no friend to the radicals. Yet its report on the proceedings praises the peacefulness of the meeting and notes the important role played by women. 'Eight caps of liberty and about forty flags have been displayed, several of which were carried to the hustings by well-dressed females.' The paper reported that some were carrying babies in their arms. Briefly mentioning meetings being held on the same day 'at London, Glasgow, and elsewhere', it described the estimated 1,500 to 2,000 people attending the London meeting as being 'of the lowest description'.[5] Given its observation that the female participants at Glasgow were well-dressed and the meeting peaceful, it would seem the reporter considered the reformers in Glasgow not to be of the lowest sort.

There is a great sense of immediacy in the *Glasgow Herald* report, reprinted in London's *Morning Chronicle* a few days later. It's headed 'Twelve o'clock' and concludes with a rather breathless, 'We have not time for other particulars.' It packed a lot of information into a short article, all the same.

> A numerous procession from the west end of the town, probably from Anderston, has just passed the Cross, preceded by a band of music, and accompanied with several flags. In the centre of the procession, a cap of liberty was carried alternately by two good looking young women. As they passed down the Gallowgate they met a squadron of the hussars coming up, when both parties passed each other in perfect good humour, and without the smallest apparent trepidation even in the heroines of liberty.[6]

Reports of radical meetings often describe what the female participants looked like. They occasionally give a brief description of the physical appearance of the men but seldom comment on whether they were handsome or not. Funny, that. The idea that the female marchers and the hussars were giving one another the eye might raise a smile. It is easy to imagine the famous Glasgow banter being batted to and fro.

The Clayknowes meeting went on for several hours. There were the resolutions and lots of music, with one band 'completely dressed in very handsome tartans. [. . .] On passing the barracks, they played the "British Grenadiers".'[7] Whether this was an ironic or a diplomatic gesture is not recorded.

The reference to 'very handsome tartans' is interesting. The band clearly saw the importance of looking, as well as sounding, good. This was more than two years before the prince regent, by then King George IV, made his famous trip to Edinburgh in 1822. Orchestrated by Sir Walter Scott, the city exploded into a riot of tartan and Highland dress, fixing the image of Scotland as a Highland one forever more. Some modern Scots dismiss much of this as 'tartanry'. The wearing of tartan had been banned after the Jacobite Rising of 1745 and was only lifted in 1782. Yet many nineteenth-century Scots, Lowlanders as well as Highlanders, were clearly proud and happy to wear tartan.

The Clayknowes meeting passed eleven resolutions. 'With feelings of the deepest horror and commiseration', there was condemnation of 'the late transactions at Manchester'. There were the familiar calls for universal suffrage, annual elections and voting to be carried out by secret ballot. There was the insistence that governments had 'to be guided and directed by the whole energy of their constituent members, THE PEOPLE'. There was condemnation too of the misery in which so many were living, a fact 'as notorious as the sun at noon-day'. The very first resolution put to the crowd at Clayknowes was this: 'That the true principle of all Government is the strength, happiness, freedom, and security of the whole people.'[8]

On Wednesday, 10 November 1819, another pro-reform meeting was held, this time in Dundee. An estimated 10,000 people came to the open space of the Magdalen Yard Green, a gentle grassy slope running down to the River Tay. It remains that today. The chairman of the meeting was George Kinloch of Kinloch. He was a local laird and landowner, instrumental in the development of the harbour at Dundee. A friend of Major Cartwright, Kinloch was also very much in favour of parliamentary reform.[9] The poster advertising the Dundee meeting read:

> A MEETING of the INHABITANTS of DUNDEE and NEIGHBOURHOOD will be held at the MAGDALEN YARD, to take into consideration the present STATE of the COUNTRY, with a view to suggest the means most likely to lead to a REFORM of ABUSES and an alleviation of the distress with which the working classes in particular are at present nearly overwhelmed.
>
> Also to express their sentiments on the late *unprovoked, cruel, and cowardly attack made on the people at Manchester,* while peaceably and lawfully assembled for a constitutional purpose.
>
> A COLLECTION will be made at the entries to the place of meeting, in aid of the fund for obtaining justice for the Manchester sufferers.
>
> Dundee, November 1, 1819.[10]

The working people of Dundee collected £16 for Manchester, a sum to which George Kinloch added £10. Concerned that the meeting should pass off peacefully, he had asked people not to bring flags and banners. Some did, all the same. They carried various slogans. 'We only want our rights in a peaceable and constitutional manner. For the sufferers at Manchester. The voice of the People is irresistible.' Other people carried poles from which hung broken tea pots, pieces of broken wine glasses, pipes and snuff boxes. This was quite common at radical meetings. They symbolised habits which some radicals believed should be rejected, both because the government taxed such products and also because the people should demonstrate they were not in thrall to such bad habits.

Addressing the crowd, George Kinloch warned them to be on their guard against government spies, 'wolves in Sheep's clothing'. Everyone knew Sidmouth had at least one spy in Dundee. The best defence against such people was to always behave well and to refuse to be led towards violent action. He reiterated the calls for universal suffrage – he did specify universal male suffrage – annual parliaments and secret ballots. Appalled by what had happened at Peterloo, he spoke passionately.

He went too far in one of the resolutions agreed on at Dundee. 'We are of opinion that, in preventing the voice of the people from reaching the Throne, the said Lord Sidmouth has been guilty of the highest species of treason, namely treason against the people and that dismissal from the Office which he so unworthily fills would be far too lenient a punishment for him.'[11]

Two weeks later, George Kinloch was arrested on a charge of sedition. On 10 December, a month after the Magdalen Green meeting, he wrote to his wife Helen from Edinburgh. He was hopeful the case against him would not come to trial. He finished his letter with a PS. 'Streets covered with snow and damnation cold.'[12]

Two days later, he became all too aware that rumours of the planned December 1819 radical rising being imminent were not going to help his case at all. He thought he would very probably be found guilty and spend time in prison. Sending his kindest love to his wife 'and the lassies', he told her that Edinburgh was still 'desperately cold and streets covered with snow'. Discovering the punishment being contemplated against him was transportation to Botany Bay, he made good his escape from Edinburgh. As a result, he was declared an outlaw.

He spent time in France before one of his daughters secured a pardon for him. She did so directly, approaching George IV when he visited Edinburgh in 1822. In 1832 Kinloch become MP for Dundee in the first parliament elected after the Great Reform Act. He did not serve long, dying two months after the parliament first assembled. His body was taken home to Meigle in Perthshire for burial.[13] His statue stands in Reform Square in Dundee.

CHAPTER 11

Web of Deceit

1816–1820

The world of secrets, spies, informers and *agents provocateurs* is a strand which weaves its tangled way through the story of Scotland's Radical Rising. As with the warp and weft of a length of cloth, sometimes it can be hard to unpick. The conviction that many, if not all, of the radicals of 1820 were the victims of entrapment by government agents is an enduring one, a belief held by many people at the time and since. Encouraged to take up arms and ready themselves to take violent action, they were then 'betrayed by infamous spies'.[1] It was believed the government had employed these mysterious characters to flush the radicals out into the open. Identify as many as possible, hit them hard and the troublesome reform movement could be dealt a body blow and a mortal wound.

Orator Hunt warned radical reformers in Scotland and throughout Britain to be on their guard and be careful what they said in public. He suggested there might be a spy in every tavern, sitting quietly in a dimly-lit corner, listening to everything being said. 'I am induced to urge this caution, from the knowledge which I have, that spies and informers are abroad, and sent amongst you. The system of espionage is now carried to such an extent, that there is not a taproom or a pot-house in the Metropolis, or scarcely in the country, without one or two of these worthies being in nightly attendance.'[2]

Hunt believed these spies were all reporting back to Home Secretary Sidmouth. 'These monsters in human form are hired and paid to make plots, and entrap the unwary into a participation of their hellish plans.'

Peter Mackenzie was a journalist who served with the Glasgow Sharpshooters in 1820 but later became an impassioned defender of the radicals. He wrote copiously about them and the spy system he claimed was working against them. Acting with the best intentions, Mackenzie sought to prove the Scottish radicals of 1820 had been sincere but innocent dupes of *agents provocateurs*. This allowed him to cast the London government and the Scottish authorities as the heartless villains of the piece, leading honest working men to their doom. Mackenzie was not alone in holding this point of view. It allowed for the radical martyrs, the three who were hanged and the nineteen who were transported to Australia after the trials which followed the rising, to become ever more exalted, transforming them into almost Christlike figures.

Unfortunately, it also took away their agency, portraying them as politically naïve, helpless pawns in a dangerous game whose rules they did not understand or were incapable of grasping. In his writings, Peter Mackenzie refers to them as simpletons and poor deluded dupes. Read the letters of John Baird, Andrew Hardie and the memoirs of other radicals and it is clear they were intelligent and quick-witted men, well capable of logical thought and deduction, even if their passion for their cause, the burning desire to bring about democracy, blinded them at a few crucial moments, leading them down dangerous paths.

There was probably some truth to the belief that a few spies helped foment the unrest, yet to put such wholesale blame onto government agents simply isn't accurate. Spies and *agents provocateurs* were certainly active in England and Scotland, especially in Manchester and the surrounding area in the run-up to Peterloo. They are mentioned in Viscount Sidmouth's papers and other official correspondence. Some were designated by coded initials.[3] Others signed their letters offering information on the radicals with their own names. A couple of the spies active in England became notorious. One went by the alias of William Oliver. His real name was Richards.[4] It was he who betrayed the radicals in Derbyshire's Pentrich Rising.

Twenty years after the events, an editorial in the *Liverpool Mercury* described the febrile atmosphere of the times. 'About twenty years ago, it required some spirit to venture to attend public political meetings, surrounded by hired Government spies, ready to catch at every word that was uttered.'[5]

In his masterly account of radical reform movements in Scotland at this time, William Roach suggests there were fewer government agents north of the border. He argued this on the basis that if the country had been 'infested with spies, had the people been persuaded by government agents to commit treason, many more leaders would have been captured and more successful prosecutions would have resulted. But as the Lord Advocate complained, the principal leaders had been allowed to escape owing to the inefficiency of the police, and presumably, the absence of efficient spies.'[6]

There is compelling evidence of some informants and a handful of spies and *agents provocateurs* in Scotland. Most are shadowy figures. This was what their roles required. Step out of the wings, make a suggestion here, drop an idea there, vanish off-stage again. The name of one man who failed to follow these rules of the game became a byword for betrayal of the Scottish radicals. He turns up by his own name in a letter from Glasgow Lord Provost Kirkman Finlay to Viscount Sidmouth, written in November 1820. Finlay served two terms as Lord Provost, from 1812 to 1814 and in 1818.[7]

Alexander Baillie Richmond was a weaver from Pollokshaws. Now a suburb on Glasgow's south side, in the first decades of the nineteenth century it was another of those weaving villages which lay outside the city. Presumably in a search for work, he moved north of the river to Anderston, becoming one of the organisers of the weavers' strike of 1812. At some point after this dispute ended, he turned his coat and started working against his former comrades.

Provost Finlay had taken a liking to Richmond at a meeting between the weavers and the magistrates in 1812. This might seem odd, given the obvious social gulf between the two men, but Sandy Richmond had ambitions to be a businessman, buying and selling cloth rather than having to sit down at a loom and make it. He had ambitions in other directions too, applying to Robert Owen at New Lanark for a post as a schoolmaster for the children who lived and worked there. He thought the annual salary of £50 was not very high, although whether he turned down the job or Robert Owen turned him down is not clear.

Like many weavers, Richmond was also hard-up, with a wife and two children to support. That Provost Finlay saw he might make use of him seems highly likely, although the use of informers could be a two-edged sword. They might well exaggerate the scale of what they were finding out with the aim of making themselves more valuable to their handlers.

Richmond pretended to still be a radical reformer and began trying to tempt other men into more extreme behaviour. It is unclear whether he was playing the role of an *agent provocateur* under instructions from his paymasters or if he was taking action on his own initiative, hoping to earn more money from his secret activities.

People soon became suspicious of Richmond. One giveaway was when he seemed suddenly to come into money. Stuart Buchanan was a weaver who had known Richmond from the time of the weavers' strike of 1812.[8] They both worked in Pollokshaws and subsequently and separately moved north of the Clyde to Glasgow. In 1816 Richmond, his wife and their two young children were renting a room on the floor above where Stuart Buchanan worked.

Buchanan remembered the Richmonds were in a 'state of nearly starvation', and that Mrs Richmond was a 'poor broken-hearted woman. [. . .] She went about in rags, and crying for victuals'. If the family really was going hungry, Richmond might well have been desperate enough to betray his friends and fellow radicals by becoming a government informer and agent. He got Buchanan to swear an oath to fight for the radical cause and instructed him how to secretly communicate this to others, how to ask, 'are you one of us?' 'The way was, draw the hand over the face and grip the left ear.'[9] Very cloak and dagger, though surely an odd, noticeable gesture. Sandy Richmond was a good talker. The oath he persuaded weaver Andrew McKinlay and some others to take was equally dramatic. Whether he composed it or not is disputed by some researchers into this subject.

In the awful presence of God, I, Andrew McKinlay, do solemnly swear, that I will persevere in my endeavouring to form a Brotherhood of affection amongst Britons of every description, who are considered worthy of confidence: and that I will persevere in my endeavours to obtain for all the people in Great Britain and Ireland, not disqualified by crimes or insanity, the elective franchise at the age of twenty-one, with free and equal representation, and annual Parliaments: and that I will support the same to the utmost of my power, either by moral or physical strength, or force, as the case may require. And I do farther swear, that neither hopes, fears, rewards, or punishments, shall induce me to inform on, or give evidence against any member or members collectively or individually, for any act or expression, done or made, in or out, in this or similar societies, under the punishment of Death to be inflicted on me, by any member or members of such societies. So help me God, and keep me stedfast [*sic*].[10]

Another weaver, Robert Craig of Parkhead, was at the 1816 meeting at Thrushgrove and met Alexander Richmond in the Trongate in Glasgow a month later. Very much in favour of the peaceful petitioning of parliament in the hope of bringing improvements to the lives of working people, Craig sat on the Calton radical committee which was now fairly openly advocating this. He resented Alexander Richmond's effort to push him into a secret society of radicals who might be willing to use violence to achieve their aims. He described Richmond as a 'demon'.[11]

Sandy Richmond does not appear to have had a subtle gene. Or much wisdom or self-awareness. He and his family began to appear ever more affluent. They had new furniture. The children who had previously been wearing little more than rags were now going around dressed 'like gentlemen's children'.[12] Richmond was accused of running a ring of spies 'whose members did not know each other', that is, if he was running a spy ring rather than operating as a lone-wolf agent, he was doing so on a need-to-know basis.

He was given money to use for bribing others, although he seems to have kept most of what he received for himself and his family. In 1817, his activities bore fruit. Andrew McKinlay, John Keith and a number of other Glasgow radical leaders were arrested on charges of the illegal taking of oaths and incitement to rebellion.[13] One of the men Richmond had bribed for information was John Campbell, a poor weaver. He was to give evidence against McKinlay. He had been offered a bribe in exchange, one which would have changed his and his family's life enormously for the better, a regular and well-paid job as an exciseman. The prospect must have been so tempting but his conscience got the better of him. Sensationally, he told the story of the bribe in open court. This rendered any evidence he might give against the defendants unreliable, and the trial collapsed.[14]

People began to realise Alexander Richmond had been involved in all of this, and that he had instigated the swearing of the blood-curdling oaths. The editor of the *Glasgow Chronicle* recalled going from his home to his office one morning in 1816 and seeing words chalked in very large letters on a wall: 'Beware of Richmond the Spy!'[15] The spy and his family had to leave Glasgow.

It might have seemed that he was now no longer useful as a secret agent. Yet in November 1820, seven months after the radical rising was over, Glasgow Lord Provost Kirkman Finlay wrote to Home Secretary Sidmouth about him.[16] He advised Sidmouth that Richmond would be satisfied with £750. This was three years after the events of 1817. The government might have been very slow payers, or could Richmond have been working undercover in another part of the country? The problem with researching spies and *agents provocateurs* is that by their very nature, veils of secrecy shield their activities.

By the end of 1819, the government in London was well aware trouble was brewing in the west of Scotland. They could hardly not be, with meetings taking place all over, in England and Wales too. As John Parkhill of Paisley observed, existing grievances were given added passion after the Manchester massacre. On 29 October 1819, a month after the big meeting held in protest against Peterloo at Meikleriggs Moor, William Rae, Lord Advocate of Scotland, wrote to Viscount Sidmouth, the Home Secretary in London.[17]

Rae had intelligence from Glasgow that the radicals in Renfrew and Lanark were holding meetings. The local committees which had grown out of the union societies such as those in Strathaven and Kilmarnock met regularly throughout the closing months of 1819. Each sent a delegate to the central committee, which met once a month in Glasgow. The government feared this underground network of radicals was plotting in secret, ready to use physical force to achieve their aims. The recollections of Paisley radical John Parkhill bear this out.

The drilling and training increased. Groups of men marching up and down and practising weapons drill wasn't always easy to hide. Indeed, there were reports in various newspapers about this. In Carlisle people claimed they were hearing pistol shots at night. Yet Parkhill did not believe the authorities had much detailed information about the radicals' intentions or any real idea of how many people were actively involved.

In the same letter in which the Lord Advocate told Sidmouth about radical meetings in Renfrew and Glasgow, Rae gave the Home Secretary another piece of news. Major-General Sir Thomas Bradford, commander-in-chief of the British army in Scotland, was now in Glasgow. Rae was sure Bradford would do everything he could 'to secure tranquillity and give confidence to the Magistrates'.

Rae wrote that he himself was not alarmed. The leaders of the reform movement were 'averse to any disturbance, and only want to ascertain their own strength'. However, if there were large gatherings, there were bound to be some individuals who would want to cause trouble.[18] Rae assured the Home Secretary that if anything violent was about to kick off, he would soon know about it, although the radical central committee, which met once a month in Glasgow, was supposed to do so in secret. Someone must have spilled the beans. Or maybe walls had ears. At Rae's request, Brown, the commander of Edinburgh's police force, dispatched two of his men through to Glasgow to infiltrate these radical circles. The undercover policemen hailed originally from the west of

Scotland so the accent in which they spoke would have helped get them accepted. Brown too was from the west. Coincidentally, John Parkhill had known him in Paisley when they were both boys.[19]

Lord Advocate Rae and the authorities in Edinburgh did not have much confidence in the Glasgow police force, which was why men from Edinburgh's police force were deployed as spies. As Rae informed Sidmouth by letter in October 1819, they were 'now members of the Secret Committee'. He wrote that he was sure the Home Secretary would keep this information to himself. Rae did not trust the discretion of Glasgow's town council either. 'Were it known to any one of the Magistrates of Glasgow I am persuaded it would get abroad and these men's lives would not only be put in peril but this most necessary source of intelligence would be lost.'[20]

On 22 February 1820, delegates to the not-so-secret Glasgow committee held a meeting at a pub in the Gallowgate. One of those delegates was a man by the name of King. He left almost as soon as he got there. Could he have been one of the undercover policemen sent through from Edinburgh?

Ten minutes after the meeting started, a maidservant ran into the room, shouting out a frantic warning. The police were coming. With no time to escape, the delegates were arrested and put into prison. The news of the arrests reached Paisley, seven miles from Glasgow, two hours later. Someone must have leapt up onto a fast horse. Although at first there was panic, reassurance followed. People reminded themselves and one another any documents the police had seized would only be scraps of paper and 'somewhat hieroglyphical'.[21]

Radicals were careful not to put too much in writing, so the conspirators were probably right to think that not much knowledge would be derived from what the police had seized. It is odd though that none of the memoirs of the Radical Rising mention delegates from local committees not coming home from Glasgow that day. What subsequently happened to the twenty-six members of the secret committee is a bit of a mystery. It provides plenty of fodder for conspiracy theorists.

There is a division of opinion here. Some believe the committee members were kept in prison for months. That might be one reason why the rising in Scotland was so uncoordinated, with those who took action seemingly not knowing what others were doing. Yet there is a mention of one member of the secret committee being back in Paisley quite soon afterwards, before the general strike and rising began.[22] Perhaps those scrappy hieroglyphs didn't provide enough evidence against them and the powers-that-be were scared of looking foolish if they brought a case against them. A lot of what was going on was dependent on who was going to blink first.

In his memoirs, government officer Henry Smith recalled being sent to arrest the radical delegates at the committee meeting in February 1820. Word spread of the arrest and a group of people began attacking the soldiers escorting the prisoners to the bridewell (prison) in Duke Street with stones, 'flying among us half as bad as grapeshot'.[23] So they didn't go quietly. People knew the arrests had taken place. To theorise that all twenty-six members of the committee were *agents provocateurs* is just not credible. If they were, why would the meeting have been raided? There would have been no need.

The Paisley radicals began to amass pike heads and pike shafts, although John Parkhill recalled people were reluctant to keep their share of them in their houses. Too incriminating, if the authorities took it into their heads to mount raids on the homes of known or suspected radicals. Meanwhile, the magistrates and the military were making their plans to meet the threat. Parkhill felt they had a false idea of their strength and were, '. . . like all the rest of the authorities, haunted by the idea that the radicals were a most formidable body of men, and if not looked after would some fine morning overturn the state; when, in fact, we could not have made ourselves masters of the porter's lodge of Dumbarton Castle'.[24]

The day after the Glasgow meeting there was also a mass arrest in London. Masterminded by Arthur Thistlewood, the plan of the Cato Street conspirators was to surprise government ministers at one of their regular Cabinet dinners in London and kill them all. A provisional government would then be set up following the principles of the French Revolution.[25]

The location was to be the house of Lord Harrowby in Grosvenor Square. As a basis for their operations, the conspirators rented a dilapidated stable in Cato Street, near the Edgware Road. This group too had been infiltrated by government spies. The conspirators' base was stormed by the Bow Street Runners. In the course of this chaotic raid, Thistlewood ran one of the Runners through with a sword and killed him.

It was a tense time. George III had died on 29 January 1820. The prince regent had become King George IV. Unpopular, and notorious for his hedonistic lifestyle, he seemed to care not one iota that so many of his subjects were starving. Attempts by local magistrates to include those subjects in the proclamations to celebrate the accession of the new king backfired in many places.

In Cupar in Fife, local radicals turned down free ale and porter. In Lanark, a large crowd attacked the Lanarkshire yeomanry. The general election which had to take place after the death of a monarch took place between 6 March and 13 April. In Scotland, the public gatherings as part of this grew rowdy in Aberdeen, Elgin and Renfrewshire.[26]

The scene was set for an almighty explosion of frustration and rage.

PART II
One Week in April

CHAPTER 12

Liberty or Death

Saturday, 1 April–Sunday, 2 April 1820

Moving stealthily through the night and into the early hours of the following morning, they put the notices up under cover of darkness. By the time people were making their way to church on the morning of Sunday, 2 April 1820, the *Address to the Inhabitants of Great Britain & Ireland* was everywhere. Produced in secret in a printer's shop in Glasgow, just over 2,000 copies were run off and fixed to churchyard gates, public wells and the gable ends of houses and taverns in Glasgow, Paisley, Duntocher in Dunbartonshire, Balfron in Stirlingshire, Johnstone in Renfrewshire, Strathaven in Lanarkshire and many more places besides across Central Scotland and Ayrshire.

Printed in a selection of elegant fonts on cream-coloured paper about the size of modern A4, the *Address* called on people to go on strike and devote themselves to recovering 'those Rights which distinguishes the FREEMAN from the SLAVE; viz: that of giving consent to the laws by which he is to be governed'.

Declaring that: 'The wishes of all good Men are with us', the *Address* called on Britons to raise the Standard of Liberty. 'LIBERTY or DEATH is our *Motto*, and We have sworn to return in *triumph* – or return no more!' It was dated at the foot, 'Glasgow, 1st April, 1820. By order of the Committee of Organization for forming a PROVISIONAL GOVERNMENT'.[1]

Those who had set their faces against reform had suspected for quite some time that a violent storm was about to break above their heads. That didn't make it any less frightening when the thunder boomed and the lightning flashed and crackled. The freeholders of Lanarkshire, the people who owned land or property, were quite clear about it. They were appalled by the demand for annual parliaments and universal suffrage. To them, these were dangerous projects, 'evils ever regarded by the wise and judicious of all parties as only names for anarchy and revolution'.[2]

The overnight appearance of so many copies of the *Address* in so many places inspired many and struck terror into the hearts of others. There was the sheer scale of it, and the planning which had clearly been necessary to spread the placards across such a wide area in such a short time. There was what those placards proposed. the *Ayrshire Advertiser* was astonished by how quickly the *Address* had been put up in their county: '. . . especially in the extensive and remote district of Carrick. Everywhere, and upon every road, these had been stuck up in the most conspicuous places before the dawn of the following Monday without leaving a trace, which, so far as we know, has hitherto led to the detection of any person guilty of this daring crime.'[3]

Describing the posting of the placards as 'this daring crime' might suggest some reluctant admiration for the effort and planning that had gone into this blanket posting. Or maybe not. At the time of the Calton Weavers' Strike over thirty years before, one description of workers coming together had described their rudimentary trade unions as 'daring combinations'. Which may have meant impertinent and unthinkable.

A report from Glasgow reprinted in the conservative London daily, the *Morning Post* on 7 April 1820 under the headline of 'Alarming Rebellious Project in Scotland', is unequivocal, describing the *Address* as 'atrocious'.

> It was supposed that the new-fangled notions which dazzled some of our people had given way to the thinking sober-mindedness: but if appearances are to be trusted, this conclusion has been too hastily drawn. [. . .]
>
> Between Saturday night and Sunday morning, there was posted upon the walls in Glasgow, Paisley,

and in all the manufacturing towns for a dozen miles around, an Address to the people of England, Ireland, and Scotland, calling upon them to come forward instantly, and to effect, by force, if resisted, a revolution in the Government. The paper is supposed to have been printed in England, and we should suppose it of English composition, from its dwelling much on Magna Charta and Bill of Rights, in which Scotland has no interest. It is probable then this same Address has been circulated through the manufacturing districts of England; and the accounts of its effects there are looked for with much anxiety by both loyal and disloyal in this part of the country.[4]

There are those who claim the *Address* was entirely the work of *agents provocateurs*. Then and now, some people agree with the *Morning Post*'s assessment that whoever wrote it must have been English and not Scottish. It was addressed not only to Scots but to all the inhabitants of Great Britain and Ireland, and as the *Post* pointed out, why would Scots refer to the English Magna Carta and Bill of Rights of 1689, since neither, apparently, was ever relevant to Scotland? Surely, this argument runs, Scots would have evoked the Declaration of Arbroath of 1320, which affirmed Scotland's right to exist as an independent nation?

Well, maybe. Study the evidence and the first-hand accounts of those who were involved in the unrest of the period of the radical rising, and a more complex picture emerges.

Scotland's heroes certainly inspired Scottish radicals. At all the large open-air meetings calling for reform the sacred name of William Wallace was frequently mentioned. Robert the Bruce was too, as were the Covenanters of the seventeenth century and those members of the old independent Scottish parliament who had spoken out passionately against the Union of the Parliaments of 1707.

At the same time, in the run-up to April 1820, Scotland's radicals were in close contact with their English comrades, particularly those in Manchester and other parts of the English North Country.

For several years before the rising, they had been reading English radical newspapers and pamphlets and sometimes listening to speeches made by English reformers. They certainly would have known about the Magna Carta and the Bill of Rights.

To muddy the waters a little more, another point can be made here. The English Bill of Rights may not have applied to Scotland, however, before the Union of the Parliaments of Scotland and England in 1707, the Scottish parliament had affirmed a Claim of Right. This was sometimes referred to as Scotland's Magna Carta. It limited the power of the monarch who was, 'by immemorial tradition, restricted by the laws and customs of the people'. It also required the monarch to frequently allow the convening of parliaments which would 'sit in order to redress grievances and to amend, strengthen and preserve the law'.[5]

At the Thrushgrove meeting in 1816, one of the resolutions passed was based on the Bill of Rights, quoting one of its clauses. 'That it is the right of the subject to petition the king, and all commitments and prosecutions for such petitioning are unlawful.'[6] It was decided that by having done everything he could to stop the Thrushgrove meeting from going ahead, Glasgow's Provost Black had 'been instrumental in preventing the inhabitants from exercising their unalienable right of petitioning the throne'. So Scottish radicals seem to have thought the Bill of Rights applied in Scotland. Even if they might have been conflating it with the Claim of Right.

There can be no doubt that when the call to action came in April 1820, many Scots workers were ready and willing to answer it, as many hands must have been at work posting up the *Address* in all the different places where it was seen that Sunday morning. They can't all have been *agents provocateurs*. The *Morning Post* report states that all the weavers in Glasgow and its suburbs were on strike. So too were all the weavers in Paisley, and the colliers and cotton-spinners in many areas had also withdrawn their labour.[7]

James Hardie was a magistrate, a justice of the peace for the county of Lanark. Some time between eight o'clock and half past eight on the morning of Sunday, 2 April 1820, he looked out of the window of his house in Duke Street in Glasgow.

What he saw was a small crowd of people gathered in the street outside around what he called a watchman's box, in other words a police box. Founded in 1800, the Glasgow police force is one of the oldest in the world. Among its main duties in those early years was keeping the peace and keeping watch, especially during the hours of darkness. They seem to have fallen down on the job on the night of 1–2 April 1820.

By James Hardie's estimation, about thirty people were studying a placard which had been fixed to the box. One young man among the crowd was reading it aloud. In this moment, one of the main players of the 1820 Radical War walks onto the stage.

Andrew Hardie, no relation to James Hardie the magistrate, lived in nearby Castle Street with his widowed mother Marion. He was twenty-six years old and a weaver to trade, as his father Thomas had been before him. Coincidentally, Andrew Hardie was born in the parish of Cadder, where Thomas Muir had been an elder of the parish kirk. He had also been at the Thrushgrove meeting.[8]

Andrew Hardie was to play a pivotal role in the Radical Rising and, five months later, end his days on the scaffold. On this Sunday morning at the beginning of April, as he continued to read out the *Address to the Inhabitants of Great Britain & Ireland*, James Hardie the magistrate burst out of his house, pushed his way through the crowd, and attempted to tear down the placard.

According to the magistrate, Andrew Hardie grabbed him by the collar and pulled him away, throwing him off the pavement. Or as James Hardie later put it, Andrew Hardie 'hustled him off the stones', helped by four or five people in the crowd. He tried to stand his ground, telling them he was a magistrate, insisting the *Address* was 'improper' and must be removed. Andrew Hardie queried his authority to do so. Could he prove he was a magistrate?

He could not, having nothing on him to show his status. Instead, he started again towards the watchman's box. He later alleged Andrew Hardie barred his way, pinioned his arms and once more threw him into the street. The young weaver averred that he 'would part with the last drop of his blood to keep the *Address* where it was'. He spoke with passion, although he later denied having manhandled the magistrate in any way. Maybe others in the crowd did, allowing Andrew Hardie to finish reading the *Address* out loud.

ADDRESS
TO THE
Inhabitants of Great Britain & Ireland;

FRIENDS AND COUNTRYMEN,
ROUSED from that torpid state in which We have been sunk for so many years We are at length compelled, from the extremity of our sufferings, and the contempt heaped upon our Petitions for redress, to assert our RIGHTS, at the hazard of our lives; and proclaim to the world the real motives, which (if not misrepresented by designing men, would have United all ranks), have reduced us to take up ARMS for the redress of our *Common Grievances.*

The numerous Public Meetings held throughout the Country has demonstrated to you, that the interests of all Classes are the same. That the protection of the Life and Property of the *Rich Man*, is the interest of the *Poor Man*, and in return, it is the interest of the Rich, to protect the poor from the iron grasp of DESPOTISM; for, when the victims are exhausted in the lower circles, there is no assurance but that its ravages will be continued in the upper: For once set in motion, it will continue to move until a succession of Victims fall.

[. . .]

Let us show to the world that We are not that Lawless, Sanguinary Rabble, which our Oppressors would persuade the higher circles we are – but a Brave and Generous PEOPLE, determined to be FREE, LIBERTY or DEATH is our *Motto*, and We have sworn to return home in triumph – or return *no more!*

There's more, including a paragraph addressed specifically at soldiers, confidently stating that they would surely not be ready to 'plunge your BAYONETS into the bosoms of Fathers and Brothers'. The *Address* then calls on them to come forward and 'Free your Country and your King from the power of those that have held them *too, too* long in thraldom'.

The *Address* insists the action to be taken will be peaceful, with no damage to people or property, no pillage or plunder. The weapon to be wielded is a general strike.

> In the present state of affairs, and during the continuation of so momentous a struggle, we earnestly request of all to desist from their Labour, from and after this day, the FIRST OF APRIL; and attend wholly to the recovery of their Rights, and consider it as the duty of every man not to recommence until he is in possession of those Rights which distinguishes the FREEMAN from the SLAVE; viz: That of giving consent to the laws by which he is to be governed.

Mr Hardie the magistrate was forced to retreat, although he soon found another copy of the *Address* posted against a pump-well. He gave evidence to this effect at the trial of Andrew Hardie for high treason. Peter Mackenzie later alleged the magistrate did not live in Duke Street but elsewhere in Glasgow. Mackenzie's contention was that Mr Hardie was going around the city knowing placards had been posted and hoping to identify radicals flushed out by this call to action.[9] This is very much the deeply flawed theory of the Radical Rising being more or less completely brought into being by *agents provocateurs*.

To many in the radical movement, the posting of the *Address* came as no surprise at all. James Paterson remembered that everyone in Kilmarnock knew the date and was waiting for it. Some were fearful. Some were eager. He quoted local woman Jenny Rowatt, found by a visiting friend bustling about doing her housework on Sunday, 2 April. Surprised, the friend asked why she was working on the Sabbath. 'Preparing for the Radical rising the morn!' was the answer.[10]

Alexander Boswell, the laird of Auchinleck, was spotted leading his troop of the Ayrshire Yeomanry through Stewarton. Radicals had a nickname for farmers and landowners like him, believing them to be profiting from the Corn Laws at the expense of the poor. They called them sour (or soor) milk jocks, soor milk being buttermilk. As Boswell and his troop rode through Stewarton, one of the village's weavers flung the taunt at him. 'Haud up your head, sour-milk Jock!'[11] Alexander Boswell jumped off his horse and chased the weaver through a close, his sword in his hand. Some of the onlookers thought that was the rising starting. Whether Boswell caught up with the weaver is not recorded.

John Parkhill was quite clear radicals and radical sympathisers in Paisley knew the rising was coming.

> The first day of April was the appointed day for the rising of the radicals, and great activity was being displayed by the leaders. There was a safety valve in the case, which, had it been attended to, would have prevented an explosion in Scotland. The ambassadors who had been sent by us to Nottingham stated that, by an agreement with the English, we were not to move until we heard that 200,000 had taken the field in England. Had we been as wise as we are generously presumed to be, we would have been perfectly safe; but we were keen to try our unfleshed swords, and the sequel showed us to be a parcel of egregious fools.[12]

The signal that the English radicals had swung into action had been agreed at the Nottingham meeting. The Carlisle radicals would stop the mail coach from London to Glasgow on the road.[13] Its non-appearance in Glasgow would indicate the rising had begun: but the mail coach did arrive on Monday, 3 April. Despite this, hundreds of Scotland's radicals decided to go ahead. They did so with clear eyes, fully aware of the risks they were running. They must have known how unlikely it was that the rising could succeed. Yet like a pan on the stove boiling over, their frustration at the lack of progress towards reform had to find an outlet.

John Neil of Paisley had been a delegate to the Nottingham meeting. He called on his friend John Parkhill in Paisley on Friday, 31 March 1820, the day before the placards went up over the course of the following Saturday night and Sunday morning. Handing him a copy of the proposed *Address*, he asked what Parkhill thought of it.[14] Could Neil have been the man who wrote the *Address*, someone perhaps heavily influenced by the rhetoric of the English reformers? Or had he brought home from Nottingham the text of an address composed by an Englishman, hence the references to the Magna Carta and the Bill of Rights?

There's a letter in Home Secretary Lord Sidmouth's papers in London from a Mr Norris in Manchester, dated 3 April 1820, with a scrawled *midnight* below the date.[15] Norris tells his lordship 'the Proclamation has appeared here similar to the one which has been placarded around Glasgow'. He thinks this is 'the signal for insurrection' and 'that in Scotland they expect the movement to commence in England and I believe that they expect the commencement in Scotland; this state of things will I hope prevent their moving in either country'.

This may be another reason why the rising was so badly co-ordinated. The Scottish and the English radicals were waiting for the other to jump first. The *Address* was posted up in Glasgow early on the morning of 2 April. Mr Norris was writing his letter at midnight on Monday, 3 April. He clearly had not long got notice from Glasgow of what had happened. The dispatch or post office express rider who brought it must have ridden hell-for-leather to get from Glasgow to Manchester in two days. Whoever sent the message to Norris, probably Glasgow Provost Henry Monteith, once more back in office, realised how serious the situation potentially was. You can imagine a breathless dispatch rider bending his head to unbuckle his leather satchel and hand over the urgent letter from Glasgow.

In reply to John Neil's question back in Paisley, Parkhill told him he thought the *Address* was well written but very dangerous, especially 'to those who might circulate it', as possibly a 'psalm in the Grassmarket' would be their reward.[16] This was a reference to the Covenanting martyrs of the seventeenth century, several of whom were hanged in the Grassmarket in Edinburgh during the years which became known as the Killing Times.

A worried Parkhill reminded John Neil they were short of guns, ammunition and military expertise. Surely it was mad to even contemplate a rising in such circumstances. Neil laughed and told him to buck up his ideas and be confident. They would soon have all the guns and ammunition they needed, money and 'a turn-out of thousands'.

Not convinced, that evening Parkhill sat in front of his fire and burned his papers, disposing of the many speeches he had written in support of reform. Despite taking this safety precaution, he tossed and turned all night. When he went out into Paisley the following morning, he found lots of people on the street but nobody seemed to know anything definite or whether the rising was going to happen.

He was, however, warned he was a marked man, considered dangerous because he had been 'actively engaged in preaching politics to the young, and that therefore I was sure to be arrested'.[17] Although this worried him greatly, he joined in with plans to make pikes at a forge near Kilbarchan.

In Langloan near Coatbridge, Janet Hamilton's father came back from an early walk on a fine April morning and got his daughter and son-in-law out of their bed.[18] He had seen a copy of the *Address* stuck on a tree in the middle of the village. Janet's husband went out and came back with the news that there were copies of the placard everywhere. The Hamiltons were alarmed. A father with several grown-up sons lived next door to them. All radicals, they had been arming themselves for some time.

On the Monday morning the next-door neighbour, Will Lightbody, came into the Hamiltons' house, where Janet's father and husband were working away at their cobblers' lasts. Lightbody swaggered in, grinning. He told Jamie Thomson it wasn't too late to join the local radicals. If he did, he would get his share of the spoils. If he didn't, he would live to regret it. Many, probably most, radicals were idealists, but as with any large movement, there were rogues in the ranks too.

Janet's husband responded to the threat by ignoring it, doggedly going on with his work. According to determinedly anti-radical Janet, her father looked Will Lightbody up and down, burst out laughing and shamed the man into beating a hasty retreat. Although the radicals were in the ascendant at this stage. By Monday, 3 April, the called-for general strike was in full swing.

CHAPTER 13

'Stop the Work!' – The General Strike

Monday, 3 April 1820

Weavers and other workers in Glasgow responded immediately to the strike call. Very few workplaces remained open. As the prosecuting lawyer said later in the year at the trial of Andrew Hardie:

> I believe there was hardly a weaver that did not shut up his house and remain idle for a considerable time. The population of that great city assembled in the streets, where they formed themselves into columns, and marched with the military step. The shops were closed, and business generally stopt. [*sic*] In short, Glasgow presented a scene which you will hear described in evidence, and which, having personally witnessed, I can safely say, was sufficient to excite serious alarm in the minds of every individual.[1]

An estimated 60,000 people in and around Glasgow, Paisley and Ayrshire answered the call to arms contained in the *Address*. Radical fervour burned fiercely in the weaving towns and villages: Paisley, Johnstone and Kilbarchan in Renfrewshire; Condorrat, now part of modern-day Cumbernauld; nearby Kilsyth; Strathaven in Lanarkshire; Milngavie, then in Stirlingshire; Balfron, also in Stirlingshire; Galston in Ayrshire.

Janet Hamilton had observed some of the local manoeuvres of drilling and marching radicals around Langloan and Coatbridge. The bleachers and cotton-spinners of Milngavie and the weavers of Balfron were also reported to have been drilling. Pikes were being fashioned at a forge in Duntocher.

These primitive weapons were centuries old but they were the simplest and cheapest to make. Potentially lethal, they allowed a man on foot to tackle mounted cavalrymen. The metal blades or points of the pikes were fixed to poles cut from trees, usually about six feet in length. Going by the many stories of their manufacture, thousands were made. A curious document in the Home Office papers is a letter included a drawing of a pike and the specifications for making one.[2]

The radicals in Johnstone in Renfrewshire were quick off the mark. Copies of the *Address* were posted up on Sunday, 2 April, and an open-air meeting called for noon on Monday, 3 April, on the School Green. Somebody shouted out a rallying cry, 'Let the friends of freedom meet at twelve o'clock!' A copy of the *Address* was read out to the crowd. They cheered at the end of every paragraph.[3] One man taking a lead at this meeting was Robert Parker. He had two nicknames, variations on a theme. Lovely Bob and Beautiful Bob.[4] Sadly, the witness who later gave this information in court was not pressed as to why Bob was lovely and beautiful. He was indicted on a charge of high treason but escaped before he could be arrested.

William Houston owned some of the thirteen textile mills in Johnstone. The town had a population of between 4,000 and 5,000. Some were weavers but most were spinners. At 10 a.m. on the Monday morning, two hours before the meeting was convened on the School Green, Houston discovered workers in several of his mills had gone on strike. He went at once to the one called the Old Mill and found a crowd gathered around the door. Going round the building to the back door and then coming through to the front, he faced the crowd and asked them what they wanted. He could see some of the people were his own workers, but others were not.[5]

There were shouts of 'Stop the work, stop the work!' Houston refused and told them to leave. They stood their ground, repeating the demand to stop the work. One man in particular, whom Houston did not recognise, was very vocal. The mill owner said he would listen if someone stepped forward and spoke to him directly, without shouting.

A man called James Walker suggested, 'We had better appoint two men to speak to Mr Houston.' The crowd formed itself into a ring and by a show of hands elected James Walker and James Speirs to be their representatives. After a further brief consultation, William Houston asked them to come to the back of the mill and up the hill behind it, where they might talk away from the noise of the crowd. James Walker was on Houston's right and James Speirs was on his left.

James Walker asked Houston if he had seen the *Address*. If not, would he like to see it? Houston said he would, but a copy could not be found. Asked again if he would stop the mill, he said no, he would not. On your own head be it, warned James Walker. If any damage is done, you will have no claim against the provisional government. Houston flashed back a response. Perhaps we can allow ourselves to imagine him giving a defiant toss or exasperated shake of the head as he did so. He had no intention of making a claim against this entity they were calling the provisional government, or James Walker either.

Andrew Logan, superintendent of another mill in Johnstone, heard this interchange. A crowd of around forty people had come to his mill at 10 a.m., making a lot of noise and trying to encourage the workers inside to come out on strike. They stayed where they were until a crowd ten times as big arrived an hour and a half later. By Logan's estimation there were 400 of them. Logan had followed this group of people to Houston's mill and then went up the hill behind it, perhaps to offer moral support to Houston. He stood very close to him, James Walker and James Speirs as they spoke.[6]

Whether they did so willingly or not, the workers came out on strike and stayed out for eight days. Almost 250 people were employed there, 30 men and 210 women and boys. On normal days, they started worked early, going home for breakfast between 9.00 and 9.45 a.m. before returning to their work.

On that same evening, a weaver at Condorrat called John Baird went to Camelon, near Falkirk and the Carron Ironworks. He bought thirteen pike-heads, made in the forges of the nailers of Camelon. Known though they were for their hard drinking and rough, sometimes brutal ways, many of the men who made nails were also radicals. There was a promise some would join the radical army if and when the call came.[7]

The Radical Rising claimed its first victim that same evening. Earlier that day Adam Cochran's father, John, had called on John Parkhill. Very upset, he asked Parkhill if he knew if Adam had taken up with the radicals. Had his son joined 'the poor fools at Gleniffer?'[8] A few hours later, his worst fears were realised.

On a trip to requisition firearms from farmhouses in Foxbar near Paisley, someone shot and killed Adam Cochran. According to John Parkhill, the musket ball which went through his heart kept travelling, on into the elbow of another young radical standing next to him.[9]

Again on the Monday night, some of the Paisley radicals headed for Kilbarchan. The plan was to set up a temporary forge for the making of pikes at nearby Pinnel Glen. 'Rather a curious party were engaged for this business. Some carried iron, others hammers, and others tools; one stout fellow had the large bellows, and two had the heavy and formidable stithy or anvil.'[10]

Making a detour to avoid meeting up with militia or government cavalry, it was after midnight before they reached Kilbarchan. By previous arrangement, they were to announce their arrival by hitting the streets with the sticks they carried. This they duly did. The response was a deafening silence.

> They accordingly rattled away till they were tired, but as not a living soul appeared, they began to make a careful scrutiny, but found there was not a light to be seen in the whole village. Every person in the village seemed to be asleep; and although Kilbarchan is famed for the best breed of terriers in the West of Scotland, not a bark was to be heard.[11]

Parkhill deduced that the weavers of Kilbarchan, 'being a shrewd set of villagers', had begun to see the rising was a bad idea, highly dangerous too. Somehow they managed to keep their dogs quiet. As night fell and Monday gave way to Tuesday, an uneasy silence settled over Glasgow, Paisley and the surrounding towns and villages.

CHAPTER 14

That Fearful Night

Tuesday, 4 April 1820

Rumours were flying. A carter brought a terrifying one to Langloan on the Tuesday evening. Fighting had broken out in Glasgow and dead bodies were lying in the streets. They weren't, but the fear engendered by this false report was very real. It was made a hundred times worse when the man claimed a band of radicals were heading for Langloan with the aim of forcing its men to join them in an attack on Airdrie. As a potential flashpoint, the Lanarkshire town was being garrisoned by the East Lothian Yeomanry, a combined force of cavalry and foot soldiers.[1]

Thrown into a panic, the women of Langloan begged their menfolk to take themselves off and hide out for the night in Drumpellier woods. It was wet and windy, so they went well wrapped up. The women were relieved the men were out of the way but were left isolated and scared. Recalling those tense hours later in life, Janet Hamilton wondered how she could 'describe the agony of terror and suspense which I and a neighbour living under the same roof endured during that fearful night'. She had been sitting with her five children, crying, when the neighbour came to join her.

The neighbour was a young woman suffering from tuberculosis, or consumption as it was then known. She took one of Janet's children onto her lap and they sat quietly in the dark, ears pricked for every sound outside the house. All they heard was the occasional sound of passing footsteps and the 'dripping sound of incessant rain'.[2] They must have jumped out of their skins when their respective husbands knocked on the window in the early hours of the morning.

As the men changed out of their wet clothes and shoes, they told the women they hadn't seen any radical army. What they had observed were two or three of their neighbours flinging muskets, bullets, powder and furled flags into a disused mineshaft at Gartsherrie. Might they still be there under the ground, or will they have rusted and rotted down there in the darkness?

A few hours later, on the Wednesday morning, it wasn't a radical army which entered Langloan but armed soldiers. They were looking for radicals and their weapons. Neither were to be found, although the houses of all known or suspected local radicals were searched. Someone had warned them to stay away and lie low for a while.

The plan hatched by the radicals for the night before had been to assemble near the local mansion of Airdrie House before attacking the town. Finding out how strong the military presence was, they had decided against it. One of Langloan's weavers, Will Marshall, had made his way to the rendezvous point and stood there in the rain for several hours before he realised nobody was going to join him. For years afterwards the wee ragamuffins of Langloan would taunt him as he passed: 'There's Radical Will'.[3]

Despite the failure of the planned attack on Airdrie House, radical passions were still running high. A party of eight soldiers taking ammunition to the Airdrie Volunteers, the local government militia, was attacked by a crowd of 700 to 800 men. They were throwing stones and calling out 'Seize the powder!' Mr Murdoch was in command of the soldiers. There were shouts of 'Kill Murdoch!' At Baillieston, a large group of militia rode to the rescue. 'Only one shot was fired, and that over the head of the mob; but some of them will doubtless feel bruises given them with the broadside of the sword.'[4]

The other Will, Lightbody the next-door neighbour, called on Janet's father pleading for a pair of stout shoes. His own were falling off his feet and he needed reliable footwear so he could take himself off for a while and lie low somewhere away from his home.

He looked rather shamefaced. Jamie Thomson took pity on him, finding him a pair of shoes that fitted. Will Lightbody promised he would 'min' the shoon' [remember he needed to pay for the shoes] once he was back weaving and earning again.[5]

In a previous century, mothers in the south of Scotland sang a lullaby to their children promising they would keep them safe from the much-feared knight known as the Black Douglas: 'Hush ye, Hush ye, Dinna fret ye, the Black Douglas willna get ye.' For a long time after the dramatic events of April 1820, the threat issued by exasperated mothers in Langloan was 'Behave yourself or the radicals *will* get you.'[6]

CHAPTER 15

'I Will Shoot All Glasgow to Please You!'

Sunday, 2 April–Wednesday, 5 April 1820

People on both sides were scared. In Glasgow, some better-off folk sent their wives and families to the presumed safety of the Clyde coast. 'Several went to Gourock, some to Largs and others to Greenock.'[1] Taking the threat very seriously, the Lord Provost of Glasgow, his magistrates and the Sheriff of Lanarkshire issued their own printed proclamation, imposing a curfew on the city.

> In Consequence of the present threatening appearances, the LORD PROVOST, MAGISTRATES, SHERIFF and JUSTICES, hereby order all SHOPS to be SHUT, this and every following night, until Tranquility is restored, at the hour of SIX, and they hereby enjoin all the Inhabitants of the City to RETIRE TO THEIR HOUSES as soon as possible thereafter, and not later than SEVEN O'CLOCK.
>
> All Strangers are hereby enjoined to WITHDRAW from the CITY before SEVEN O'CLOCK at Night. PARTIES or GROUPS of PEOPLE, Standing Together, or Walking the Streets after the hour of SEVEN, will be deemed Disturbers of the Peace, and will be dealt with accordingly.
>
> If the LAMPS ARE PUT OUT, the Inhabitants are desired immediately to ILLUMINATE THEIR

WINDOWS with as much lights as they can conveniently command.

God Save the King.

Glasgow, 3rd April, 1820.[2]

On the following day, Tuesday, 4 April, the authorities gave notice of a reward to anyone who could give information leading to the arrest of the people who had posted up the placards over Saturday night and Sunday morning. They described the *Address* as 'wicked, revolutionary and treasonable' and the reward promised was £300. This was a huge amount of money, the equivalent of four years' wages for an experienced weaver.

The authorities clearly believed the radicals posed a credible and large-scale threat. Regiments from the British army had been deployed in and around Glasgow, Paisley, Ayrshire and other potential flashpoints. They included men from infantry and cavalry regiments, the Rifle Brigade and the Royal Artillery. In addition, many local yeomanry militias were on standby. Total numbers are estimated to have been in the thousands.[3]

Glasgow was an armed camp, with possibly up to 2,000 soldiers patrolling the streets. They were guarding potential targets such as local government buildings, the High Court and all the banks. Guns were sited on the bridges over the Clyde.[4] In addition to the soldiers in the barracks near Glasgow Green, the Glasgow Light Horse were stationed in St Vincent Street, the men of the 500-strong Armed Association were standing by in St Enoch Square and the 700 Glasgow Sharpshooters were in George Square.[5]

One local wag mocked the city's panic, describing Glasgow as 'Gotham in alarm'.[6] The name Gotham goes back a long way. It originally meant a farmstead where goats lived, and came to mean a place whose inhabitants were always fearful. It was Washington Irving, American author of *Sleepy Hollow*, who later gave the name to New York.

Gotham in Alarm was also the name of a three-act farce which had been performed in Glasgow after the Thrushgrove meeting. An extended satirical sketch, it mocked Lord Provosts Black, Monteith and Kirkman Finlay. Black was given the name of Lord Fungus in the play and is depicted as being only interested in feathering his own nest and having absolutely no sympathy for the plight of the poor. Another more sympathetic character, called Steadfast in the play, is believed to represent James Turner, who allowed the big reform meeting at Thrushgrove to happen.

Lord Fungus (Black) is given these words: 'But I will keep my distance, stand aloof, strut, and look big, and awe them into silence, and as long as in my power keep down the noses of the ragged sooty knaves, at rough oppression's grindstone.' When a servant comes in to announce that 'four most ugly men' have called to see him, Lord Fungus asks if they are weavers. 'Two of them are too fat for weavers,' answers the servant.

Outraged that 'the swinish multitude' has the temerity to want to hold a meeting, another character declares: 'Mobocracy must be kept down or none of us are safe.' Despite their best efforts, the meeting goes ahead and attracts a huge audience. A journalist given the name of the Pig of Knowledge reassures Lord Fungus and the Glasgow magistrates about that. 'They say 40,000; but in my report I'll say 4,000; and if any noise is made I'll say 'twas a small mistake, an omitting of a cypher – an error of the press.'

The Glasgow Sharpshooters were commanded by Samuel Hunter, editor of *The Glasgow Herald* and implacable enemy of reform. The notice of reward was printed at the newspaper's offices, which were then in Bell Street, off the High Street and just up from Glasgow Cross. Many in this and similar government militias seem to have been young bucks enjoying themselves playing at soldiers.

Brimming over with excitement and enthusiasm, the Sharp-shooters drilled early in the morning and in the evening too. They did a lot of this indoors, in buildings which included the Trades Hall in Glassford Street, in what was then Stirling's Library and is now Hutcheson's Hospital, Glasgow headquarters of the National Trust for Scotland. They also practised their drills in several ware-houses belonging to Glasgow merchants, including one in Miller Street. They lined up on Glasgow Green to be inspected and fought a mock battle or two. It is easy to imagine the career soldiers who were there looking on with a jaundiced eye, having experienced the real thing at Waterloo, Talavera and other bloody battles.

At the end of the review, Samuel Hunter addressed the young gentlemen. They whooped and cheered at everything he said. Hunter pointed his sword in the direction of the Cathkin Braes and told them he 'was confident that if any *Treasonable* ragamuffins shall dare to approach the city, you will give them *a warm reception*'.[7]

The Sharpshooters were very proud of their uniforms. Gentlemen's outfitters in Glasgow made a killing, supplying 1,000 well-heeled young gentlemen with very fancy threads. They wore:

> a beautiful green jacket, of the finest Yorkshire wool, fringed richly with silk and cotton tambouring, with three rows of dark covered buttons on the breast; white vest, green trousers to match the pretty jackets, with fine white linen ones for field or summer, or gala days; polished Wellington boots, then new in fashion; the rich silken cravat, as worn by George the Fourth, unfolding to view the spotless shirt, with the finest lace or cambric ruffle attached to it, nowhere now to be seen; and then in a ball-room [. . .] their white or cream-coloured embroidered *silken* stockings – rarely do we see any of them now – displaying the green trig ancle [*sic*], encased in the pumps or the shoes with their brilliant buckles, which made the very floors to creak with animation.[8]

They wore very tall hats too, surmounted with a tuft of black horse hair. Yes, the chocolate soldiers were having a whale of a time – but it could have come to bloodshed. They were ready for any attack, with fixed bayonets and guns kept in the entrance vestibules of a couple of the city's churches. The weather helped the defenders of Glasgow. On Wednesday, 5 April the city's streets were kept clear by relentless downpours. It was a day when you would only go out if you absolutely had to. Older Glaswegians said it was one of the wettest days in living memory. Some called it 'the Radical wet Wednesday'.[9]

In the regular army there were heroes, honourable men and some rotten apples. There are a few stories of swaggering braggadocio and boorish behaviour. One played out on a Sunday evening in Glasgow a few months before the rising. Drunk as lords at the door of the Buck's Head Inn, which stood on the corner of Argyle Street and Dunlop Street, some hussar officers were swearing their heads off. People walking home from evening church services stopped to look. They took a dim view of such behaviour, especially on the Sabbath.

At this point 'one of these doughty champions of the whisker took a segar [*sic*] out of his mouth, which he had been smoking, and squirted his unsavoury saliva into the face of one of the spectators'. Gilbert McLeod wrote this story up in the *Spirit of the Union*. With savage sarcasm, he described 'this act of courtesy' being followed by more swearing. The Glaswegian onlookers began to hiss, a common way of expressing disapproval at the time. The drunken hussars responded by insisting they were gentlemen. They muttered a threat or two, that they had 'troops at hand'. Which they did. Their horses were stabled in the yard behind the inn.

'Shortly after, these *gentlemanly* venerators of the sanctity of the Sabbath, Bacchanalian props of Church and State, and whiskered *defenders* of the people, as a never-to-be-forgotten proof of their prowess, knocked down a decent looking man, who was walking peaceably along, and in no expectation of such an attack.' When the people watching looked as though they might be inclined to retaliate, the hussars '*courageously* sneaked off'.[10]

There's another story about two members of a local militia feasting on 'beef-steak, ham and onion' and having rather too much to drink at an inn in the suburbs of Glasgow. They called the landlady and claimed to have no money to pay the bill. What's worse, after she was forced to let them leave without paying, they came back and demanded she hand over her day's takings. It came to court but they got off when the sheriff discovered they were members of the local militia: '. . . the whole then became a *frolic* . . .'[11] Just a joke. Youthful high spirits. One law for the powerful and one law for the powerless.

One of the Glasgow Sharpshooters who probably did not indulge in such boorish behaviour was Peter Mackenzie. He was in his early twenties at the time. In the years to come he was to use his journalistic skills to write about the radicals of 1820. In his defence of them he became very much a conspiracy theorist, convinced the rising had been provoked by 'infamous spies'.[12] He thought all these troop movements had been part of a concerted plan to paint the radicals as a huge danger to respectable citizens and a threat to the peaceful running of society.

The Glasgow Sharpshooters were trained by the regular soldiers of the Rifle Brigade. The company which had already been garrisoning Glasgow was from the 7th Hussars. The man who later became Lieutenant-General Henry Smith spent a few years in the city, witnessing the radical ferment. Known to his friends as Harry, he did not find Glasgow an easy posting. To his mind, the city was more full of foes than friends. He had married Juana, his Spanish wife, while serving in the Peninsula. For a period, he felt it safer to send her to Edinburgh.

When he wrote about he and his men being attacked by a stone-throwing mob after they had arrested the secret committee members he described Glasgow's magistrates as 'horribly timid'. They were scared the soldiers would retaliate by opening fire on the crowd. Peterloo had happened only six months before.

Lord Advocate William Rae had no such reservations. He was in Glasgow that day and was furious with Harry Smith for *not* ordering his men to open fire. The stone-throwing crowd had insulted His Majesty's troops. '*I am surprised, sir*,' Rae said with outraged emphasis. 'Why did you thus tamely act?'[13]

Smith's account of how he ordered his men to respond does not sound all that tame. He told them to use the flats of their swords to 'make the heads of some ache'. He stood his ground with the Lord Advocate, telling him he had not responded with more vigour because he was acting under the instructions of Glasgow's magistrates. 'They would not act, and I did not desire to bring upon my head either the blood of my foolish and misguided countrymen, or the odium of the Manchester magistrates.'

Which unfortunately rather suggests Glasgow's magistrates were covering their own backs, rather than acting out of humanity towards their fellow citizens. Standing up to the angry Lord Advocate, Harry Smith told him he had done his duty and taken every member of the radical committee into custody without any blood being shed. If the Lord Advocate wanted to give him a written order, Smith would 'march through Glasgow with the same party of soldiers and my prisoners. A mob will soon attempt the rescue, and d—me, my lord, but I will shoot all Glasgow to please you!' Hopefully he was joking.

CHAPTER 16

The March to Carron

Tuesday, 4 April–Wednesday, 5 April 1820

Despite the increasingly large military presence in Glasgow, many of the city's radicals remained on high alert, ready and willing to act. A series of covert meetings were held throughout the day on Tuesday, 4 April. Journalist and former Glasgow Sharpshooter Peter Mackenzie later claimed four of the radical leaders were government agents. He alleged that they had wildly exaggerated the extent of radical activity in England and had told the west of Scotland radicals a French army would soon be arriving to support them.[1] He said that Kinloch of Kinloch, the radical laird at that time in exile in France, would be with them.

In a bizarre flourish, this army was to be led by James or Jacques MacDonald, Marshal of France. He was the son of Neil MacEachainn, loyal companion to Charles Edward Stuart while he was being pursued by the redcoats through the Highlands and Islands after the failure of the 1745 Jacobite Rising. Given how severely radical thought was at odds with the House of Stuart's belief in the Divine Right of Kings, this seems strange. The radicals categorised this regal philosophy as 'the right divine of kings to govern wrong'.[2] In addition, many of the Lanarkshire and Ayrshire radicals came from Covenanting stock. They had little love for the Stuarts, their forebears having been persecuted during the reigns of Stuart kings.

According to Peter Mackenzie, Duncan Turner of Glasgow was a government agent. He persuaded Andrew Hardie to lead an expedition to the Carron Iron Works. In his own account of the events of that rainy Tuesday night, Hardie wrote that he went out of Glasgow with two men, 'whose names I forbear to mention'. They rendezvoused with a small band of other radical volunteers waiting near Glasgow Cathedral, on the hill now covered by the Necropolis, Glasgow's Victorian city of the dead.

Hardie had been assured he was doing the right thing. 'I was made to understand . . . that the whole city would be in arms in the course of an hour afterwards . . . and that the coach would not be in the following morning; and that England was all in arms, from London downwards, and everything was going on behind our most sanguine expectations; and declared that there were no soldiers to oppose us betwixt that and Edinburgh; and further that the whole was ready to receive us, and well armed, and those that wanted get arms by the road, refreshments and every thing necessary.'[3]

This confirms the story that the non-arrival of the mail coach from London was to be the agreed signal the rising had begun. The Carlisle radicals would have seized it and its crew, stopping it from travelling any further.

Despite the assurances of plenty of support, marching out of Glasgow late on a rainy night after a long day of high tension seems rather ill-advised, to put it mildly. It was dark, of course, which would conceal them and their purpose. Perhaps it was also a quixotic act. Maybe Andrew Hardie felt he had to do something, stand up for his passionate belief in democracy.

He asked who was to command the group. 'You, until Condorrat,' he was told, with a promise they would be joined there by upwards of fifty or sixty more men. He was further instructed to call at the house in Condorrat where John Baird lived. Like Hardie, he too had served in the British army. Baird had been with the 95th Rifles and had fought in Argentina and Spain.

Andrew Hardie seems to have been a natural leader. A mile out from Condorrat, the men he was with, of their own accord, appointed him to take charge, '. . . which I did by forming front and rear rank, and sized them accordingly, and likewise numbered them the same as a guard; my reason for doing was because we

Thomas Muir of Huntershill (1765–1799), the father of Scottish democracy. (Courtesy of East Dunbartonshire Leisure & Culture Trust; bust by Alexander Stoddart)

Eliza Fletcher (1770–1858), falsely accused of guillotining chickens in her back garden in Edinburgh so as to be prepared if Britain followed the example of the French Revolution.

James Turner of Thrushgrove (1768–1858), who enabled the huge pro-reform meeting of 1816 to take place on his estate in what is now Royston, north Glasgow. (Courtesy of Glasgow Museums)

Janet Hamilton of Langloan (1795–1873), writer, poet, wife, mother of ten and critic of the radical reformers.

Granny Duncan (dates not known), who smuggled letters from and to Andrew Hardie and John Baird in Stirling Castle hidden in and under bowls of porridge.

James Wilson (1760–1820), hanged and then beheaded in Glasgow for his participation in the 1820 radical rising. (Courtesy of the National Galleries of Scotland)

William Howat in a photograph taken in later life but showing him dressed and armed as he was when he marched out with the radical Strathaven Pioneers.

John Fraser of Viewfield, schoolmaster, radical, musician, loving husband and father. (Courtesy of Renfrewshire Archives)

ADDRESS

TO THE

Inhabitants of Great Britain & Ireland;

FRIENDS AND COUNTRYMEN,

ROUSED from that torpid state in which WE have been sunk for so many years, We are at length compelled, from the extremity of our sufferings, and the contempt heaped upon our Petitions for redress, to assert our RIGHTS, at the hazard of our lives; and proclaim to the world the real motives, which (if not misrepresented by designing men, would have United all ranks), have reduced us to take up ARMS for the redress of our *Common Grievances.*

The numerous Public Meetings held throughout the Country has demonstrated to you, that the interests of all Classes are the same. That the protection of the Life and Property of the *Rich Man*, is the interest of the *Poor Man*, and in return, it is the interest of the Rich, to protect the poor from the iron grasp of DESPOTISM; for, when its victims are exhausted in the lower circles, there is no assurance but that its ravages will be continued in the upper: For once set in motion, it will continue to move till a succession of Victims fall.

Our principles are few, and founded on the basis of our CONSTITUTION, which were purchased with the DEAREST BLOOD of our ANCESTORS, and which we swear to transmit to posterity unsullied, or PERISH in the Attempt.—Equality of Rights (not of Property,) is the object for which we contend; and which we consider as the only security for our LIBERTIES and LIVES.

Let us show to the world that We are not that Lawless, Sanguinary Rabble, which our Oppressors would persuade the higher circles we are—but a BRAVE and GENEROUS PEOPLE, determined to be FREE, LIBERTY or DEATH is our *Motto*, and We have sworn to return home in *triumph*—or return *no more !*
SOLDIERS,

Shall YOU, Countrymen, bound by the sacred obligation of an Oath, to defend your Country and your King from enemies, whether foreign or domestic, plunge your BAYONETS into the bosoms of Fathers and Brothers, and at once sacrifice at the *Shrine of Military Despotism*, to the unrelenting Orders of a Cruel Faction, those feelings which you hold in common with the rest of mankind? SOLDIERS, Turn your eyes toward SPAIN, and there behold the happy effects resulting from the UNION of Soldiers and Citizens. Look to that quarter, and there behold the yoke of hated Despotism, broke by the Unanimous wish of the People and the Soldiery, happily accomplished without Bloodshed. And, shall You, who taught those Soldiers to fight the battles of LIBERTY, refuse to fight those of your own Country? Forbid it Heaven! Come, forward then at once, and Free your Country and your King, from the power of those that have held them *too, too* long in thraldom.

FRIENDS AND COUNTRYMEN, The eventful period has now arrived, where the Services of all will be required, for the forwarding of an object so universally wished, and so absolutely necessary. Come forward then, and assist those who have begun in the completion of so arduous a task, and support the laudable efforts, which we are about to make, to replace to BRITONS, those rights consecrated to them, by MAGNA CHARTA, and the BILL OF RIGHTS, and Sweep from our Shores, that Corruption which has degraded us below the dignity of Man.

Owing to the misrepresentations which have gone abroad with regard to our intentions, we think it indispensably necessary to DECLARE inviolable, all Public and Private Property. And, We hereby call upon all JUSTICES of the PEACE, and all others to suppress PILLAGE and PLUNDER, of every description; and to endeavour to secure those Guilty of such offences, that they may receive that Punishment, which such violation of Justice demand.

In the present state of affairs, and during the continuation of so momentous a struggle, we earnestly request of all to desist from their Labour, from and after this day, the FIRST OF APRIL; and attend wholly to the recovery of their Rights, and consider it as the duty of every man not to recommence until he is in possession of of those Rights which distinguishes the FREEMAN from the SLAVE; viz: That of giving consent to the laws by which he is to be governed. We, therefore, recommend to the Proprietors of Public Works, and all others, to Stop the one, and Shut up the other, until order is restored, as we will be accountable for no damages which may be sustained; and which after this Public Intimation, they can have no claim to.

AND We hereby give notice to all those who shall be found carrying arms against those who intend to regenerate their Country, and restore its INHABITANTS to their NATIVE DIGNITY; We shall consider them as TRAITORS to their Country, and ENEMIES to their King, and treat them as such.

By order of the Committee of Organization,
for forming a PROVISIONAL GOVERNMENT.

GLASGOW, 1st April, 1820.

Britons.—God.—Justice.—The wishes of all good Men are with us.—Join together and make it one CAUSE, and the Nations of the EARTH shall hail the day, when the Standard of LIBERTY shall be raised on its *Native Soil.*

Address to the Inhabitants of Great Britain & Ireland, posted up in and around Glasgow and Ayrshire. (Courtesy of the National Archives, London)

The Radical Dyke, around which a small force led by Andrew Hardie and John Baird fought the 10th Hussars and the Stirlingshire Yeomanry.

Pikes used by the radical army at Bonnymuir, picked up off the field and taken to Stirling Castle. The weapons are now in the care of Historic Environment Scotland.

The Radical Pend, through which the captured and wounded radicals were brought away from the field at Bonnymuir after the battle.

Above left. Bonnymuir memorial, placed there by the 1820 Society.

Above right. The coat and axe worn and used by the headsman of Wilson, Hardie and Baird. (Courtesy of the Stirling Smith Art Gallery and Museum)

Left. The plaque in Broad Street, Stirling, which marks the spot where Hardie and Baird were hanged and then beheaded.

Right. The plaque in Condorrat marking where John Baird lived. The house is still there.

Below. A replica flag in front of the memorial to James Wilson on the site of his home, Strathaven.

JOHN BAIRD
LEADER FOR
REFORM AND FREEDOM
IN SCOTLAND AS
COMMANDANT,
CONDORRAT RADICALS

MARTYR TO THE CAUSE OF LIBERTY
AND SOCIAL JUSTICE

HANGED AND BEHEADED
AT STIRLING AS A 'TRAITOR'
SEPTEMBER 8 1820

SCOTLAND FREE
OR
SCOTLAND A DESART

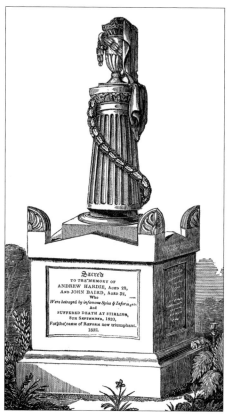

The original Thrushgrove memorial, which stood close by the present-day Royston Road and Royston public library.

The Sighthill memorial in Springburn, Glasgow to Baird, Hardie and Wilson, erected in 1847 largely on the initiative of journalist Peter Mackenzie, chronicler of the Scottish radicals of 1820.

Above. Greenock memorial, remembering those who were shot dead and wounded by the Port Glasgow militia in a successful attempt to free radical prisoners from Greenock prison.

Left. The Weaver's Cottage, Kilbarchan, illustrating how 19th-century Renfrewshire weavers lived and worked.

HARDIE
AND
BAIRD.

On the 8th of September, the bell had toll'd one,
A solemn procession in Stirling began ;
When the Magistrates and Sheriff to the Castle did repair,
To demand from the Governor brave Hardie and Baird.

When the prisoners were called, for they soon did appear,
Grace marked in their countenance, quite banished was fear ;
No guilt in their bosoms for what they had done,
But happy to think that their last hour was come.

So mournful and solemnly they marched through the hall,
And only one hour left for mercy to call.
But I hope they are treasur'd in that blest abode,
Where martyrs for ever sing praises to God !

They viewed all the instruments of death with a smile,
Soon to be relieved from all sorrow and toil ;
And bring them I trust to that world so fair,
Where they will be relieved from all sorrow and care.

But methinks that I hear their poor mothers weep,
That oft times have dangled their sweet babes to sleep ;
But when that to manhood their children had grown,
They were drag'd from their bosom and murder'd and torn.

If they had been like villains that lurk in the wood,
Determined for murder or thirsting for blood,
Then few would bewail them, few cries would be heard,
But they've murder'd these two hero's brave, Hardie & Baird.

Now farewell to those martyrs, they have signed their discharge,
And I hope that in heaven they are pensioned at large,
Where no perjured villains will e'er find a place,
But banished will be from his God with disgrace.

Farewell to those martyrs, and in peace may they rest,
Until that great day, when the souls of the blest
Shall behold their bright Saviour, whose flag gently waves
To welcome them home from their cold bloody grave.

Printed and sold by JAMES LINDSAY Jun,, Stationer, &c.
9 King Street, Glasgow.

12

Hardie and Baird: a broadside lament for their execution. (By permission of University of Glasgow Library, Special Collections) were all strangers to one another, and did not know our names, that if anything was wanted, we might answer to our numbers'.[4]

His military training was clearly proving useful. At Condorrat, he went on ahead with a man called Kean to where John Baird lived with his brother Robert and Robert's wife. They found John King there. He was the man who had made a suspicious early exit from the meeting of the Glasgow radical committee. As Andrew Hardie later put it: 'This King belongs to Glasgow, but what he is I do not know, but this I know, that he acted a very unbecoming part with us.' King promised John Baird 200 well-armed men were coming out, all veterans and experienced soldiers.

Andrew Hardie was not yet beginning to smell a rat. After he'd helped fix the pike-heads made by the nailers of Camelon onto their shafts, he left Kean with Baird and went with the other Glasgow men to a nearby pub, where he had 'one glass of whisky, and a bit of bread'. It was a bitter disappointment when only six men joined the group at Condorrat.

Now numbering around twenty-five, the little army moved on through the wet night, stopping at an inn at the Castlecary Bridge for a rest and some breakfast. They drank porter, a dark beer, and ate one bread roll each. They paid for the food and drink and asked for a receipt.

King had gone on ahead of them at Condorrat, claiming he was going to make sure the people who would be joining them at Camelon and Falkirk would be ready. So as not to miss these new recruits, Hardie and four or five men went by the road and John Baird led the main party by the towpath along the Forth and Clyde canal.

The party marching along the road met a few people. They advised a man on horseback who was heading for Glasgow to turn around because there was 'sad work going on there'. At this stage they clearly believed what they had been told about plenty of men in the city coming out in support of the radical cause. The rider kept heading for Glasgow but shortly afterwards came back and passed them, telling them he'd decided to take their advice.

Going a short distance off the road, they went to a house and requisitioned a fowling piece. They offered a receipt for this but the owner of the gun turned them down. Andrew Hardie noted that both the man on horseback and this man were 'very civil'.

Their next encounter was with Thomas Cook of the 10th Hussars, although at that stage they did not know his name. He too was civil – or seemed to be. They called on him to stop, which he did, although they didn't really give him much choice. The five or six men surrounded man and horse and took hold of both sides of the animal's bridle. They asked Cook to hand over any dispatches he was carrying. When he told them he wasn't carrying any, they asked for his ammunition. He managed to talk his way out of that,

> . . . and told a very good story that he was a friend to our cause, that he was a weaver, and had a wife and five children & etc. I told him it was no matter what he was, we should do him no harm; he answered every question we put to him very correctly; said he was going to Kilsyth, and that he had fallen behind his detachment.[5]

When he told them he too had been a weaver, as most of them were, they all shook hands with him. Brothers in the craft. They asked if he could read. When he said yes, one of the radicals by the name of Henderson took a roll of handbills out of his pocket and handed one up to Cook. It was the *Address to the Inhabitants of Great Britain & Ireland*. They advised him to read it and to let his comrades read it.

Thomas Cook rode on to Kilsyth. He went to an inn before he reported for duty and had a stiff drink. Perhaps he needed it to steady his nerves. His encounter with the radical army could have gone very badly wrong, even fatally wrong. After he'd finished his drink he did his duty and showed the *Address* to his superior officer, Lieutenant Hodgson of the 10th Hussars.[6]

About a mile and a half past Bonnybridge, where the canal towpath and the road are not very far apart, the group being led by John Baird signalled to Hardie's group to join them. King had advised them to go up onto nearby Bonnymuir and wait for the promised reinforcements from Camelon.

They accordingly went to the right, going under the canal via the Ironstone Pend. This tunnel for men and women on foot, possibly sometimes driving cattle and sheep through to the other side of the waterway, has now almost completely silted up, although a section of its top arch is still visible. Once on the other side of the canal the radical band followed a drove road and walked up the hill for about a mile, where some of them sat down and others lay flat and stretched out.

They occupied a breathtaking vantage point, where they could see for miles. Even from down the hill at the modern memorial which marks the site of the engagement you can see way over to the distinctive outlines of Ben Lomond and the peaks of the Trossachs. To get to Bonnymuir they had walked through layers of history, reaching back 2,000 years and more. They crossed the Roman Antonine Wall, constructed in the second century AD. The Wall's fortlet of Rough Castle was no distance away. William Wallace and Charles Edward Stuart had fought battles at nearby Falkirk.

The Forth and Clyde canal which had guided their footsteps to Bonnymuir had been dug some thirty years before to facilitate trade between Glasgow and Edinburgh. Known as the Great Canal, it was a potent marker of the modern age, a much more efficient means of transporting goods than by horse and cart along rutted and often muddy roads. Speeding forward in time to our own days, the Falkirk Wheel and the stunning Kelpies sculptures, two steel horses rearing up into the sky, are also close by. Did John Baird, Andrew Hardie and their companions know they would write another page in this long history?

With time to reflect, and beginning to realise no reinforcements were coming, they came to the decision to stay where they were for the day before returning home to Condorrat and Glasgow.[7] They would wait till evening fell, hoping they would not be noticed. That was the plan. It didn't work out that way. About an hour after they'd thrown themselves down onto the grass, they spotted the cavalry coming towards them.

CHAPTER 17

The Battle of Bonnymuir

Wednesday, 5 April 1820

The cavalry and yeomanry approached at a canter, although they had to ride in single file. The ground was marshy. One of the soldiers of the Stirlingshire Yeomanry knew the area and indicated a path through the bogs where the horses might place their pounding hooves on more solid ground. Lieutenant Ellis Hodgson of the 10th Hussars led the way. It was still fairly early in the morning, about half past nine.[1] The militia soldiers fighting at Bonnymuir under Hodgson's command belonged to the Kilsyth troop of the Stirlingshire Yeomanry.[2]

The radicals at the top of the hill scrambled to their feet, ready to meet the cavalry. Andrew Hardie suggested the classic military tactic of forming a square. His fellow veteran John Baird said no, better to take up a defensive position behind a stone dyke a little way down the hill. A private in the approaching yeomanry saw them take their hats off and wave them in a circle above their heads in combined agreement of Baird's suggestion. After that they ran down to the dyke. When they got there, they gave three cheers and moved into position.

There was a gap in the dyke, what was then called a slap. Eight of the men armed with pikes gathered there, all down on one knee presenting their pikes to the cavalry. This was another classic tactic, a way in which men on foot might offer resistance to men on horseback, although it only worked if the cavalrymen came close enough.

The five radicals who were carrying muskets and the requisitioned fowling piece rested the barrels of their weapons on top of the dyke, which was nearly five feet high. They fired first. Two or three shots cracked out, then two or three more. Undaunted, Hodgson rode right up to the dry stone wall and called on the radicals to lay down their arms. He did so repeatedly, six or seven times in all.

At close quarters, Hodgson observed two of the men to be better dressed than the others. These were Hardie and Baird. The latter was wearing 'a brown shooting jacket, a black silk neckcloth, and worsted trowsers [sic] and boots'.[3] When the radicals refused to drop their weapons, there was more shooting. The cavalrymen attacked the slap in the dyke, got through it, but were forced back. They sat on their horses sufficiently far away to be out of reach of the pikes, except for one rider. When he approached the dyke again, one of the radicals 'made a stab at him'. The hussar shot him and as Hardie recounted, the man 'fell forward on his face'.

The hussars mounted another charge and got through the dyke. The radicals fought back, both sides inflicting wounds on the other. When Hodgson again called on them to surrender, promising they would not be harmed, some dropped their weapons and ran for cover. A few got away. One was Henderson, the man who had handed hussar Thomas Cook a copy of the *Address to the Inhabitants of Great Britain & Ireland*. Did the two men make eye contact across the field of battle? It is a sobering thought that at least two of the combatants had fought on the same side at Waterloo: John Baird and Ellis Hodgson.

Some of the radicals got away, but Alexander Hart was not among them. He was twenty-six years old and came from Old Kilpatrick, downriver from Glasgow. Andrew Hardie was shocked by the treatment meted out to him.

> ... and it was truly unbecoming the character of a
> British soldier to wound, or try to kill any man, when
> he had it in his power to take him prisoner, and when
> they had no arms to make any defence. One of the
> Yeomanry was so inhuman, after he had sabred one
> of the men sufficient, as he thought, to deprive him

of life, as to try and trample him under his horse's feet; but here, my friends, the horse had more human- ity than his master, and would not do as he wished, but jumped over him, in place of trampling upon his wounded and mangled body . . .[4]

The man who so savagely slashed his sabre relished the deed. Hardie described this member of the Stirlingshire Yeomanry as boasting in braid (broad) Scots that he had left Alexander Hart 'wi' his head cloven like a pot'. Hart survived but bore the scar between his eyebrows for the rest of his life.

Both Lieutenant Hodgson and his horse were wounded. The ani- mal was attacked first, a pike thrust into its hindquarters. Hodgson took a less serious pike wound to his hand. The horse was his own mount, not one borrowed from the yeomanry.[5] Both injuries might understandably have made him thirst for immediate revenge but it seems he wasn't that kind of a man. Perhaps, as a professional sol- dier, he took the same view as Andrew Hardie. Once the battle was won, you did what you could for your own men and the defeated enemy. Using the flat of his sword, he stopped the men under his command from inflicting further wounds on the radicals. They had wounds enough already. One man had his face cut so deeply you could see the white of his jawbone.[6] One sergeant in the 10th Hussars and three members of the Kilsyth Stirlingshire Yeomanry troop were wounded.[7]

Alexander Johnston was the youngest of the radical army's little band of soldiers, barely fifteen years old. Although he ran away towards the marshy ground, he turned and continued to fire his pistol at the hussars and the yeomanry. Spotting him, Lieutenant Hodgson bellowed out an order: 'Save the life of that spirited boy!'[8]

Chasing a fleeing radical called Black, another hussar showed mercy. Twisting the pike out of his hands, he told him to take to his heels.[9] Unfortunately for Black three of the yeomanry soldiers were not so merciful, one cutting him badly with his sabre. Leaving him for dead, they rode off, but Black was still alive. He was found and rescued by Alexander Robertson, whose farm of Damhead was nearby.

Robertson got Black back to the farmhouse and sent for a doctor. When some soldiers went to the farmhouse looking for fugitives, the doctor told them he wasn't well enough to travel. The soldiers said they would be back the next day but with the help of his uncle and cousin, Black was spirited away from the farmhouse that night. He recovered and managed to escape retribution.

For Baird, Hardie and sixteen of their comrades there was no escape. The two leaders being uninjured, they helped the wounded. A cart was found to put them in for the journey to imprisonment at Stirling Castle. The rest had to walk. They left the moor via a different aqueduct under the canal, subsequently renamed the Radical Pend. With a burn running through its cobbled base alongside a raised walkway, it is still used as a shortcut today. The wall around which the Battle of Bonnymuir was fought has been known ever since as the Radical Dyke. Substantial remnants of it are still there.

Lieutenant Hodgson quizzed Andrew Hardie directly after the engagement as to who their captain was, specifically asking if his name was Baird. It was immediately clear someone had betrayed the plans and location of the radicals to the militia. That someone must have been John King. It now seemed clear Duncan Turner had sent them off into a trap.

Hodgson's horse managed to carry him as far as a tavern in Bonnybridge. As Andrew Hardie later wrote in his account of the skirmish, the animal was 'so wounded it could carry him no farther'. The lieutenant stopped to find another horse and to do his paperwork. He wrote up a brief report of the engagement, a list of the weapons collected and a description of all the prisoners. His horse died that night.

The prisoners had no choice but to keep going. Lieutenant Davidson of the Stirlingshire Yeomanry was temporarily in charge of them. Exhausted through lack of sleep and the stress and exertion of the fight, Andrew Hardie asked if they could stop somewhere to get a drink of water. The yeomanry officer refused. When Hodgson caught up with them, Hardie put the request for water to him and it was immediately complied with. 'Although my enemy,' wrote Hardie, 'I do him nothing but justice by saying that he is a brave and generous man.'[10]

Hardie and Baird were of the same stamp. When they arrived at Stirling Castle, Baird stepped forward, ready to take any punishment on his own shoulders. He addressed Major W. Peddie.[11] 'Sir, if there is to be any severity exercised towards us, let it be on me. I am their leader, and have caused them being here. I hope that I alone may suffer.' He added, 'They have not had much to eat since they left Glasgow. I beg you will be kind enough to order food for them.' John Baird continued to make himself responsible for his fellow prisoners for as long as he was able.

Sir Thomas Bradford, in overall charge of government forces in Scotland, wrote a general order from Edinburgh on 19 April 1820 commending his troops and passing on the approval of the new monarch George IV, the former prince regent, who had now succeeded to the throne on the death of his father.

> The Major-general, commanding the forces in North Britain, has great satisfaction in acquainting the troops of the line, yeomanry and volunteer corps, who were employed on the late occasion, particularly those who repelled a party of rebels on the 5th instant, between Kilsyth and Falkirk, and made prisoners a great proportion of the assailants; that His Majesty has been graciously pleased to express his entire approbation of their conduct.[12]

The pikes and other weapons picked up off the field at Bonnymuir were taken to Stirling Castle along with the prisoners. Lieutenant Hodgson detailed what they were and supervised them being put into sealed boxes. 'I think there were sixteen pikes and one pike handle, and a pitchfork, and five muskets or guns of different kinds, and two pistols.'[13] The radical army had no swords.

A number of the pikes wielded at Bonnymuir still exist and are in the care of Historic Environment Scotland. Sit looking at them for a while and a number of charged and emotionally conflicting images and thoughts spring to mind. The pike-heads are of different designs. One looks like a Lochaber axe. Others are slimmer, pointed spikes. Some are roughly hewn, others more finely made. They are all vicious, potentially lethal to man and horse alike. Yet they were made for and by men who had such high hopes, getting their courage up as they readied themselves to go out and fight for their rights.

CHAPTER 18

Tae Fecht for the Rights o' Auld Scotland

Saturday, 1 April–Thursday, 6 April 1820

Strathaven is a small market town in Avondale in South Lanarkshire. Made a burgh of barony in medieval times, it's an attractive place. There's an old castle, an extensive and verdant park, picturesque houses, churches and public buildings, all nestled within rolling hills and green fields. In 1820 as many as 800 of its inhabitants worked at looms. They are remembered today in the name of one of the local pubs, The Weavers.

Robert Hamilton was the local delegate to the Glasgow radical committee, which had apparently re-formed after the arrests at the end of February. On Saturday, 1 April, he came back from Glasgow with a couple of hundred copies of the *Address to the Inhabitants of Great Britain & Ireland*, and these were posted all around Strathaven.

On Monday, 3 April, many local weavers and other workers responded to the strike call contained in the *Address*. Some time after ten o'clock that night, a meeting was held at Three Stanes Farm, a little way outside the town. About fifty people were addressed by two men, William Robertson and John Stevenson. Their speeches were stirring. Robertson told the assembly,

> Our cause is just. We have counted the cost of this contest, and find nothing so dreadful as voluntary slavery. We have bowed our heads to the yoke too

long; let us resolve this evening to draw our swords in defence of our liberties, and if we do so, we must throw away the scabbard. There must be no compromise; there can be none. Our tyrants will leave no mode of retreat for us – we must go on – liberty or death must be our rallying-word.[1]

Robertson went on to evoke 'the glorious field of Bannockburn' where 'our gallant ancestors' fought for freedom. He said their motto should be 'Scotland free, or a desert'. Here he was referring back to Tacitus, the Roman historian, who attributed similar words to Calgacus, the hero of Caledonia who fought back against the invading Romans. 'They make a desert and call it peace.'

Stevenson was equally passionate. It is interesting that he mentioned 'the red flag of defiance' in his speech. The red flag as an emblem of socialism was many decades in the future.

Are our hands always to be tied, and our backs bowed down with hunger and labour? Are degradation and misery to be our sole inheritance? Are we to be effectually, and are our children and our children's children to remain eternally, the tools and victims of a villainous aristocracy who have shed the blood of three millions of men in the late revolutionary wars, and who would still shed the blood of half the human race to perpetuate their desolating usurpation of the rights of man? Forbid it, heaven!

We must and shall have justice; our petitions must no longer be insulted; [. . .] we must unfurl the red flag of defiance and trust to God and our own right arms for salvation for ourselves, our families and the fatherland.[2]

There were roars of approval and unanimous agreement to the proposal that when word came from Glasgow, 'we would muster at once and march to the western metropolis, and assist our friends in the deadly struggle which we anticipated would take place between them and the military'. The next day they started making bullets, lead shot and pikes. Houses and one shop where they knew there to be guns were visited and the weapons commandeered. The atmosphere was electric and rumours abounded. So did fear, especially among the women and older men of Strathaven. One rumour these terrified people helped spread was that the Duke of Wellington himself had arrived in Glasgow and 'was smiting the Radicals hip and thigh'.[3]

At least one mature man did throw himself into the preparations. Purlie Wilson's home became the headquarters of the incipient radical regiment of Strathaven. More than twenty years later one of those radicals, returning to Strathaven after years spent in the West Indies, anonymously wrote up his account of what happened in Strathaven during the first week of April 1820.[4]

As 'class leader' of the Strathaven Union Society, James Wilson either made a flag or had one made. On one side it read *Strathaven Union Society, 1819*. The other side bore the bold statement: *Scotland Free, or Scotland a Desart*. This was an accepted alternative spelling of the word at this time. Strathaven Union was much more than an innocuous evening class and discussion group, although this does not necessarily mean James Wilson and other local radicals favoured more than robust moral force campaigning.

On the afternoon of Wednesday, 5 April, a messenger who said he was from the secret central committee in Glasgow arrived in Strathaven. James Shields was a Paisley weaver, a brother craftsman. The news he brought was trusted, and it was electrifying. An attack was to be made on the government troops and local militia occupying Glasgow on the following day, Thursday, 6 April. As much manpower as possible was needed. Shields told the Strathaven men the Glasgow radical committee wanted them to march to the Cathkin Braes south of Glasgow, where they would join a well-armed radical army of over 5,000.

To the north of Glasgow, Shields said that a similarly well-armed body of men was mustering on the Campsie Fells, ready to attack the city from that direction. Fired up, the Strathaven radicals chose John Morrison to be their leader. Another former soldier, he had served for several years in Spain.

The readying of weapons ramped up a gear. Wilson's house could be accessed via its back door by coming through the churchyard on the hill above and climbing down a ladder into the garden. Despite this option, the would-be radical soldiers made little attempt at discretion. Several of Wilson's near neighbours saw men going in and coming out of the front door late on Wednesday evening.

It was a wild night, dark, wet and stormy. Perhaps they thought the weather might camouflage their movements. It didn't cover up the noises a neighbour heard coming from the Wilson house between ten and eleven o'clock. James Thompson lived just across the road. He thought it sounded like a smithy, with lots of banging and hammering going on.[5]

Despite the howling gale, more trips were made in the hunt for guns and volunteers. They didn't have much luck there. James Wilson stayed at home, keeping the fire in. As day dawned on Thursday morning their woes were compounded when they realised some of their number had disappeared back to their own homes. The diehards sat on the floor in Wilson's house quietly discussing the situation.

William Howat was all for going through with the plan, saying, 'If liberty is worth the having, it is surely worth the fighting for.' Morrison agreed. The discussion was interrupted by someone knocking at the front door. They were all surprised to see who was standing there. It was Matty, the local spaewife. Nowadays we would call her a psychic.

Known as she was for predictions of death and disaster, Stravonians treated her with wary respect. The Wilsons had always been kind to her, often feeding her and giving her the shelter of their home and hearth on cold winter nights. Matty was tall and skinny and she made a dramatic entrance into the house, spinning around as she sought James Wilson. Jamie Russell irritably demanded to know who had asked her to breenge in. She gave him short shrift.

> Ye're a young head-strong gomeral, Russell; you an'
> the rest o' thae braw chiels are gaun awa' to fecht
> for the rights o' auld Scotland, but ye'll no prosper
> at this time; it'll be threety years before Scotland be

able tae right hersel' and smite her oppressors – ye'll
be a' scattered like sheep wantin' a shepherd lang
before the sun gae doon . . .

The dire prediction got even worse. She had come 'in the name
o' Him wha rides on the whirlwind' to warn James Wilson to stay
safely at home. Blood was going to be shed on the scaffold and
she specified it would be at Glasgow and that the blood would be
his. During the storm which had raged through the night, 'a terrible flash' of forked lightning had shown her a vision of his 'gory,
ghastly head in the kirkyard'. She drove home her message with a
final warning. 'Dinna ye gang a step wi' these armed men, or ye'll
lie a bluidy mangled corpse in that kirkyard before sax months.'

This final warning was the last prediction Matty the spaewife
would ever make. She stood there with staring eyes, laughing hys-
terically. Then she dropped dead, falling like a stone to the floor. A
stunned silence descended on the room and the men within it. It's a
melodramatic story, one that is impossible to verify. It appears only
in the account given in *The Pioneers* and the parish records for
Strathaven do not record the death of any woman named Matty,
Matilda or Martha. On the other hand, there is so much detail, and
what Matty said and how she spoke sounds authentic.

According to *The Pioneers*, Rab Hamilton said he hoped 'the
turf will lie light on her old head'. James Wilson said 'Amen'. With
tears in his eyes, he said he was sorry his old friend Matty had
given them such a terrible warning not to march. 'But march we
will: we are seeking nothing but what our forefathers bled to main-
tain – we deserve freedom – and if are to die, we cannot lose our
lives in a juster or holier cause; but we will put our trust in Him in
whose hands are the issues of life.'[6]

We cannot know if any of these words were put into James
Wilson's mouth. The teller of the story was writing his account
many years after the event. Wilson seems to have been an agnostic,
if not an atheist, but they were about to rise in armed rebellion.[7]
This was a hanging offence and they all knew it. Maybe he was
advising trust in God on the same basis that you don't find many
atheists in a lifeboat. His words about their going out in a just

cause ring absolutely true. He had been a supporter of reform for thirty years and more.

As they were all sitting there staring in shock at Matty's dead body, a second caller arrived at the Wilson house. It was Shields, the Paisley weaver who had brought the news from the secret committee in Glasgow. The Strathaven men were wanted at the Cathkin Braes by twelve noon. We might wonder why he didn't tell them that the night before. They didn't ask. Pulling themselves together, they told him they were ready to go.

> William Watson went out and waved our flag with the celebrated inscription, 'SCOTLAND FREE, OR SCOTLAND A DESART,' in front of Wilson's house. We rallied under it, and after saluting this 'emblem of Liberty,' we marched for Cathkin with the firm step and bold bearing of men who had made up their minds to encounter the perils, and grapple with the real difficulties of such a hazardous undertaking.

The anonymous author of *The Pioneers* made the point that they were all 'quiet, inoffensive, industrious men'. It was the tyranny and intransigence of the government which had driven them to arm themselves and rise in rebellion. They set out from Strathaven at eight o'clock on Thursday morning, about twenty-five of them. Almost the whole population of the little market town turned out to watch them go as they headed towards the Glasgow road.

William McIntyre joined them when they were about a mile along it. He had been delayed by his wife hiding his hat in an attempt to stop him from marching out with the impromptu army. Clearly it was unthinkable to embark on a journey or rise in armed rebellion without first putting your hat on. McIntyre found his headgear and left his worried wife.[8]

They were still looking for weapons. They knew Gavin Cooper had 'an excellent gun'. Mr Cooper, however, had hidden his excellent gun away where the raiding party could not find it. Losing patience, they threatened to shoot him with one of the guns they already had with them 'and brought him out of the house for that fell purpose'.

'Howat, who was a young dare-devil, advancing close up to the old man, said we had turned out to fight for the liberty of Scotland, and could not afford to lose our errand – and to decide at once whether he would give up the gun, or get an ounce of lead through his old stupid forehead . . .'

As he made the threat, William Howat slowly raised his own rifle, pressing the muzzle against Gavin Cooper's cheek. Cooper was shaking like a leaf but still refused to say where he had hidden his gun. Luckily for him, Howat had second thoughts. Stevenson too said they had not left their homes to make war on old men. Their aim was 'to better our own conditions, and that of our oppressed starving countrymen'.

James Thompson, who had heard all the noise the night before, passed them on the road. He was a carter to trade, going about his usual business. He recognised several of them, some carrying pikes and some carrying guns, noticing that William Watson was carrying the flag.[9] He spotted shoemaker John Walters. He was James Wilson's son-in-law.

James Wilson was bringing up the rear and looked rather melancholy. Small wonder if the story of Matty the spaewife is true. He was carrying a sword but it was an old broken one which had been propping up a corner of his loom. It seems likely he was doubting the wisdom of the whole venture.

That doubt was reinforced when they met two men in a carriage about a mile outside the place known then simply as Kilbride. The men told them the military were in control of Glasgow and they had heard nothing about any radical army encamped at the Cathkin Braes. The group rounded on Shields, the messenger from the Glasgow committee. He told them he had done nothing wrong and had acted in good faith. If they had been fooled, then so had he.

They kept a close watch on him all the same, the atmosphere in the group growing tense. They were jumpy, 'expecting every moment to be pounced upon by the cavalry from Hamilton'. The threat was doubled when one of the men they had sent on ahead as a scout reported back that the local yeomanry was waiting for them at Kilbride.

Yet the knowledge also provoked a defiant reaction. Yeomanry troops were often composed of local farmers. There was little love lost between the soor-milk jocks and artisans like weavers. They felt farmers were growing rich at their expense, their incomes protected by the Corn Laws. Morrison had been involved in hand-to-hand and house-to-house fighting against the French in the towns and villages of Spain. He laughed at the very idea of the local yeomanry posing much of a threat. He gave the men who'd elected him their captain a brief but rousing pep talk. The yeomanry might well rue the day they ever met the Strathaven Pioneers of 1820. 'Wallace and Bruce had often fought and conquered in the glorious cause of liberty, and he was proud to see a few Scotchmen [*sic*] leave their homes to tread in the footsteps of their illustrious countrymen.'

Buoyed up, laughing and joking, they marched on to Kilbride, where they found the yeomanry 'had scampered off to Hamilton'. At this stage James Wilson made the decision to proceed no farther. He had begun to realise it was hopeless. There was no radical army waiting for them on the Cathkin Braes and if the story of old Matty's death and last prediction is true, it wasn't to be wondered at if this was weighing him down.

He went into a change-house. These were pubs and coaching inns, where riders and coach drivers could hire fresh horses. James Wilson and the landlady knew each other. Agnes Richmond was the wife of Robert Hamilton, a different one to the man of the same name in the Strathaven Pioneers. Like James Wilson, she too was a hosier. For a while they discussed the technique of making stockings. She gave him tea and a bread roll and he smoked a pipe of tobacco. When he left he made a point of saying that if anyone came asking about what had happened this Thursday morning, would she please say the two of them had been talking business. Sounds like he was already looking for an alibi to defend himself against the charge of rising in armed rebellion.[10]

The other Pioneers marched on, reaching Cathkin between noon and one o'clock. To find no radical army of 5,000 men waiting for them was a bitter blow. To make matters worse, they were all aware that by marching out bearing arms they had committed treason. With one last defiant flourish they planted their flag on the hilltop overlooking Glasgow. One man went to Glasgow in the forlorn hope of hearing from the central committee that substantial numbers of the city's radicals might yet join them.

It was four hours, the length of the April afternoon, before the messenger returned. Glasgow was too well-guarded. Known radicals were being arrested and the authorities would soon be aware the Strathaven Pioneers had raised a radical flag on the Cathkin Braes. If they were not going to be arrested too, they needed to leave now. With heavy hearts, they lowered and folded their flag and all but one of them hid their incriminating weapons about the hill.[11] James Shields, the messenger from the Glasgow committee, was still with them, and one of the last to reluctantly hide his pike. Quite a number of the weapons were later discovered, hidden in Cathkin woods.[12]

So as not to arouse suspicion they split up, going down the brae in twos and threes. Some went into a cottar house where women were boiling potatoes. They begged for a few, 'which they fell upon like as many hungry dogs. Nothing could exceed their wretched and alarming experience.'[13] In the meanwhile, James Wilson had returned to Strathaven. He was readying himself to leave again and go into hiding when he was arrested.

William Howat had held on to his weapons and ammunition. Returning to Strathaven and spotting that soldiers were already approaching the town, he hastily hid his gun, bandolier, coat and hat. Then he went calmly back on to the road, pretending to be a weaver out taking a leisurely evening walk. Hooking his thumbs through the armholes of his waistcoat, he made his way past the soldiers. He got away with it and was not arrested.

Little more than a week later, on 13 April 1820, Home Secretary Viscount Sidmouth wrote to Alexander Boswell in Auchinleck, expressing his satisfaction with the outcome. 'The Disaffected in the West of Scotland have received a severe Blow. I trust it will be followed up by the customary punishment of the principal leaders.'[14] His wish was soon to be granted.

CHAPTER 19

Radicals Arrested at Milngavie

Tuesday, 4 April–Sunday, 9 April 1820

Radicals were being arrested everywhere, and the crackdown started early. They came looking for John Parkhill in Paisley on Tuesday, 4 April. He wasn't at home but local sheriff William Motherwell, at the head of a group of soldiers and constables, ransacked his house looking for pikes and any incriminating papers.[1] Motherwell, who was a published poet, asked Mrs Parkhill if there were any pikes or guns in the house. No, she said sweetly, but I do have a pretty long spear. Motherwell politely asked to see it. She told him Spear was her maiden name. He laughed and asked where her husband was. She told him she had no idea and the raiding party left the Parkhill home. John Parkhill went off on the tramp, lying low until he finally went to Greenock and took passage for Montreal in Canada. He returned home to his wife and family about a year later.

Duntocher was taken by surprise on the morning of Wednesday, 5 April. A village of cotton-spinners and blacksmiths, it might have considered itself to be way out in the country. Its houses, textile mill and forge clustered on the lower slopes of the Old Kilpatrick hills. There was farmland between the village and the River Clyde, an expanse known as the Barns o' Clyde. It was decades later before the town of Clydebank grew up around John Brown's shipyard and the Singer sewing machine factory.

The soldiers and the militia set off in the early hours. They arrived at Duntocher at six o'clock in the morning and proceeded to surround it. Bursting into houses, they arrested eight men while they were still in their beds. They knew who they were looking for. The prisoners were taken to Dumbarton Castle. A search produced pikes hidden behind a hedge and one musket and ammunition hidden in a pigsty.[2] They also took away three sets of bellows, allowing locals to nickname the military raid the Battle of the Bellows. On Thursday, 6 April, it was the turn of Bridgeton and the Calton in Glasgow. After stationing sentries at all potential escape routes through closes and wynds, the search began. The soldiers found some pikes and arrested several people for what they had done 'in the late atrocious proceedings'. Over the next few days there were further raids in Paisley, Anderston and Milngavie.[3] Some suspects were also taken at Garscube on the River Kelvin.[4] There were mills, bleaching fields and farms here, with the associated cottages for the workers. Paisley radical John Parkhill had spent a year of his childhood here when his father worked briefly on the banks of the Kelvin. Dawsholm Park and the University of Glasgow College of Veterinary Medicine now occupy the site of the Garscube estate.

Now a pleasant suburb of Glasgow, Milngavie in 1820 was a large village of cotton-spinners and bleachers. The newspapers reported that as many as 400 to 500 of those workers had still been drilling on the Friday but had 'fled' by the Saturday. Where they might have fled to is not stated, although they could have gone up onto Drumclog moor at Mugdock, a large expanse where they could quite literally go to ground. The soldiers came back from Milngavie with 'five prisoners, seven guns, and about 300 rounds of ball cartridges'. The cartridges had been hidden in a haystack.[5]

By the end of the week, the authorities were confident they were once more in control of the situation. 'Our streets have again resumed their wonted quietness', the *Caledonian Mercury* could not resist gloating. 'There is no longer any talk of civil war. On the contrary, the fear of punishment is now strongly depicted in every Radical countenance. It is a strange feature of the infatuation that many of the individuals who turned out with arms on Wednesday were seen the very next morning, going about as if they had done nothing amiss!'[6]

While the villagers of Duntocher had been enthusiastic supporters of the radical cause at the start of the week, they had baulked at
committing acts of violence. By the end of the week their numbers
were 'quite contemptible'. Gloating yes, but also a huge combined
sigh of relief. Glasgow's middle classes and establishment had been
scared witless by the radical threat.

James Turner of Thrushgrove, who had allowed his fields to
be used for the mass meeting in 1816, was also arrested.[7] As at
Duntocher, it was a dawn raid. Turner was woken by an almighty
hammering on the front door and his alarmed dogs barking in
response. It was five o'clock in the morning on Sunday, 9 April.
When he opened the door he was astonished to see Procurator
Fiscal George Salmond standing there. By his side was Calder, the
sheriff-officer. They'd brought some muscle with them, a party of
soldiers who surrounded the house.

Salmond told Turner he was being arrested for high treason.
He waved a warrant at him but would not let him read it. A copy
surfaced later and a terrifying document it was too. Lord Advocate
William Rae requested the warrant on the grounds that:

> the petitioner has received information that James
> Turner of Thrushgrove is guilty of high treason,
> actor or art and part, by having joined in the pres-
> ent insurrection, being possessed of and have borne
> arms in furtherance thereof, and of levying, and
> of inciting the subjects of our Lord the King to
> levy war against his Majesty within his realm, in
> order to effect the overthrow of the Constitution by
> law established.[8]

Salmond began raking through Turner's writing desk. He found
a bayonet and demanded to know if there were any more weapons
in the house. His captive told him he had the gun that went with
the bayonet, a pair of pocket pistols he carried while travelling and
a few ball cartridges which had been in his desk for nigh on twenty
years. They dated back to when he had served as a volunteer in the
Glasgow Armed Association militia. With what sounds very like

exasperated sarcasm, Turner suggested Salmond take his uniform from back then too.

The procurator fiscal confiscated the weapons but declined the uniform. He went through the papers in the writing bureau, taking away the guest list for the funerals of Turner's parents. The inference was that anyone who was a friend of James Turner was also under suspicion of being a radical.

The soldiers were dismissed and Turner went quietly. They called in at his tobacconist's shop in the High Street. He had told Salmond he had one larger pistol there and it too was confiscated. The procurator fiscal also seized some of Turner's business correspondence and several copies of *Cobbett's Register*, a popular English radical journal.

At the offices of Glasgow police, he was given into the care of Captain Mitchell, the Paisley man who had been sent through from Edinburgh to strengthen the Glasgow police force. Mitchell and Turner knew each other of old and Mitchell was kind. He let Turner's son George spend most of the day with him. He allowed Turner's friend William Lang to send him in a good meal. Lang was a Glasgow printer who had been one of the speakers at the Thrushgrove meeting.

Turner asked if he could write to his old colonel in the Glasgow Armed Association. He'd bought his weapons from Cunningham Corbett back in 1802 and the colonel would be able to corroborate that. Mitchell agreed as long as he could read the letter. Helpfully, he went off to the police coffee room to find Corbett's address before taking the letter to the post office. With the same proviso of reading them through, Mitchell permitted Turner to write letters to a friend and to his wife.

When Mitchell got orders Turner was to be transferred to prison, the police officer 'begged for God's sake that I would say nothing about his permitting me to write these letters, for if it were known he durst not consent to it'.[9]

Turner and twenty other prisoners were taken to the prison in what he described as a grand procession. Each man was escorted by a police officer and they were surrounded by soldiers on foot, with mounted hussars flanking them on each side. A very unsubtle message was being sent: we're catching all the radicals, they won't escape our net. We have the situation back under control. We can all sleep soundly in our beds tonight.

It was eleven o'clock at night before they got to the prison. For James Turner, it had been a very long day. Half an hour after he got there, James Wilson was brought in from Strathaven. Turner reckoned there were as many as a hundred radical prisoners, an estimate reached by other contemporary observers. For the next six days, until the following Friday, Turner was held on his own in a cheerless, cold cell with a stone floor and no fireplace. On the first day of his prison stay he was allowed pen, ink and one sheet of paper. He wrote to the Lord Advocate giving some facts in defence of himself and William Lang, who by now had also been arrested. They had always done everything they could to keep the peace. They were not 'the friends of disorder'.[10]

He requested permanent access to writing materials but on Tuesday morning the pen and ink were removed. Fortunately, the police officers of the day before had suggested he put a few sheets of paper into his pocket – and he had a pencil. He wasn't giving that pencil up for love nor money.

> Just think what my feelings were when my *pencil* was demanded. I told the man who was sent [with] this message that I knew he was a servant, and of course it was his duty to deliver his message; however, I begged he would have the goodness to inform his employers that I would not part with my pencil. Upon this he went away, observing that he would say no more about it until he got farther orders. Indeed, I would rather have parted with a five pound note than my pencil, for it was the only treat they had left me in my solitary cell.[11]

Given that he was in a cell on his own and not allowed to send any messages out, you wonder how his gaolers knew he had the pencil. Had one of them seen him writing with it through a spy-hole in the door? Or did everyone carry a pencil in their pocket in those days? How did he sharpen it? If he also had a penknife in his pocket, would he have been allowed to keep that? These are questions which history books probably cannot answer.

History lovers can only be grateful for the existence of this humble writing implement. It allowed Turner to document his imprisonment. As important for him, it gave him something to do to pass the time, allowing him to pour his worry and anxiety onto the page. He suspected his gaolers were questioning all the other prisoners before they interviewed him and Lang, hoping to find evidence that would incriminate the two of them. He was confident they wouldn't find any, but there was no guarantee that would see him set free again.

That evening he requested 'half a glass of good whisky' with his dinner. He didn't get it. At six o'clock he was cheered up by the arrival of some 'necessaries' his wife had sent in. At nine he waxed lyrical. 'Night hath again spread her sable curtain over that part of the globe which we inhabit. This hath been a very solitary day.' He was a gregarious man. Being forced to endure prolonged solitude was torture.

His Christian faith giving him strength, he prayed to God to guide not only him but his interrogators. The following morning he was cast down again by witnessing through his cell window the arrival of more radical prisoners. He described them as 'poor creatures' who had been duped into aggressive action by 'hired spies and informers'. Like so many at the time, James Turner was convinced it was *agents provocateurs* who had entrapped all those radicals who chose to take direct and armed action. He himself had always deplored the use of physical force to secure political reform.

> I hope that I shall soon be set at liberty, for I can solemnly declare, in the presence of the Searcher of Hearts, that I never saw a weapon intended for the mad business that has taken place, till after I was a prisoner in the police office – and that I did not know a single individual who was to take any part in it. God knows this to be truth. I have now had a bit of dinner, and feel quite comfortable.

Although he spotted two of his friends through his cell window, they weren't allowed in to visit him. He got some consolation when a bottle of wine and 'a can of marmalade' were sent in that evening. During the Napoleonic wars, canned food had been pioneered first by the French and then the British with the aim of providing armies on the move with a reliable food supply. Turner was thankful his friend inside the prison had also had some liquid refreshment. 'I have had information that Mr Lang has also got a little wine. I hope it will do him good.'

He spotted one of William Lang's daughters outside the prison, hoping to catch a glimpse of her father. He longed to see his own wife Jean and his family but counted his blessings. The Turners were comfortably off, with no problem putting food on the table. Most of his 'poor fellow prisoners' had wives and families who were 'almost on the point of starvation'. He saw some of them from his window. Bewildered women and children were standing around outside the prison hoping to catch a glimpse of their imprisoned menfolk.

One of those men was Alexander Rodger, poet and satirist. Although he hadn't taken any active part in the rising, he was suspect because of the pieces he had written for the *Spirit of the Union*. Like James Turner, Sandy was outraged that he had been thrown into prison. He wrote a poem about the experience. The title was not subtle: 'Lines Written in a Certain Bridewell, by a State Prisoner, in the Month of April, 1820'. Here's a taste of it.

> Pent up within this horrid cell,
> How heaves my breast with anger's swell!
> To think what I must suffer here,
> Cut off from friends and freedom dear;
> Reft of the truest joys of life,
> The joys o' hame – my bairns, my wife . . .[12]

Even a Cherokee would show mercy to poor prisoners like them, wrote Sandy, would surely 'draw back, his scalping knife and tomahawk'. Even a cannibal would relent and 'throw aside his bloody knife'. The poem goes on to celebrate those who refused to praise a rotten system of government, even if they did end up in prison as a result.

In the same building but being treated rather better, James Turner spotted his servant and found he had brought him in more tasty treats, 'some biscuits and a mug of jelly'. The interview he was dreading came on Friday evening. The first question was about the *Address to the Inhabitants of Great Britain & Ireland*. Had he had a hand in it at any stage or given money towards the printing costs? No, he said, he had not.

He was asked if he had been involved in the Committee of Organization for Forming a Provisional Government or if he belonged to a union society. No to both questions, was his reply. He was quizzed about a couple of individuals, including Mr Brayshaw, the radical reformer from Yorkshire who had made campaigning visits to Scotland.

On the Friday evening Turner was closely questioned by John Hope, the Advocate Depute, and Sheriff Hamilton. They wanted to know how many reform meetings he had helped set up and what he might have said in speeches at those meetings. They also wanted to know what he thought about the other men with whom he had been confined for almost a week.

He could say very little as he hadn't spent much, if any, time with the other prisoners. His answers seemed to satisfy his interrogators. He was told he would be allowed writing materials and to see his friends. Several came, his son George a frequent caller.

James Turner was released on bail on Tuesday, 18 April, the tenth day of his imprisonment. When he left the prison and walked into the High Street a cheering crowd was waiting for him. He had to keep stopping because so many people wanted to shake him by the hand.

Outraged by his imprisonment, he subsequently took his case to the Westminster parliament, sending a petition and a letter to several MPs. He gave them a summary of his arrest and his time in prison. He mentioned his pencil and the attempt to take it away from him. That petty cruelty continued to rankle.

> From this brief statement of facts I trust you will see that in my person the rights of a British subject have

been grossly violated, and that I have been made a victim of tyrannical power and malignant persecution, for which it appears there is little or no chance of redress, and that merely because I have not concealed my being friendly to the cause of Parliamentary Reform, which I only sought to have accomplished by legal and constitutional means.[13]

Turner's MP was Lord Archibald Hamilton. A year later, in May 1821, he raised the case in the House of Commons. The Lord Advocate would accept no blame being laid at the door of Glasgow's magistrates. The events of the first week of April 1820 had constituted an emergency. If extreme measures had been taken, they were justified by the nature of the crisis. Glasgow had been in real danger.

He denied most distinctly that in any of the transactions in Scotland the spy-agent or informer had been employed. His Lordship then alluded to the disorderly state of Glasgow, to the proclamation for a general rising, which had obtained implicit belief, and to the marching of masses of men in military array, to the terror of the loyal inhabitants. The shops were shut up for some days, but tranquillity and confidence were restored by a timely exercise of the powers of Government.[14]

Turner had approached another local MP for help. He was John, later Sir John, Maxwell of Pollok. Contradicting the Lord Advocate, he said it was the general belief in Scotland that spies had been employed to promote the rising.

In Turner's petition to parliament he called for an inquiry into the powers of the Lord Advocate and for these to be limited by law. On a more personal note, he wanted the Lord Advocate to be obliged to admit who had laid false information against him, leading to that dawn raid on Thrushgrove. He never did find that out.

James Turner had the last laugh. He stayed active in politics, continuing to call for reform and a strengthening of the links between middle and working-class reformers. After the Great Reform Act of 1832, he was elected to Glasgow Town Council. Fourteen years later, he was made a bailie. There is a very handsome portrait of him dressed in his official robes in Glasgow's civic art collection.

The Turner family left Thrushgrove in 1838 because of encroaching railway and industrial development. It must have been very poignant for them to see their much-loved home and the fields around it disappear so completely. Yet they could take comfort from how crucial Thrushgrove and James Turner had been to the reform movement. He died in 1858, a man who made a difference, a man who left the world in a better state than he found it.

CHAPTER 20

'Remember Manchester!' – The Greenock Massacre

Saturday, 8 April 1820

Many of those arrested during and after that eventful first week of April were apprehended only on suspicion of being involved in radical activities. This was the case in Kilmarnock, whose inhabitants were woken up on the morning of Saturday, 15 April by the clopping of horses' hooves.[1] The town was being surrounded by a troop of hussars. They were the cavalry of the Edinburgh Yeomanry, who had marched all night so as to reach Kilmarnock by daybreak.

A number of the smartly dressed soldiers were noticed to be almost nodding off in their saddles. Waking up, they made a few arrests before heading back to Edinburgh. The cavalrymen joked about their visit to Kilmarnock, calling it the 'Western Campaign'. One of them wrote a satirical ballad about it which was later published in the *Scots Magazine*.

> Let us sing of the heroes that marched from yon town,
> To keep liberty up, to put Radicals down,
> With their long spurs and sabres so bright.
> Their majestic manoeuvres in cross-road and lane,
> Their walk on the hill, and their trot on the plane,
> The butts that were shed, and the beeves [complainers and trouble-makers] that were slain,

Stamped immortal renown on the western campaign,
And the long spurs and sabres so bright.[2]

Apparently they used to belt this out in the officers' mess in Edinburgh for quite some time afterwards. It was modelled on and sung to the tune of 'Black Joke', which was a popular bawdy song of the time. A week before, things had taken a more serious turn in Paisley, another well-known hotbed of radicals and reformers. As the gaol there filled up, the decision was taken to move some prisoners to Greenock, several miles down the Clyde.

The Port Glasgow militia were detailed to provide the escort and duly set out from Paisley for Greenock around eleven o'clock in the morning on Saturday, 8 April 1820. The militia approached the port with drums beating and fifes playing, which might not have been the most brilliant of ideas. Triumphalism trumped tact, not to mention wisdom and a sense of self-preservation. The music and the marching naturally attracted attention.

Shortly before five o'clock in the afternoon, the party entered Greenock at Cartsdyke at the town's east end. The Port Glasgow militia found all the shops already shut, their windows boarded up. A crowd had gathered in front of those shops, watching as the militia and their five radical prisoners rumbled into the port. The prisoners were being transported in a cart. The Port Glasgow Volunteers were wary, alert lest a rescue attempt might be mounted.

No such attempt was made at this stage. The Cartsdyke crowd did call out encouragement to the prisoners: 'You will soon be free of your present difficulty!' George Robertson was a merchant whose house stood on the main road into Greenock. He was having dinner with his wife and children and his cousin, Dr Archibald Robertson. One of the servants came into the dining-room and told them a party of prisoners was being brought into the town.[3] Everyone rose from the table and went upstairs to watch the prisoners and their guards going past. They were astonished to see how big the following crowd was. It was growing increasingly hostile.

John Fish was a sailmaker. He had left his sail loft to go down to the old east quay on business and also saw the crowd passing. Experiencing some difficulties of their own, the militia were struggling to make it through to the centre of Greenock and the bridewell in Bank Street. George Robertson felt sure the crowd did not know the muskets were primed and loaded and they were risking being shot on the spot. He urged his wife to take their children through to the back of the house for safety and came out onto the street. People were picking stones up off the ground, ready to use as ammunition. Robertson tried to persuade them not to. He was hit by a few himself.

One woman stepped in front of one of the soldiers guarding the cart in which the radical prisoners were being transported. Looking Adam McLeish straight in the eye, she told him they were all 'ill-looking blackguards. If there is any spirit in Greenock not one of you will return home this night.' He told her to get out of his way.

At the square in the centre of Greenock, a carter with a load of wood was caught up in the mêlée. Some in the crowd tried to force him to keep going up Bank Street, hoping to drive the horse into the Volunteers and scatter the soldiers. Andrew Ramsay urged the carter to resist. 'Turn your horse's head Sir, and let me see who will stop you.' The Volunteers succeeding in delivering the prisoners to the bridewell and the crowd swung into action, following them as they marched away. An anonymous eyewitness described what happened next.

> Mr Denniston, one of the Magistrates, happened by chance to come to the square, and went to the jail, when some persons (said to be strangers) threw some stones at the Volunteers, who fired two shots in the air with intention of intimidation; this however had the contrary effect; and on Mr Denniston remonstrating with the crowd, he was hustled, and with difficulty rescued from amongst them. The Volunteers then marched off, and got the length of the Rue-end, when the mob began pelting them with stones, by which several were severely cut. Thus assailed, a file of them faced round and fired among the crowd, when several people fell.

One of those people was Andrew Clephane. Aged forty-eight, he was a silversmith by trade. He lay in the street, dying of gunshot wounds. Another was Archibald McKinnon, a seventeen-year-old butcher's boy. He had been throwing stones at the Port Glasgow Volunteers. Another eyewitness gave a chilling description of how he died. He 'saw a man in the near section with a long green Coat, and the second from the left turn round and take a double aim at a Butcher boy who was at the distance of about ten or twelve yards, and shot him, and the boy fell'.

The same witness saw a woman and a younger boy standing about three feet away from Archibald McKinnon as he was shot. They too were shot. The woman was Catherine Turner, who was sixty-five years old. She survived but her leg had to be amputated. The boy was James McGilp. Just eight years old, he was the youngest victim of the Greenock massacre.

Archibald McPhedran was another Greenock merchant. He had followed the Volunteers, their prisoners and the growing crowd into Greenock as far as the White Hart Inn. He was taking shelter in the pub's coffee room when he heard the first shot being fired. He looked out of the window and saw a stone flying through the air. One of the Volunteers levelled his musket in response and fired into the very dense crowd. The man was not aiming at the direction from which the stone had been flung. McPhedran thought the soldier and several other Volunteers were drunk. He based that opinion on 'their ferocious look and swaggering appearance'.

Roused to fury, the crowd redoubled its attack on the men of the militia. A running battle ensued, musket fire against hurled stones and bottles. Some of the latter were thrown from windows and closes. The Port Glasgow Volunteers fought their way back through to the eastern end of Greenock and the road home. By the time they did, the crowd in Greenock had been swollen by people coming out of their work at six o'clock. Voices in the crowd called for pursuit of the Volunteers. They should 'Lay Port Glasgow in ashes!' A group led by a bagpiper were all ready to mount the pursuit.[4]

Robert Sinclair, another Greenock businessman, went into the crowd and tried to persuade people to disperse. He didn't succeed.

Tempers were running high. One stone cut through Sinclair's hat, 'just at the place where the brim joins the crown'. The impact of the stone caused him a brief moment of concussion. Realising calming words weren't going to stop the stone throwers, he retreated. As he left, he heard a shout go up that instead of chasing the militia back to Port Glasgow the mob should storm the prison instead. The cry was 'Bridewell! Bridewell!'

John Denniston also tried to calm people down. Greenock's chief magistrate was assisted in this endeavour by seven or eight other men. They walked round the square in front of the prison, talking to different groups in the crowd. For half an hour or so, it seemed wise words and cooler heads would prevail, taking the heat out of the situation.

In the end, people were too angry for that. When they were assured there would be a full inquiry into the deaths they retorted that the people of Manchester had got no redress for what had happened at the Peterloo massacre the year before. There were cries of 'Remember Manchester!' and the mood again grew restless. The seven or eight gentlemen 'buttoned their coats' and, linking arms, stood in front of the prison doors. Did they button up their coats as a very rudimentary form of protection against stones?

As daylight began to fade, someone did throw a stone, breaking the lamp and some windows above the door of the prison. At this point all hell broke loose. The crowd had found a scaffolding plank. The gentlemen in the buttoned-up coats beat a hasty retreat.

Some of those wielding the battering ram were sailors, easily recognisable by their short navy-blue jackets and canvas trousers. After a 'long thumping' the doors of the prison broke open. The crowd ran up the stairs and swiftly came back out with the five radical prisoners, leaving the other prisoners where they were. The radicals were spirited away and never caught again.

An hour or so later, Greenock was silent. As the letter writer to the *Glasgow Herald* put it: '. . . by 11 o'clock the town was as quiet as ever I saw it'. Although presumably people with troubled faces were sitting by their firesides talking in low, shocked voices about the tragic events of the early evening, while others were grieving for their lost loved ones and tending to the wounded.

Despite the apparent quietness hanging over the town that Sunday evening, there was concern that trouble might flare up again at any moment. An express rider was sent to Paisley and Glasgow to request military support. A troop of hussars got there by one o'clock on the morning of the Sunday. 'Some riflemen and other soldiers' arrived by nine o'clock that same morning, using the most modern of methods of travel: they sailed down the Clyde from Glasgow, 'by steam-boats'.[5]

The *Glasgow Herald*'s correspondent emphasised it had all been very frightening while it had been happening but that everything was all right now. 'For a considerable time, the alarm was great, fearing they might attack private property; but no such thing was attempted, not even a pane of glass broke, nor was any insult offered to any of the inhabitants.'

Apart, that is, from those who were killed and wounded by the Volunteers. On the front page of their edition of Friday, 14 April 1820, the newspaper posted a casualty list, the names of the dead and wounded set out in table form. There are eighteen names on the list and the newspaper's information came from the doctors of the town who had tended to the casualties.

Six were dead, all of gunshot wounds: Adam Clephane the silversmith, aged forty-eight; Archibald Drummond, aged twenty; James Kerr, aged seventeen; Archibald McKinnon the butcher's boy, also aged seventeen; John Boyce, aged thirty-three; William Lindsay, aged fifteen. He died instantly. The death toll rose, adding John McWhinnie, aged sixty-five, and young James McGilp, just eight years old. As well as Catherine Turner, one young boy had to have his leg amputated as a result of his injuries. Hugh Paterson was fourteen years old.

Many more people had been hurt or suffered gunshot wounds. Most of the dead had been hit in the head, chest or stomach. Many of the wounded were shot in the leg. Assailed by stones, the sergeant-major and the adjutant of the Port Glasgow militia were badly injured. Many of the other Volunteer soldiers 'received such severe bruises as to confine them to bed'.

Assurances were subsequently repeated in the many newspapers which reported on the 'affray at Greenock', that the port was normally considered 'the most loyal of towns'. The trouble was blamed on mysterious and unidentified strangers. Greenock being the departure point from Scotland for many leaving by sea, mysterious strangers were easy to blame. A local estimated 200 people had arrived in the port that weekend, ready to board the ships which would take them to a new life overseas.[6]

The official line was that the affray was absolutely not the fault of Mr Denniston and his colleagues. Which to be fair, it wasn't. 'No blame whatever is attachable to our Magistrates, who did everything in their power to preserve the peace.'[7] The *Glasgow Courier* and other newspapers blamed 'artful incendiaries and rebels' from outwith the port for provoking the trouble.[8] The Port Glasgow Volunteers bore no ill will to the people of Greenock. 'It is to be hoped that this forgiveness will be reciprocated on the part of the people of Greenock, that they will consider the Volunteers as having been employed in a laudable and imperative duty, and that the events of the 8th of April 1820 will be for ever buried in oblivion.'

Not a chance.

PART III
Aftermath

Chapter 21

Levying War against the King

Stirling, July 1820

On Monday, 10 April, barely one short week after the Radical Rising had erupted, the *Glasgow Herald* was smugly sure it was all over.

> There have been no radical demonstrations here since our last that deserve notice, and the business appears to be over for the present, and we trust is over forever. None of the public works, as far as we can learn, are yet going, the Proprietors adhering steadily to the determination of taking back none of the workers till a thorough investigation be made, and the names of the leaders given up. This insurrectionary movement has been put down with such an admirable promptness, that the danger already begins to appear like a dream; it is proper, therefore, to recall to our minds some of the leading circumstances.[1]

The paper goes on to list those circumstances. There were claims that weavers, spinners and other artisans were intimidated into going on strike. That may be true, offers the *Herald*. Yet if a 'system of terror' intimidated so many people, that was as dangerous as people choosing of their own free will to come out on strike.

Furthermore, with only a slight dropping of the smug triumphalism, it had been seen that thousands of men answered the call and armed themselves, ready to fight. The military had had to take strong measures to suppress this, they had had no other choice. Nor was their work finished. 'A number of persons have been apprehended since our last, both in this city and neighbourhood, and the military have been much employed in searching for arms and scouring the country.'[2]

Another newspaper, under the headline, *Disturbances at Glasgow, &c.*, reported that there had been 'numerous arrests of disaffected persons', in Glasgow, Paisley and nearby towns and villages. There was dismay as to what the writer had read in the Edinburgh and Glasgow papers:

> We understand among the persons apprehended for treasonable practices in Glasgow and the neighbour-hood, are several persons above the common ranks of life; and some who, from their employments, might have been expected to have acted differently; a clerk in a public office, and a serjeant in a respectable corps are said to be of the number, and some who, by industry, have raised themselves to a respectable station in life.[3]

Not being able to put all the blame on the lower orders made some people uneasy.

As with James Turner, those in custody were subjected to intense interrogation. Andrew Hardie's letters and account of Bonnymuir show him to have been scrupulously fair. He recorded that at Stirling Castle they were told they might answer only those questions they chose to answer. Although he did mention that '. . . on the other hand, I was plied with wearied importunity by Captain Sibbald, which was not his duty to do . . .'[4]

He told Sibbald nothing, even when the army officer told him in gloating terms that he was probably going to be hanged. These sound like tense and intense encounters. Hardie was convinced now the whole story was already known. He knew who had done it too. They had been betrayed by one of their own who had turned King's Evidence.

He does not name him in his account but states that the man had already 'made no less than fourteen pages of declaration before we left Stirling, beside what he gave in Edinburgh, which I suppose was much more'. Captain Sibbald had promised this man his thirty pieces of silver, saying he would find him work in Edinburgh as a reward. The bargain was not kept.[5]

Andrew Hardie answered questions put to him by other interrogators, using the opportunity to state the radical case.

> After being in Stirling Castle a day or two, we were all examined, and on being the reason why I was in arms, I told them I went out with the intention to recover my rights; they then asked me what rights I wanted? I said annual parliaments and elections by ballot. Question – what reason had you to expect these rights? Answer – because I think Government ought to grant whatever the majority of the nation requested, and if they had paid attention to the people's lawful petitions, the nation would not have been in the state it at present was . . .[6]

It's interesting to note that at no point did Andrew Hardie say he wanted a Scottish parliament in Edinburgh. In fact, in the reports of all the meetings, speeches and in the memoirs of Scottish radicals, the idea of re-establishing Scotland's parliament in Edinburgh is never mentioned. Nor is there a single word said about this in any of the trial transcripts. The evidence that they did want a reinstatement of the Scottish parliament is based on two supposed letters from Mitchell, Glasgow's Master of Police, to Lord Sidmouth.[7] Despite extensive research in several possible sources, I have been unable to find these letters. Other researchers have also had this difficulty.[8]

One hundred years later, Red Clydesider Davie Kirkwood said the workers had no country; they make common cause with workers in all countries. On the other hand, Kirkwood put a bill to parliament in 1924 that the Stone of Destiny should be removed from Westminster Abbey and returned to Holyroodhouse in

Edinburgh. He was a proud and passionate Scot. So were Andrew Hardie, John Baird, James Wilson and their fellow radicals of 1820.

We cannot put words into their mouths. We cannot know if they wanted Scottish independence as a result of political reform. We do know the vast majority of ordinary Scots were opposed to the union with England of 1707. On the day the Treaty of Union became law, the bells of St Giles in Edinburgh played a tune called *Why am I so Sad on my Wedding Day?*

We might allow ourselves to speculate that for Hardie, Baird, Wilson and all the others, the desire to reinstate the Scottish parliament in Edinburgh was an ambition which lay farther down the line. They were all patriotic Scots. They showed this in their frequent evoking of Scotland's heroes, their singing of 'Scots Wha Hae', and in the imagery they used, the thistle a recurring symbol. The flag carried by the Strathaven Pioneers read 'Scotland Free, or Scotland a Desart'. They often referred to themselves as the heirs to Wallace and Bruce and called themselves the sons of Caledonia.

John Stevenson of the Strathaven Pioneers insisted the workers had every right to reclaim their rights. The radicals of 1820 clearly saw strength in numbers: if they worked with their English, Welsh and Irish counterparts, the despotic government in Westminster could be brought down. That might have been only the start.

Andrew Hardie, John Baird and the other men who fought at Bonnymuir were tried in Stirling on Thursday, 13 and Friday, 14 July 1820. Trials of other radicals were also held in Glasgow, Dumbarton, Paisley and Ayr. All the trials were held under English law, under a Special Commission of Oyer and Terminer, which meant 'to hear and to determine'. In England, the Cato Street conspirators had already been tried and found guilty. Arthur Thistlewood and four of his fellow conspirators were hanged and then beheaded outside Newgate Prison in London, where the Old Bailey now is. There were some gruesome prints made showing the scene.

Baird and Hardie had legal counsel because advocate Francis Jeffrey offered his services *pro bono*. Through him, they were allowed to challenge the proposed jurors without any explanation of why they did not want them. They took advantage of this opportunity several times. The pool from which the jurors were drawn was known quite far in advance of the court cases. Evidence at another of the radical trials in Paisley shows the friends of the accused did their research to establish who the jurors were and whether they were likely to be sympathetic or unsympathetic to the men in the dock.

The same shorthand writer, Mr Green, took notes at all the Scottish state trials and these were published in three volumes in 1825. There were also reporters in attendance, although the press was warned not to publish anything until after all the trials were over. From under his horsehair legal wig and his exalted position on the bench, the Lord President at Hardie and Baird's trial issued a dire warning: any breach of this would be met with 'the severest penalties that this Court can inflict'. He claimed this was essential if the ends of justice were to be served. What was the point of keeping witnesses out of the court apart from when they were giving their own evidence if they could read everything that had been said there in the following day's newspaper? Mr Knapp, the clerk of arraigns, asked the prisoners individually whether they were pleading guilty or not guilty. Then the question was 'How will you be tried?' The expected answer was 'By God and my country'. To which the clerk responded, 'God send you a good deliverance'.

Jeffrey challenged the use of English law in a Scottish court but without success. There was a good deal of discussion as to what constituted treason in the context of the radical rising. The *Address to the Inhabitants of Great Britain & Ireland* was read out many times and dissected in minute detail. The court and the jurors heard how the placards had appeared overnight 'betwixt the night of Saturday, the first of April, and Sunday morning, the second . . . all over the town of Glasgow and in various parts of the adjoining country, etc'.[9]

It was also asked whether the prisoners by their acts had shown themselves to be determined 'to imagine or compass the death of the King' and 'of levying war against the King'. It is easy to get lost in the legal arguments put forward at the Stirling trials. Much was made of how the prisoners were getting a fair and impartial trial. They weren't. At least one witness, possibly two, committed perjury.

If a man 'imagines the death of the King' and does nothing about it, that cannot be judged in any court. If the same man acts on those thoughts, then that's treason, even if it doesn't lead to the death of the king.

> Gentlemen, by the construction of all the lawyers whose authority is listened to in England, this is not confined to the actual imagination to put the King to death; but it applies to every attempt indirectly by which that life may be put in danger; to all attempts against the government of the country; for every one must feel how impossible it is to carry into effect any proceeding having for its object the overthrow of the government of the country, with putting the King's life in peril . . .[10]

The prosecuting lawyer, Mr Serjeant Hullock, went on to beat the jurors over the head with his main argument. Surely it was only common sense to recognise that going out in an armed insurrection against the political status quo was in fact levying war against the king. He quoted the recent trial in England of Arthur Thistlewood, of the Cato Street conspiracy. He and his fellow conspirators had not intended to kill the king, but his ministers. Yet it was decided by the English judges that in attacking the king's government, the Cato Street conspirators had committed 'treason, by levying war'.

The lawyer read out extracts from the *Address*, describing it as 'this extraordinary manifesto', and stating that he had to connect it with the prisoners at the bar. First though, he described what it had provoked. The jury's reaction was clearly expected to be one of horror.

> . . . though previous to that time the inhabitants of Glasgow were quietly employed in their occupations, and all the manufactories at work, yet the consequence of that manifesto was, that upon the Monday, the whole of the manufactories, with the exception of one or two, were stopped; and I believe there was

hardly a weaver that did not shut up his house and remain idle for a considerable time. The population of that great city assembled in the streets, where they formed themselves into columns, and marched with the military step. The shops were closed, and business generally stopt. In short, Glasgow presented a scene which you will hear described in evidence, and which, having personally witnessed, I can safely say, was sufficient to excite serious alarm in the minds of every individual.[11]

Mr James Hardie the magistrate was called to the witness box. He alleged that when he tried to tear down the copy of the *Address*, Andrew Hardie forcibly stopped him from doing so and 'hustled me off the stones'. This is a charge Andrew Hardie denied. They agreed that Andrew Hardie had challenged James Hardie on his authority as a magistrate. Also that Andrew Hardie had sworn 'that before he would permit me to take down that paper, he would part with the last drop of his blood'.

Did Mr Hardie the magistrate lie under oath? Peter Mackenzie later claimed he did, although he did not dispute that the magistrate had witnessed Andrew Hardie reading out the *Address* in Glasgow that morning. Much was made of the part of the *Address* he had heard from Andrew Hardie. Mr Hardie the magistrate was asked to read it out in court. This was the section appealing to soldiers, stating that surely they would not be prepared to plunge their bayonets into the hearts of fathers and brothers and calling on them to help free their country and the king from the evil counsellors of a corrupt government.

The lawyer made a second connection between Andrew Hardie and the *Address*, alleging he had given a copy of it to Thomas Cook, the lone hussar they met on their way to Bonnymuir and who was called as a witness at Stirling. Although it wasn't Hardie himself who had handed the *Address* up to Cook, he had watched this happen. As he was the leader of the group which had met the hussar, he was therefore complicit in spreading a call to commit treason.

The lawyer had detailed the skirmish at Bonnymuir, stating 'that there cannot be a doubt of those being the self-same individuals who were engaged in this gross and traitorous outrage . . .'[12] In the indictment, the Bonnymuir men were charged that they had,

> in that part of the United Kingdom of Great Britain called Scotland, maliciously and traitorously, with guns and pistols and other firearms, then and there loaded with gunpowder and leaden bullets, and with swords, bayonets, pikes, pike-heads, pitch-forks, and other offensive weapons, shoot and fire at, charge, thrust, strike at, and wound the said troops, soldiers, and faithful subjects of our Lord the King [. . .] and did then and there maliciously and traitorously attempt and endeavour, by force and violence, to subvert and destroy the government and constitution of this realm, as by law established, in contempt of our said Lord the King, and his laws, to the evil example of others . . .[13]

Clearly they had not had 'the fear of God in their hearts, but being moved and seduced by the instigation of the devil, as false traitors against our said Lord the King, and wholly withdrawing the love, obedience, fidelity, and allegiance, which every true and faithful subject of our said Lord the King should, and of right ought to bear, towards our said Lord the King . . .' This was in no way a fair trial. These words, read out by the clerk of arraigns when he listed the charges of which the prisoners were accused at the start of the trial, make it clear they were going to be found guilty.

The person who had turned King's Evidence was not called as a witness. In any case, in the eyes of the court Andrew Hardie had damned himself out of his own mouth. Under interrogation he had said he wanted annual parliaments and universal suffrage. The crucial point was that he had taken up arms in an effort to bring those changes about and reclaim his rights.

The witness who definitely lied was Nicol Hugh Baird, a private in the Stirlingshire Yeomanry. He swore under oath that on his way home to Kelvinhead near Kilsyth on a short period of leave, he had come upon a dozen or so members of the radical army. He doubled their actual numbers at that point, trying to make himself look brave.

Francis Jeffrey almost resorted to violence himself during the trial. He and Hullock, the English barrister, were verbally sparring with each other. Jeffrey felt some of the comments Hullock made were insulting to Scotland and the Scots. He struggled and failed to hide his fury.

The Sheriff of Stirling was the splendidly named Ranald Macdonald of Staffa and Iona. Hullock's remarks made him angry too. He scrawled a note, leaving out the expletive, and threw it across to Jeffrey. 'Challenge the . . . ; I'll be your second, anywhere out of this county.'[14] Jeffrey reached out over the table and shook Macdonald by the hand. Spotting that he was indeed very close to challenging Hullock to a duel, the judge intervened and instructed the English barrister to apologise.

John Baird was tried the following day. Witnesses testified they had seen him buying pike-heads in Camelon on the Monday night and that he was seen to be the leader of the men who fought at Bonnymuir.

Francis Jeffrey did his eloquent best to get the charges against both men confined to sedition. That he failed to do so has less to do with his legal abilities than judges who had already made up their minds the defendants were guilty. He cross-examined the witnesses but did not call any for the defence. He had some character witnesses lined up but decided against using them. He must also have advised Baird and Hardie to say as little as possible. They were offered the chance to suggest a question their counsel might put to several of the witnesses but always politely declined. Possibly Francis Jeffrey realised from the outset that they were going to be found guilty. Their best hope for clemency was to appear penitent.

The sixteen other Bonnymuir men and boys changed their pleas from not guilty to guilty. One man each from St Ninian's near Stirling, Balfron and Camelon also pleaded guilty. They were all initially sentenced to be hanged, drawn and quartered. Except for Hardie and Baird, this was commuted to transportation to

Australia. What terror they all must have felt before that happened, as they listened to the judge pronounce the awful sentence
on all of them.

> The sentence of the law is, – That you, and each of
> you, be taken to the place from whence you came,
> and that you be drawn on a hurdle to the place of
> execution, and there be hung by the neck until you
> are dead, and afterwards your head severed from
> your body, and your body divided into four quarters,
> to be disposed of as His Majesty may direct; and may
> God, in his infinite goodness, have mercy on your
> souls. I have only to intimate now, that a warrant
> will be signed by the court for your execution, on
> Friday, the eighth day of September. [The Prisoners
> were then taken from the Bar.][15]

The official transcript of the trial records states that before
sentence was pronounced, the prisoners were asked if they had
anything to say. They said nothing, only bowed to the court.[16]

CHAPTER 22

The Trial of James Wilson

Glasgow, 20 July 1820

The travelling court moved on to Glasgow. At preliminary hearings there at the end of June, twenty-three men were indicted on a charge of high treason. They came from Strathaven, Anderston and Parkhead. Only eight of them were in custody. James Wilson was tried on Thursday, 20 July. On trial with him in the High Court of Justiciary on the north bank of the Clyde, the same building that is there today, was William McIntyre. He was the man whose wife had unsuccessfully tried to stop him from leaving Strathaven by hiding his hat. Both men pleaded not guilty.

The case against William McIntyre and the men from Anderston and Parkhead was dropped because of lack of evidence and also perhaps for fear of a backlash.[1] There was a balance to be struck here between justice – or what passed for it – and bloodthirsty wholesale revenge.

James Wilson faced a formidable array of lawyers. There was the Lord President, the Lord Justice Clerk, the Lord Advocate, the Solicitor-General and Mr Serjeant Hullock. Defending Wilson and McIntyre were Messrs Murray and Menteith. This trial too was a complete set-up, the indictment long and wordy. There was repetition *ad nauseam* of various phrases. One of the most irritating to Scottish ears was the accusation they were being charged with offences committed 'in that part of North Britain known as Scotland'.

Two of the Strathaven Pioneers were not in custody. In their absence, William Robinson and William Watson were charged along with Wilson and McIntyre. Their alleged crimes were sedition, reading seditious news-sheets, joining the general strike, rising in armed rebellion and conspiring to threaten the life of the king. This they had done 'with divers other false traitors, arrayed and armed in a warlike manner, that is to say, with guns, muskets, blunderbusses, pistols, swords, bayonets, pikes, pike-heads, pitch-forks, clubs, and other weapons'. They were accused of visiting violence on their neighbours and of seizing a large and unrealistic number of weapons, hundreds of muskets, pistols and swords.[2]

It took a long time to read all this out and almost thirty witnesses were called. Jean Hamilton of Strathaven was questioned by Mr Serjeant Hullock. She was married but followed the Scottish custom of continuing to go by her maiden name. Her evidence was that she had called at the Wilson house on the morning of Thursday, 6 April. She had gone there looking for her brother Robert Hamilton and had tried hard to dissuade him from going off with the Pioneers. Failing to convince him, she had turned to James Wilson and told him he was going to get them all killed.[3]

What she said after that was damning. Wilson had responded that 'they could not die in a better cause', which to him was the cause of radical reform which he had advocated throughout his adult life. Jean Hamilton flashed back an angry retort: if they didn't get themselves killed they'd end being transported and never come home again. James Wilson replied 'that they were seeking the rights of their forefathers, and he hoped they would get them'.[4]

Hullock asked what she had in her hand. She gave it to him. Hullock told the judge, oh-so-casually, before swiftly moving on: 'It is only a certificate of her own character, My Lord.'[5] James Wilson's lawyer had a go at that. Why had the witness felt the need to bring along a character reference? Nobody else had. Was it because her testimony might be suspect?

Two statements made earlier by James Wilson were also read out, although not detailed in the trial transcript. By the time the court got through all that it was ten o'clock at night. It was midnight before

John Murray finished giving his opening speech for the defence. The court was adjourned and the jury of twelve men, as was the number under English law, were taken in coaches to their overnight accommodation and a meal. The Lord President had warned them at the outset not to talk about the trial to anyone who was not present at it. They were put up at the Black Bull Inn in the Trongate at the foot of Virginia Street, not too far from the court. Today, a plaque on the side wall of Marks & Spencer shows where the inn stood.

Court resumed at ten o'clock on Friday morning. Five witnesses were called for the defence. They gave evidence that James Wilson had not willingly gone off with the Strathaven Pioneers. These five painted him as a nervous old man who feared for his life and his house if he didn't go along with them. This was patently untrue but it was the only desperate hope there was of getting him acquitted.

One of those witnesses was Margaret Barr, who lived next door to the Wilsons. She was also James Wilson's sister. The judge suggested the jury might therefore not rely too strongly on her testimony. She painted quite a picture of Wilson being threatened and herself being so scared she had run two doors along the road to her daughter's house. James Wilson's niece was apparently so frightened of these threatening men she had slipped her sugar tongs and her spoons into her pocket, protecting her prized valuables from the menacing radicals.

Mr Murray argued that the famous flag reading 'Scotland Free, or Scotland a Desart' was in no way treasonable. As he said, surely every Scot would agree with that sentiment.

The jury retired to consider its verdict at 7 p.m. on the second day of the trial. It took them two hours to decide. James Ewing was chairman of the jury. A well-off Glasgow merchant with a fine house at the top of Queen Street, now vanished under the railway station of the same name, Ewing was no friend to the radicals. When people spotted him in court, it seemed depressingly clear to James Wilson's friends that he was not going to get off.[6] One other juryman did his utmost to persuade his co-jurors to find Wilson not guilty of treason. He did not succeed but he did get them to agree to give their guilty verdict with a recommendation for clemency.

They found James Wilson guilty on the fourth charge of which he was accused, 'of compassing, imagining, inventing, devising, and intending to levy war against the King within his realm, in order, by force and constraint, to compel him to change his measures and counsels – accompanied by such overt acts as appear to you to be proved . . .'[7]

The Lord President said he would make sure the recommendation for clemency would be 'transmitted to the proper quarter'. Only the Crown could grant that clemency. He then thanked the gentlemen of the jury and told them they might be needed for the trials which were to follow James Wilson's. A Mr Smith begged to be excused any further duty. 'My Lord, I left my house on fire and smoking, and my wife and family of six children were in a different house.'[8] The Lord President took pity on the juror, telling him he was excused.

If James Wilson spoke any eloquent and defiant words from the dock, they are not recorded in the official trial transcript, nor in the newspaper reports or any other contemporary accounts of the trial. The *Glasgow Herald* said only that he stammered out 'a few incoherent words'.[9] There's a bit of a mystery here. It is entirely possible that what he said was censored. In the trial transcript it is recorded that he was asked if he had anything to say as to why 'the Court should not give you judgment to die according to law?' He is not shown as giving any reply to that. The transcript moves straight on to sentence being pronounced by the Lord President. It is certainly curious that there is not even a 'No, my lord'.

A quite different version is given in *The Pioneers*, the pamphlet published more than twenty years after the events of April 1820. When the judge asked James Wilson if he had anything to say, he stood up and did so, at some length.

> My Lords and Gentlemen, I will not attempt this mockery of a defence. You are about to condemn me for trying to overthrow the oppressors of my country. You do not know, neither can you appreciate my motives. I commit my sacred cause, which is that of freedom, to the vindication of posterity. You may condemn me to immolation on the scaffold, but you cannot degrade me. If I have appeared as a Pioneer

in the van of freedom's battles – if I have attempted
to free my country from political degradation – my
conscience tells me I have only done my duty. Your
brief authority will soon cease, but the vindictive
proceedings of this day shall be recorded in history.
The principles for which I have contended are as
immutable, as imperishable, as the eternal laws of
nature. My gory head may, in a few days, fall on the
scaffold, and be exposed as the head of a traitor, but
I appeal with confidence to posterity.[10]

Wilson went on to say that he hoped some 'future historian
[will] do my memory justice' and that his 'name and sufferings
[would] be recorded in Scottish story'.

After the judge had pronounced the sentence of hanging, drawing and quartering, the writer of *The Pioneers* has the condemned
man having the final word.

Wilson heard the sentence with heroic firmness,
drawing himself up to his full height, and looking his
judges full in the face, he said: 'I am not deceived. You
might have condemned me without this mummery of
a trial. You want a victim; I will not shrink from the
sacrifice. I neither expected justice nor mercy here.
I have done my duty to my country. I have grap-
pled with her oppressors for the last forty years, and
having no desire to live in slavery, I am ready to lay
down my life in support of these principles, which
must ultimately triumph.'[11]

While Wilson was in prison awaiting his sentence, James Turner
of Thrushgrove had visited him. James Wilson asked for his help in
drafting a statement. Turner wrote this out and went back to the
prison with it. However, he was not allowed to show it to Wilson.[12]

What he might have wanted to say in this statement we cannot
know. It could have been one last defiant statement, matching what
he had said in the dock if the account given in *The Pioneers* is

accurate. On the other hand, his defence team would undoubtedly have advised against that or any subsequent statement. Any hope of getting him off would have been dashed completely by provocative words in praise of the radical cause. At the end of June, one month before his trial, he was certainly hopeful of being acquitted. On 27 June he wrote to his wife Helen. He called her Nelly. He told her not to despair and to find out what she could about the witnesses against him, although she was not to talk to them directly. He also asked her to bring him some tobacco for his pipe on her next visit. 'Do not fail to come on Friday, I remain, Your Loving Husband, James Wilson.'[13]

Eleven years later, James Ewing wrote to Peter Mackenzie about the trial.

> As to the trial of poor Wilson, I can only repeat that while I felt the most painful reluctance in the voice which I gave as a juryman on oath to administer the law as it stood, I have the testimony of my own conscience as to the purity, the independence, and the clemency of my conduct, *that I exerted all my humble efforts subsequently to spare his life;* and if I erred, I did so in common with all the rest of the jury.[14]

A petition was sent from Glasgow to Viscount Sidmouth, asking for mercy to be shown to James Wilson. It went with several letters of support from individuals. Sidmouth and Hobhouse, Sidmouth's secretary, both sent replies to the lawyers in Glasgow who had sent the petition, the Lord Justice Clerk and Lord Provost Kirkman Finlay. The answer was stern and cold. The law had to take its course. Sidmouth did not even forward the petition to the new King George IV. He did not consider James Wilson 'a fit object for any extension of the Royal Mercy'.[15]

We might be tempted to think someone had it in for James Wilson. The reality may well be that he was a pawn in a game of chance. He had come very close to being acquitted. The government could not afford to risk any more trials where acquittals might result. That could make them look foolish and undermine their authority. On 25 July 1820, the Lord Advocate wrote from Glasgow to Viscount Sidmouth in London saying exactly that. The evidence they had against people tried or due to be tried in Glasgow was weak and too many of the relevant radical leaders in these cases 'had been allowed to make their escape'.[16]

The Lord Advocate was sure the man who tried to persuade his fellow jurors to go for an acquittal for James Wilson was politically a radical. The trouble with Glasgow juries was that too many of the jurors were likely to have radical tendencies. So it would be better to wind proceedings up with one last conviction and sentence of death. Seen from this point of view it is clear that James Wilson was never going to be reprieved.

The juror who tried so hard to get him acquitted failed. Persuaded to compromise in the hope of royal mercy, he must have been bitterly disappointed when this was refused. Yet he may have helped save the lives of other radicals.

CHAPTER 23

'We Apprehend You on a Charge of High Treason!'

April–July 1820

The Special Commision court decamped to Dumbarton. The men in Duntocher who had been arrested in their beds were held at the castle there. One of them, Robert Munroe, was tried at Dumbarton on 26 July. Despite those pikes hastily thrust under hedges, there wasn't enough evidence to convict him or his five fellow villagers of high treason.

Moving on again, the lawyers sailed by steamboat from Dumbarton the short distance up the Clyde to Paisley. Seven men were indicted on a charge of high treason but five had evaded capture. Of the prisoners who remained in gaol at Paisley, James Speirs and John Lang were charged with treason. James Speirs was the man who had persuaded the workers in the mills at his native Johnstone to come out on strike.

Speirs shared a tiny cell in the bridewell at Paisley with fellow natives of Johnstone, Alexander Thomson and John Fraser. The fourth cellmate was John Neil, the Paisley weaver who had been the delegate to the radical meeting in England. On the afternoon of the Saturday before the *Address to the Inhabitants of Great Britain & Ireland* was posted up across Central Scotland and Ayrshire, James Speirs and a man called John Dunlop, both weavers, had gone to John Fraser's house with a request.[1]

Fraser was a schoolmaster. Self-educated after starting his

working life as a weaver while still a boy, he went on to teach. His first job was at a small country school before he was offered the position of teacher at a bigger school in Johnstone. Well respected and well liked, he earned quite a decent salary there. Speirs and Dunlop wanted him to make two fair copies of a letter they had composed. This was addressed to two local ministers, advising them to tell their flocks on Sunday not to offer any resistance to the rising. If they obeyed this instruction, no harm would come to them or their property. That evening Speirs passed John Fraser, who was standing outside his father's shop. Mr Fraser senior was an apothecary. Speirs handed Fraser a printed copy of the *Address*. Speirs came back on the Sunday and took the handbill away with him.[2]

According to John Parkhill, by Monday night people had heard that the radicals in England had not risen. Despite the success of the general strike in Central Scotland and Ayrshire, there was widespread despondency and a sense of betrayal. That is understandable but not justified. It was difficult for radicals to communicate between different groups and areas when there was no fast method of getting in touch. There certainly wasn't the wholesale response promised by some radical leaders north and south of the border, but many English radicals were poised to take direct action. Some already had. On the evening of Friday, 31 March between 1,500 and 2,000 radicals assembled at Huddersfield in Yorkshire. They were surprised by government soldiers, with 100 pikes seized.[3]

On the night of Saturday, 1 April and Sunday, 2 April, placards were posted up around Carlisle. Purporting to have been printed in Glasgow, they offered encouragement to the radicals of the border city. 'The Reformers of Scotland, animated with the untameable spirit of their forefathers, have just exhibited themselves in an arduous struggle against their oppressors, and in a manly vindication of their usurped rights.'[4]

There were reports from Manchester of radicals drilling on the moors surrounding the city, waiting for the word. At Durham, some coal miners voluntarily surrendered their pikes. In the week following Scotland's Radical Rising, blacksmith Thomas Forester in Newcastle and his wife were arrested. He was charged with forging pike-heads, she of selling them around the collieries.[5]

On 11 April, some 200 to 300 men from Barnsley marched to Grange Moor, near Kirklees, with the intention of taking nearby Huddersfield. They were hoping to rendezvous with men from Wakefield and Huddersfield itself but they didn't appear. Fearing a group of dragoons were heading towards them, they abandoned their makeshift weapons and dispersed. There were protests and marches at Sheffield, Halifax, Wigan and other places too.[6] Twelve Yorkshire radicals were tried and transported to Van Diemen's Land (Tasmania). Twelve were imprisoned at home for various lengths of time.

When the arrests started in Scotland there was panic and mounting fear. Local radicals got word that John Dunlop had escaped by sailing for America. James Speirs took off south, to Ecclefechan in Dumfriesshire, where he got himself a job weaving.

Three weeks later, Speirs wrote to John Fraser, telling him where he was and asking for a message to be passed on to his wife. He was safe and she wasn't to worry. The letter never reached Fraser. He and his correspondence were being watched. When the letter was intercepted at Johnstone post office, men were immediately dispatched to Ecclefechan to arrest John Speirs. The next day a dawn raid was mounted on John Fraser's house. Loud hammering on the front door woke him from sleep.[7]

He opened the door to find his house surrounded by cavalrymen. Mr Brown, the Paisley fiscal, headed the party. A court official stood there with a drawn sword in his hand. Somewhat bizarrely, the landlord of the local Black Bull pub was also there. Or perhaps John Fraser meant the landlord's son.[8] He was a lawyer and had been on snooping duty at the post office when the letter from John Speirs had arrived.

> 'We apprehend you,' they exclaimed. 'For what?' 'On a charge of high treason. Get ready to go with us.' Drawers and desks were rifled, every scrap of paper with writing on it seized and taken away. In the midst of a troop of Scots Greys, I had to walk to Paisley Jail, not understanding the cause of my apprehension.[9]

Fraser was a young married man in 1820. It is not clear if he and his wife were living in the same house as his parents. His mother certainly heard the dragoons, jumped out of her bed, looked out of the window and ran to the desk. There was another copy of the *Address* there, given to John's father by a friend 'as a historical curiosity'. Mrs Fraser senior threw the incriminating piece of paper in the fire. Smart thinking. Those words were enough to hang Andrew Hardie and John Baird.

The day after his arrest, John Fraser was interrogated by the Paisley sheriff. Because John Speirs had written to tell him he had sought refuge in Ecclefechan, the authorities assumed John Fraser was involved in the radical plot. Not only that, John Lang had turned King's Evidence and given information that he had seen John Fraser with the *Address*. Fraser was asked if he had written it. No, he said, but he could not deny he had read it. Lang had already told them that.

Fraser was then accused of writing the warning letters sent to the local ministers. They were laid in front of him and he was instructed to write a few lines on a separate piece of paper so the handwriting could be compared. However, he had had a cunning plan when he wrote them, altering his handwriting so it would not be recognised as his. It seemed to work. He denied any knowledge of the letters, salving his conscience over the lie by telling himself that as all he had done had been to copy the text, morally he was innocent. He was also acutely aware that any of this might be enough to hang him.

A couple of days after this interview, Fraser again protested his innocence, this time via a letter to the sheriff. He had had no involvement in the rising. He had committed no crime, therefore he must be released. This missive provoked Sheriff Campbell into visiting him at the gaol. He spoke sternly. 'Mr Fraser, I have received a letter from you, demanding your liberation and maintaining your innocence. The time will come when you will get an opportunity of proving your innocence. You are the very man we want to make an example of. Your position should have taught you not to mingle yourself up with such political, disorderly affairs.'[10]

Yet when Fraser's wife Marjory visited Sheriff Campbell a few days later, he smiled at her and said they really had no evidence against her husband. It would do him good to cool his heels in prison for a while all the same, a statement which must have taken Marjory Fraser's breath away. Other people tried to get her husband released but to no avail. The sheriff said the decision was for the Lord Advocate to make. No prisoners were to be released until after all the trials were over.

John Fraser spent four months in prison. Shortly after he arrived at the bridewell in Paisley, James Speirs turned up, full of remorse for having landed his friend in so much trouble by sending him that letter. The cell the four men shared was so small they couldn't all stand up at the same time. They took it in turns, two lying on the bed while the other two walked the short stone floor to give themselves some exercise. They were not allowed newspapers but there were other channels of communication. Prisoners who were in for non-payment of debts were allowed to move around the building during the day. They whispered through the keyhole of the four-man cell.

They were four or five storeys up, with a small barred window overlooking Paisley High Street. Looking out at the people walking past helped pass the time. Many looked back up at them. A Mr Carlyle, whom John Fraser described as a young gentleman and manufacturer, was allowed to visit, as a sort of official prison visitor. He brought them in books, including Thomas Paine's *The Age of Reason*. Somewhat ironic, when Paine was considered such a radical and dangerous thinker. Mr Carlyle also brought in a book on the law of treason. They all studied that one very carefully.

The schoolmaster went back to school, John Fraser applying himself to 'Murray's Grammar'. He was proud of himself for learning so much from it. The Scottish desire to educate yourself as far as your brains will take you burned strongly in the radicals. Young Mr Carlyle was a religious man and he and John Neil had some robust discussions about scripture. Neil remained unconvinced that you could always believe what you read in the Bible.

The head gaoler was strict, but his assistant Robin was not. He was a kind man and he gave the prisoners paper, pen and ink, brought them candles to read and write by at night, and smuggled letters in and out. The court came to Paisley initially on 1 July

1820 to establish who should be indicted for high treason. They sat in St George's Church. As happened elsewhere, there was a procession of legal officers to the building.

Dressed in their legal wigs and gowns, guarded by soldiers and accompanied by music played on trumpets and drums, the pompous procession moved along Paisley High Street towards the church. Hearing this, Fraser and his friends decided to join in, gathering around the barred window and singing 'Scots Wha Hae' at the tops of their voices. Everyone down in the street turned their faces up to stare at these defiant radicals.

Punishment was swift. The stern head gaoler came up to their cell, his keys rattling as he opened the door and yelled at them. 'Ye're a wheen [o'] deevils; I'll put you in chains and shut you up in darkness.' As John Fraser wryly remarked: 'That was the reward we got for Scottish patriotism.'

Speirs was to be tried. The other three were removed from their cell to the attic floor of the prison. There was more room there but it was swarming with beasties and creepy-crawlies of several varieties.

> We were horrified. Every seam in the floor and every crack in the walls was crowded with the vile vermin. We had to lay our mattresses on the bare floor. In the morning the mattresses, blankets and our personal apparel were covered with the bloody tribe, from which there was no escape. The following night we tried to surround our bed with a rampart of water laid on the floor, but the assailants managed to surmount the barricade. There was no hope for us but submission to the conquering enemy. They were too numerous to be exterminated.[11]

He made light of it but the situation must have been well-nigh intolerable. John Fraser was a sensitive person. Musically gifted, a year or so before his incarceration in 1820 he had attended an oratorio in Paisley Abbey. A large choir sang the Hallelujah Chorus and the Chorus of Angels from Beethoven's Mount of Olives. It was the first time Fraser had ever heard an organ being played and he was deeply moved by the experience as the sound reverberated around the ancient walls of Paisley Abbey. The music echoed around his head for weeks afterwards.

By means of the smuggled messages and their study of the law of treason, the prisoners made some suggestions to solicitor Peter Jack, who was preparing the case for the defence. Jack had been supplied with a list of possible jurors and another friend on the outside went around the area. It was quite a large one. The task he had volunteered to take on was to find out as much as possible about the political views of the potential jurors and whether they might be sympathetic to radicals.

John Mitchell came back with notes on each juror and the recommendation of several among them who it would be good to have on the jury. They definitely wanted Bailie John McNaught of Greenock. He was 'a most liberal man and stern radical'. It seems not to have occurred to the prosecutors that this careful planning was going on. They underestimated their opponents. Like the defence, they were allowed to challenge any jurors and did, but not the ones they should have done if they wanted a conviction.

John Fraser and his cellmates were pleased too when Robin, the kind gaoler, brought them the names of the jurors. They were delighted, especially by the confirmation of the selection of Bailie McNaught of Greenock. 'We burst out into wild, enthusiastic cheers, prolonged far beyond three times three; and exclaiming "Speirs is safe!" we cheered again and again. The plotting prisoners thus outwitted the Crown, and almost certainly saved their lives.'

The trial took place on 22 August and John Fraser was called as a witness. He took the opportunity to plead his own case, addressing the court. 'My Lords, I have been falsely imprisoned nearly four months on a charge of high treason, – my business ruined, my aged parents and family thrown into trouble and distress; and I want to know the position in which I now stand before giving any evidence.' By his business he meant the school at which he taught.

His words electrified the court and the people who had come to St George's to see the proceedings. He was ordered to leave the witness box and the court. When he was called back in, he was told he would be set free as soon as he had given his evidence. He testified that he had got a copy of the *Address* from James Speirs and said he had had nothing to do with any plans for a radical rising. They 'badgered' him for a while but he stuck fast to the line he had chosen and was dismissed from the court and told he was now free to go.

On the way out, he met his wife Marjory coming in. She too had been called as a witness. John Fraser hugged and kissed her, 'my heart in my lips'. Fraser later proudly commented: 'The Crown counsel tried to bamboozle her; and she happened to make a witty remark at their expense, which created a laugh against them, and they thought the better way was to let her go, and ask no more questions.' Reunited after four weary and anxious months, husband and wife walked home together to Johnstone along the canal bank.

The next day, the jury found James Speirs not guilty. Charges against John Lang were dropped. Paisley's radicals celebrated that night with a wee soirée in a local hall.

At Ayr, trials were also held in a local church. As elsewhere, there were two preliminary hearings before the trial itself, spread over several weeks. On Tuesday, 1 July, a grand jury of twenty-three minor gentry and gentlemen, the latter defined by the inclusion of Esq. after their names, were sworn in. They listened to the charges the Lord President had prepared and decided who was to be indicted for high treason. The accused faced four specific charges: compassing, which meant imagining or contemplating the death of the king; levying war against the king; conspiring to dethrone the king; conspiring to levy war against the king, to compel him to change his measures and counsels.

Seven men from Stewarton were on the list. Five were not in custody. Two were, Thomas McKay and Andrew Wyllie. Eight Galston radicals were indicted, a ninth man was not. None of the eight men were in custody. Two men from Mauchline were indicted, John Dickie and Hugh Wallace. At a second sitting in Ayr on Saturday, 29 July, in front of the Lord Justice Clerk, the Lord Chief Baron and the same grand jury, Thomas McKay, Andrew Wyllie, John Dickie and Hugh Wallace all pleaded not guilty to the charges of levying war against the king. The *locus delicti*, or scene of the crime, was stated to have been Stewarton and Mauchline respectively. It would have been a neat trick to have accomplished all this, especially of conspiring to dethrone the king, from two small villages in Ayrshire.

The final trial was held in the same venue on Monday, 9 August. Thomas McKay was brought to the bar, coming up before the Lord Justice Clerk and the Lord Chief Baron. He had been persuaded to change his plea to guilty. As his lawyer Mr Grant put it, McKay was ready to throw himself upon the mercy of the court.

The Lord Advocate moved that the three other prisoners be acquitted. What the men indicted in Ayrshire had done was not as serious as what had occurred elsewhere. Those offences had led to twenty-four people being convicted of the capital offence of high treason. Unfortunately, the trial records reveal nothing of what the men tried at Ayr had done. 'And, viewing the proceedings of this Commission, as calculated to influence not a particular county, but the whole of Scotland, I think enough has been done to answer the great end in view . . .'[12]

So enough was enough. The mailed fist could not slip back inside the velvet glove quite yet. Thomas McKay found himself becoming the scapegoat, forced to endure a long lecture from the judge on the evil of the crimes he had committed. He should look into his heart and kneel at the feet of Almighty God to beg forgiveness. Continuing with pompous gravitas, the judge told McKay that even if mercy should be extended to him, he should use the stay of execution well:

> I trust, whatever may be the issue of your fate, if it shall amount either to a full and free pardon, or to a recognition of the dreadful sentence which I am about to pronounce on you, it will have its effect in producing a thorough reformation in your life and future conduct – that you do return a loyal, virtuous, and peaceable subject, determined from henceforth to avoid all those circumstances that have brought this dreadful calamity upon you, and that you will,

by your example, shew [sic] to others, that although the laws of this country are powerful to punish the guilty, they are, nevertheless, administered with mercy, and with due regard to the magnitude of the guilt of those who are brought under its operation.[13]

After this remarkable piece of oratory, the judge sentenced McKay to be hanged, drawn and quartered. The sentence was not carried out. Probably it was never going to be. As it was the king alone who had the power to commute a death sentence, this allowed for the fiction that the monarch was showing mercy towards a condemned man. Thomas McKay could not have known that as he stood there listening to those dreadful words. They must have made him tremble with fear.

One radical who evaded punishment was Moses Gilfillan of Balfron. He went to America, where his son James Gilfillan later became the chief treasurer of the United States. His signature appears on dollar bills of the 1870s and early 1880s.[14]

Another radical who escaped was William Jenkins, a nailer from Camelon near Falkirk. He had cast bullets for the little radical army which fought at Bonnymuir. A newspaper report following his death in 1893 at the age of ninety-three stated that when he realised that the rising had ended in failure, he took the bullets and their moulds and cast them 'at night in the Milton Bog on the field of Bannockburn, where they are believed to remain to this day'.[15]

CHAPTER 24

'Did Ye Ever See Sic a Crowd, Tammas?'

Wednesday, 30 August 1820

James Wilson was executed on Wednesday, 30 August. As the *Glasgow Herald* reported, it was a fine summer's day and a large crowd gathered to witness the hanging and subsequent beheading. The gallows were set up in Jail Square, in front of the High Court where he had been tried, facing Glasgow Green. This was to be another lesson from the scaffold.

There is an old Glasgow saying: 'You'll die facing the monument.' It meant you would come to a bad end, facing the tall obelisk which stands on the Green between the High Court, the Saltmarket and the People's Palace. It was placed there in 1806 in honour of Admiral Lord Nelson, fourteen years before James Wilson died facing the monument.

He had said his farewells to his family the previous day. During the short visit from his wife, daughter and grandchildren on the Tuesday, everyone was very stoical. In their account on Friday, 1 September 1820, the *Glasgow Herald* gave this a sanctimonious nod of approval: 'all parties conducted themselves in the most becoming manner, but none of that excess of feeling so common on these distressing occasions was displayed by any of the parties'.[1] So that's all right then. No unseemly emotion as your husband, father and grandfather, a man who had harmed nobody, was torn away from you in the most hideous way. Or so the newspaper of the Glasgow establishment thought.

More than a decade later, journalist Peter Mackenzie claimed James Wilson had written a dying declaration ten days before his execution and given it to his wife. It is a peculiar document, with Wilson claiming he had been forced out and coerced into joining the other Strathaven radicals, yet declaring: 'I die a true patriot for the cause of freedom for my poor country'.[2] John Stevenson, one of the Strathaven Pioneers, completely rejected the idea of this dying declaration.

Stevenson published a pamphlet – price twopence – in which he angrily refuted the suggestion that Wilson had been forced out. Wilson's grandson, John Walters, denied the existence of any dying declaration. If his grandfather had given such a paper to his grandmother, she would have told him about it. John Walters Junior recounted what happened when the family said their farewells to Wilson the night before his execution. He told his grandson he had no parting gift for him except his tobacco speuchan (a speuchan was a leather pouch). Wilson said he hoped John would keep this homely object for the sake of his unfortunate grandfather. After a pause, he added a few poignant words. 'I hope that my countrymen will at least do my memory justice.'[3]

Shortly after two o'clock on Wednesday, 30 August, Glasgow's Lord Provost, magistrates and sheriff took their places on the bench of the courtroom where Wilson had been tried. He followed them in, walking with 'a firm step and an undaunted countenance' to the chair that had been placed for him in front of the magistrates' bench. He was dressed in white, his clothes trimmed with black. This was the prison uniform. He had been offered the choice to be hanged wearing his own coat but declined, declaring this to be the waste of a good coat.[4] Definitely a weaver's point of view.

James Wilson's behaviour in his final days and hours was, the newspaper wrote, 'very decent'. He listened attentively to the ministers who stayed with him the night before he died. At the religious service which preceded his execution, he was observed to be more composed than many others in the courtroom.

Mr Ewing, the minister who conducted the service, called on the members of the public packed into the courtroom's benches to emulate Wilson's composure, so 'the unfortunate prisoner might not be disturbed on this most solemn occasion, who in so short a time was to undergo the awful sentence of the law in the judicial separation of his soul and his body, and was so soon to appear before his God'.[5]

Throughout the *Glasgow Herald* article, there is an uneasy mix of pity for the putting to death of a respected older man and an insistence that the government had to defend itself against radicals and others who sought to change the political status quo, especially by means of an armed rising. Referring to Wilson as 'this poor man', the minister nevertheless felt the need to issue a warning.

> ... the sacrifice that was now to be made, was intended to teach the evil-designing not only that all private property was to be respected, but that the peace and safety of the public at large were not to be disturbed with impunity, and without the most awful examples being made; for that no Government could allow itself to be assaulted, and look passively on, when it had the ability to protect itself from insult.[6]

Reverend Dewar of Glasgow's Tron Kirk delivered 'a most energetic prayer' before directly addressing James Wilson, urging him to throw himself on the mercy of God and to join in with everyone in singing Psalm 51.

> Have mercy on me, o God, According to your unfailing love,
> According to your great compassion blot out my transgressions.
> Wash away all my iniquity and cleanse me from my sin.
> For I know my transgressions, and my sin is always before me.[7]

The condemned man was offered and drank a glass of wine. Reverend Dewar read several pages from the Bible before part of Psalm 51 was sung again, from the seventh to the tenth verse. As before, James Wilson joined in with the singing, 'with considerable earnestness, frequently making a slight inclination of his head as the words appeared to suit his situation'.[8]

Purge me with hyssop, and I shall be clean:
Wash me, and I shall be whiter than snow.
Make me to hear joy and gladness;
That the bones which thou hast broken may rejoice.
Hide thy face from my sins,
And blot out all mine iniquities.
Create in me a clean heart, O God;
And renew a right spirit within me.

Hyssop is a herb belonging to the mint family. In its wild form it was used in ancient Jewish purification rituals. Once the religious service was over, the public benches were cleared before Wilson was escorted outside, where his executioner was waiting for him. As was customary, he was dressed in black, his face shielded by a mask. In his right hand the headsman held a large axe, in his left a knife.

He and Wilson were drawn together by horses to the scaffold in a hurdle, usually a cart without wheels which had to be dragged along. This had been usual at public hangings for centuries. Being dragged to your death served to underline the humiliation of what you were about to undergo. The hurdle too had been painted black for the occasion.

The tension must have been mounting to an almost unbearable level. Yet James Wilson showed no fear. He addressed a comment to the man carrying the axe and the knife. 'Did ye ever see sic a crowd, Tammas?'[9] For there were thousands of people waiting there on this lovely August afternoon to see him die.

The executioner was Thomas Young and he was twenty years old.[10] Since James Wilson addressed him by an affectionate Scottish diminutive of his first name, he must have previously been introduced to him. It was traditional for hangmen and the man who struck the blow to ask forgiveness from the man whose life they were about to end. It was a long time since anyone in Scotland had been beheaded. Young may have been a medical student who had been asked to do the job.[11]

James Wilson mounted the scaffold a few minutes before three o'clock. The noose was placed around his neck, a black hood put

over his head and a cambric handkerchief put into his hand. This
was for him to drop as a signal that he was ready, composed before
he met his death. As he held the square of white cloth, the crowd
began to hiss and call out. 'Murder,' they cried. 'He is a murdered
man!'[12]

James Wilson gave the signal and the trapdoor beneath his feet
fell open. At that same moment, some people on the outer edges
of the huge crowd yelled out that the cavalry was moving at speed
towards Jail Square. A few moments of panic ensued. A fair few
folk were injured by falling over and being trampled, not by horses'
hooves but by human feet.

It was a false alarm. The *Glasgow Herald* was convinced the
shout had gone up from pickpockets in the crowd, seeking to take
advantage of the situation. When it quickly became clear there
were no hussars thundering towards them, sabres slashing, attention swung back to James Wilson. The *Glasgow Herald* might have
called his execution 'this horrid business' but it supplied a compre-
hensive word picture of exactly what happened.

> About five minutes after the body was suspended,
> convulsive motions agitated the whole frame, and
> some blood appeared through the cap, opposite the
> ears, but upon the whole he appeared to die very
> easily. At half past three, after hanging half an hour,
> his body was lowered upon three short spokes laid
> across the mouth of the coffin, his head laid on the
> block with his face downwards, and the cap taken
> off, when there was again a repetition of the disap-
> probation of the crowd.[13]

Upon the whole he appeared to die very easily. Chilling words.
Thomas Young had retreated into the High Court as Wilson
mounted the scaffold. You wonder what the young headsman was
thinking about during that half hour while he waited. According
to the *Glasgow Herald*, he appeared calm as he severed the head
from the body. 'The headsman appeared to be about 20 years of
age, of a genteel appearance, and executed his obnoxious task with

the most determined coolness.' The young man held up Wilson's head, calling out the customary, 'This is the head of a traitor.' The crowd disagreed. 'It is false,' they called back in impassioned and sorrowful response, 'he has bled for his country.'[14]

Purlie Wilson was buried in common ground at Glasgow Cathedral, then more often called the High Kirk of Glasgow. That night his daughter and his niece exhumed his body, possibly with the connivance of those who were supposed to be guarding the grave. He had expressed a wish to be 'buried in the dust of his fathers'. What a macabre task this must have been for the two distraught women. They lifted the coffin up onto the wall of the burial ground. On the other side of that a farmer from Avondale was waiting with a horse and cart. Mrs Walters, her cousin and the farmer brought the body home to Strathaven where a group of locals had gathered. Wilson was buried in the kirkyard at the back of his house. The house is no longer there but a monument in his memory marks its location, where Strathaven's Castle Street gives way to North Street.

On the morning of the execution, more placards had appeared in Glasgow. The *Glasgow Herald* described them as 'inflammatory'. 'May the ghost of butchered Wilson ever haunt the relentless pillows of his jurors. Murder! Murder! Murder!'[15]

James Wilson was put to death a few days before his sixtieth birthday.

CHAPTER 25

'I Die a Martyr to the Cause of Truth and Justice'

Stirling, Friday, 8 September 1820

Whilst imprisoned in Stirling Castle in July and August 1820 awaiting his execution, Andrew Hardie wrote his own account of the march to Carron and the Battle of Bonnymuir.[1] He denied much of the evidence presented in court. That he did so with some sarcasm is entirely understandable. This evidence had condemned him to death, proving him to be guilty of the charge of 'levying war against the king'. At least to the satisfaction of the court.

He was scathing about the hussar who claimed to have been threatened by the radicals on the road. He described him as a coxcomb, meaning a vain, preening man. According to Andrew Hardie, Nicol Hugh Baird wasn't even there.

> In the name of common sense, what could tempt this coxcomb to swear a notorious lie like this – to face and frighten ten or twelve well armed men; he is worthy of being classed with Sir William Wallace. I am astonished that, after such a feat, he did not petition the officer of the Hussars to fight the whole of us on the moor himself; but he had done enough for one day. But the truth of the matter is this, we never saw him on the road at all.[2]

In the letter he sent from imprisonment in Stirling Castle on 1 August 1820 Hardie apologised for 'the ungrammatical manner and style in which it was written, when you consider that while I was writing it, I was always in fear of being discovered, as it is against orders'.

He was only able to get it and other letters to his friends by smuggling them out via a woman known to everyone in Stirling as Granny Duncan. She lived hard by the castle. Also known as a slap, the narrow close of houses is no longer there. It ran off to the right at the foot of the esplanade, heading down the brae towards Ballengeich. Granny Duncan made a few shillings by selling coffee to the soldiers garrisoning the castle. She also took porridge in to the Bonnymuir prisoners.

The story goes that she allowed the porridge to cool, turned the resultant fairly solid lump of oatmeal and water out, placed a letter in the bottom of the bowl and then put the porridge back on top of it. Coming back out, she hid Andrew Hardie's letters in the now empty bowls. It is thanks to her running this risk that we have a record of his thoughts and feelings during his final few weeks of life.[3]

In an earlier letter written from Edinburgh Castle on 22 April 1820 to his mother and siblings, he asked them to give his regards to everyone he knew, including the men with whom he had formerly worked. 'Give my kind compliments to my shopmates; I know they will miss me – I hope they take care of my poor bird, which you may allow to remain with [them] if you please.' He had kept a canary in a cage beside his loom at the weaving shop where he worked.[4]

He asked in the same letter if his good wishes could be passed on to his friend Walter, wondering if Walter had been able to speak with Jean MacKechnie. 'I saw her at the door as we passed through Queen Street, Stirling, on our way to the steam-boat.' Who helped get the letters from Edinburgh out we don't know. Perhaps he was allowed to write letters in this different prison. He expressed his gratitude for the good treatment he received at Edinburgh Castle, which was a lot better than he had expected. 'I have a Bible, which I use with attention, a good bed and fire, with an allowance of a shilling a day to keep me; and for these favours I give the civil authorities of Edinburgh my sincere thanks.'

His family was not idle during his months of imprisonment. A petition was got up, pleading for mercy for both Hardie and Baird.[5] Hardie's cousin, John Goodwin, did everything he could to get signatures. Several Church of Scotland ministers refused to sign the petition, but Thomas Chalmers, a popular and charismatic minister, did sign it, and added a note of support. He was very much against any violent action taken by the radicals and had prayed aloud about it on Sunday, 1 April, asking God 'to protect this kingdom, we humbly beseech thee, from the horrors of civil war, apparently approaching us in this city'.[6] Chalmers went on to become the first moderator of the Free Kirk of Scotland after the Disruption of 1843, when 450 ministers of the Church of Scotland, disputing the Church's relationship with the State, would break away to establish the Free Kirk. Reverend Marshall, minister of Glasgow Cathedral, also signed the petition. Some Glasgow factory owners signed too.

John Goodwin called on Henry Monteith, the Lord Provost of Glasgow. Like his father before him, Monteith had once been a weaver himself, but there was no fellow-feeling for a guild brother. He told Andrew Hardie's cousin the law had to take its course, and that in any case, Hardie deserved the death penalty. Goodwin pleaded with the provost: his cousin had been deceived by spies. All to no avail. 'Upon this, his Lordship stormed like a fury, and in the most ungentlemanly manner frowned us from his presence.'[7]

The petition was forwarded to Home Secretary Viscount Sidmouth. He gave the same curt response as Glasgow's Lord Provost: the law must take its course.

Whether Andrew Hardie was deeply religious before he found himself staring death in the face we do not know. Some radicals and weavers were. Others, in their questioning of all kinds of authority, were free-thinkers, agnostics if not atheists. Hardie certainly grew very religious while in prison. In letters to his mother, his brothers and sister, his grandfather, his friends and his girlfriend Margaret MacKeigh, he expressed himself passionately on this, telling them he was ready to meet his saviour. His faith gave him comfort in his unimaginable situation. He remained committed to the radical cause.

> My suffering countrymen! As I am within view of being hurried into the presence of my Almighty Judge, I remain under the firm conviction that I die a Martyr to the Cause of Truth and Justice, and in the hope that you will soon succeed in the cause which I took up arms to defend; and I protest, as a dying man, that although we were outwitted and betrayed, it was done with a good intention on my part, and I may safely speak for the whole of those that are here in the Castle, that they are in the same mind; I have had several interviews with them, and I was happy to find them all firm to the cause.[8]

He wrote that he had thought he might speak at some length on the same subject when he stood on the scaffold but had thought better of it because he was too passionate and 'a little quick in temper'. Like many weavers, including at least one of his fellow prisoners, Hardie put pen to paper to write a poem. It had the simple title of 'Bonnymuir' and it described the skirmish.

> Then to the moor we went with speed
> And on the heather laid our head:
> But here we did not long remain
> Until we saw a dreadful train.
>
> Men and horses in armour bright,
> Advancing speedy in our sight.
> Up we sprang, to arms we flew
> And this we then designed to do.
> Close to the dyke to run with speed
> And then to face the prancing steed
> To keep them back as long's we could
> Or in the cause to shed our blood.[9]

While they were in Stirling Castle, the radical prisoners were visited by several local ministers. Hardie was upset by one of the clergymen, who raised the subject of the French Revolution, criticising what he saw as its 'fatal effects'. Hardie disagreed vehemently. The conversation preyed on his mind. Despite this disagreement, all the ministers were moved by the strength Baird and Hardie were demonstrably taking from their Christian faith.

On Thursday, 7 September 1820, the day before the execution, there was an annular or partial eclipse of the sun. William Wordsworth wrote a poem about it, not perhaps one of his best. With startling originality, he gave it the title of *The Eclipse of the Sun, 1820*. In Stirling, surgeon Dr Thomas Lucas wrote about it in his diary, noting with true Scottish resignation: 'The Day was cloudy of course.' Despite this, he managed to make some observations. The moon appeared to cover seven-eighths of the diameter of the sun and the eclipse lasted from nine minutes past midday till three minutes past three that afternoon.[10]

That evening Andrew Hardie signed and dated a letter to Isabella Condy of Stirling, his 'dear young friend'. She must have visited him and the other radical prisoners. 'Before this reaches your hand, I will be immortal, and, I trust singing to the glory of God and the Lamb among the spirits of those who have washed their robes in the precious innocent blood of our Lord and Saviour, Jesus Christ . . .'

He wrote to Isabella that he hoped 'our next meeting will be in glory'. He must have been aware or at least hopeful that the executions of John Baird and himself would be remembered in history. The way he addressed the letter to Isabella shows that.

> From Andrew Hardie to Isabella Condy, as a token of gratitude for her kind attention to him while a prisoner in Stirling Castle, who fell a Martyr to the cause of Truth and Justice on the 8th of September, 1820.
>
> Stirling Castle, Thursday night at 10 o'clock, 7th September, 1820.
>
> To Isabella Condy, Stirling.[11]

He wrote to his girlfriend that same day, to 'my dear and loving Margaret'. It is an eloquent letter, in which he expresses his love for her. 'Could you have thought that I was sufficient to withstand such a shock, which at once burst upon me like an earthquake, and buried all my vain earthly hopes beneath its ruins, and at once left me a poor shipwrecked mariner on this bleak shore, separated from thee, in whom all my hopes were centred?'[12]

He hoped she would not 'take it as a dishonour that your unfortunate lover died for his distressed, wronged, suffering and insulted country; no, my dear Margaret, I know you are possessed of nobler ideas than that ...' She had always known how strongly he felt about this subject. He told her he needed to lay down his pen, 'as this will have to go out immediately'. Granny Duncan must have been waiting to take the letter, neither she nor Andrew Hardie wanting to arouse suspicion by her lingering too long.

He finished the letter to Margaret by asking his sweetheart to give his 'dying love' to her parents, 'James and Agnes, Mrs Connell and Jean Buchanan'. He expressed another wish and reassured her on one point.

> I hope you will call frequently on my distressed and afflicted mother. At the expense of some tears I have destroyed your letters. Again, farewell my dear Margaret, may God attend you still, and all your soul with consolation fill, is the sincere prayer of your most affectionate and constant lover while on earth.
> Andrew Hardie.

There is no record of Margaret's feelings. Grief, certainly. You wonder if she was angry at him for risking his life in the way he had. All her hopes for the future had been dashed too.

John Baird also wrote letters. Some were sent from Edinburgh Castle, where the radical prisoners were taken for further interrogation. They travelled by steamboat, the new and exciting development in transport, from Stirling to Newhaven. Perhaps, as practical men with inquiring minds, they were able to take some pleasure in that, albeit qualified. One of the paddle steamers plying

the Stirling, Alloa, Newhaven route in 1820 was *The Lady of
the Lake* and this is the one on which they made the journey to
Edinburgh and back.[13] The name comes from Sir Walter Scott's
epic poem. The Wizard of the North was a high Tory and despised
the radicals, describing them as dogs and scoundrels.[14]

In a letter John Baird wrote to his brother Robert from
Edinburgh on 9 May 1820, he told him they were being very well
treated. The prison governor at Edinburgh Castle was 'a very fine
man', as the governor's wife was a fine woman. She arranged to get
their washing done and charged them nothing for this kindness.
'The Colonel of the 80th Regiment is one of the best of men; he
has given each of us a fine shirt as a present.' Baird too was taking
comfort from his Christian faith. 'When God is with us, who can
be against us?' He told his brother: 'Go and prosper. Give my kind
love to all inquiring friends.'[15]

He admitted he hadn't always been so religious, nor a stranger
to sin, and mentioned his 'former ways'. He wrote this in a letter to
his brother on 14 August 1820. The prisoners were back in Stirling
and had been tried, found guilty and sentenced to death. He hoped
his brother was not too distressed.

> If you knew the state of my mind, you would envy
> my situation. My hopes are not in this world – I
> look for a better. The sentence of death had as little
> impression on me as if the Lord President had read
> an old ballad. As this is an unpleasant subject to you,
> I will say no more about it; but, oh! God prepare me
> for thy will and my duty.
>   Your affectionate brother
>   John Baird

Again, you wonder how Robert Baird must have felt. It was
at his house in Condorrat that Andrew Hardie and the men from
Glasgow had called on that very wet night in April. Robert had
advised waiting to see if more men turned up to swell the ranks of
the little radical army. Did he blame Andrew Hardie for leading his
brother into such terrible danger?

On 28 July, John Baird wrote a consoling letter to his sister, Mrs Leisham. On the same day, without any apparent irony, he told their brother Robert, 'I am in good health at present, thanks be to the giver of all good, for it.'

Although letters were forbidden, kindness was shown to them at Stirling Castle too in their final weeks. Among the two men's last words was a request to the sheriff to pass on their thanks to General Graham, lieutenant-governor of the castle, and also to Major Peddie. With the job title of fort-major, he had day-to-day supervision of the prisoners. Baird and Hardie wanted 'to express to General Graham and Major Peddie our sense of gratitude for the humanity and attention which they have always shown to us'.[16]

This kindness allowed some of Baird and Hardie's relatives to spend their last night with them. The names of those who did so are not recorded. Since Andrew Hardie had written to his girl-friend Margaret the day before, it seems unlikely that she was there. Perhaps she did not trust herself not to break down and was keeping a lonely vigil of her own, at home in Glasgow.

Baird's elderly father, three sisters, their husbands and his two brothers spent time with him that evening. His father was eighty years old. Baird was calm and composed, although at one point he came close to breaking down. He brought out his snuff box, made from horn trimmed with silver, and presented it to his father. 'Let me offer you this – you will perhaps look at it, when you cannot look at me!'[17]

Baird, Hardie and their relatives talked, prayed and read passages from the Bible. Calm and composed, Hardie asked his folks if they had a strong coffin in which to carry his body back to Glasgow.[18] A brave question but how painful it must have been for his loved ones. He inspected the winding sheet. As a weaver, he would have been casting an experienced eye over the length of linen.

The two condemned men slept for a couple of hours until they were woken at 6 a.m., as they had requested. They washed and dressed before singing part of the 51st Paraphrase. John Baird read from 1 Corinthians 15:51–53: 'Behold, I shew you a mystery; We shall not all sleep, but we shall all be changed, In a moment, in the twinkling of an eye, at the last trump: for the trumpet shall sound, and the dead shall be raised incorruptible, and we shall be changed. For this corruptible must put on incorruption, and this mortal must put on immortality.'

After that, he engaged 'in an agony of prayer'.[19] Praying out loud, he asked God to be with them and keep them strong as they faced death and underwent their ordeal. The ministers who had been visiting the men regularly were moved to tears.

At one o'clock, an hour before the time for which the execution was scheduled, John Baird and Andrew Hardie were allowed to say farewell to their comrades. Hugs were given and received. The two youngest members of the little radical army were distraught at the parting. Bookbinder Andrew White from Glasgow was only sixteen. Alexander Johnson was even younger, just fifteen. He was the boy who kept firing at the hussars and the yeomanry and whose life Lieutenant Hodgson had called on his men to spare. Both lads clung on to Andrew Hardie until they were ordered to let him go and return to their cells.

> This scene was touching in the extreme. Some eight-een or twenty youths were grouped around the windows of their prison, and both Hardie and Baird addressed them in most affectionate and endearing terms, assuring them that, though suffering, they were not evil-doers; and that the cause for which they suffered would sooner or later prevail. After this they were all permitted to embrace each other, and it was with considerable difficulty that some of them were torn away from that sad and solemn embrace.[20]

A horse-drawn hurdle was waiting at the gates of Stirling Castle to draw them to Broad Street, a little way down the hill. A scaffold had been erected in front of the Tolbooth and a large crowd had gathered. Fearing trouble, perhaps a riot in protest against the executions, soldiers of the 13th Regiment of Foot and the 7th Dragoon Guards were in attendance.[21] They might also have feared a rescue attempt. Hardie stepped out of the hurdle, looked up at the gallows and declared, 'Hail, harbinger of eternal rest!'

Offered refreshment, he drank a glass of sherry and John Baird took a glass of port. About 2,000 people looked on as the two of them mounted the scaffold. For a moment they knelt together in prayer. Then, leaning over the bar that ran around the platform, Andrew Hardie called out: 'Granny, are you there?' 'Aye,' replied Mrs Duncan, 'Andrew, my poor young laddie, I'm here.' She had promised him she would lay him out in his coffin, make him look at least peaceful before his loved ones saw his dead body. 'Bide till the end, then,' he said to her.

Both men addressed the crowd from the scaffold. John Baird said that what he had done, and what had brought him here to the scaffold, had been for the cause of truth and justice. He had never hurt anyone and had always led an innocent life, which rather contradicts what he had said before. Perhaps he did not mean innocent in the sexual sense. 'I am not afraid of the appearance of this scaffold, or of my own mangled body, when I think of the innocent Jesus, whose own body was nailed to the cross, and through whose merits I hope for forgiveness.'

Hardie agreed with Baird and said his own few words. 'My dear friends, I declare before my God, I believe I die a martyr in the cause of truth and justice.' A great roar of approval went up from the crowd and the nervous soldiers moved in more closely. When they unsheathed their sabres, excitement turned to fear. There were screams of terror and panicked movement among the crowd. With more to say, Hardie was confronted by the sheriff who had been present at their trial, Ranald Macdonald of Staffa, running up to the scaffold. If he did not stop talking in this vein, the order would be given to the executioner to go at once about his business.[22]

Hardie bowed politely and contented himself with one final statement addressed to the crowd. 'My friends, I hope none of you have been hurt by this exhibition. Please, after it is over, go quietly home and read your Bibles, and remember the fate of Hardie and Baird.'[23]

The two men kissed and shook hands as well as they could when their arms were pinioned. They had agreed beforehand who should give the signal to the hangman that they were ready. Hardie held a white cambric handkerchief. He spoke his final words, quoting Corinthians once more, in a firm and calm voice. 'Oh death, where is thy sting? Oh grave, where is thy victory?' Then he dropped the handkerchief and the trapdoor fell away beneath their feet. 'The bolt fell, and the last moving sight of them was swinging together, and momentarily and convulsively attempting to catch each other again by the hands, but in vain.'[24]

They were allowed to hang for half an hour, when they were lowered and laid flat. The headsman lifted his axe and severed each head. It was clumsily done. He took two strokes to behead John Baird and three to separate Andrew Hardie's head from his body. As at James Wilson's execution in Glasgow, he lifted each head by the hair and pronounced the required words. 'This is the head of a traitor; this is the head of another traitor.' Dr Lucas, who had written about the eclipse of the sun in his diary the day before, was watching and listening.

> They both addressed the Spectators and declared that they were Murdered for the cause of justice truth and liberty. The crowd shouted out Murder. After hanging 35 minutes a fellow in disguise severed their heads from their bodies in a very bungling and awkward manner by several strokes with an axe to each of them. The Hangman, headsman, Hurdleman, Hurdle and the horse were all from Glasgow.[25]

Dr Lucas also wrote that the coffins with the bodies in them were taken back to Stirling Castle before being buried in the grave-yard of the nearby Church of the Holy Rude at about nine o'clock that night. They were interred in common ground, given paupers' burials. Soldiers guarded the grave to stop Baird and Hardie's relatives from exhuming them and taking them for burial in their home parishes. Judging by Hardie's query as to whether his relatives had a good strong coffin to carry his body home to Glasgow, neither man had expected to be buried in Stirling. Although several of their gaolers had been kind to them, this seems like one last mean and vindictive act on someone's part. Their deaths were noted in Stirling's parish records, with the cause of death listed as 'Executed for High Treason'.

The man who beheaded them was the same Thomas Young who had been the headsman at James Wilson's execution. He was paid £40 for his work in Stirling, although he had to write several letters to the sheriff substitute before he got his full fee.[26] He wore a long black coat treated with a glazed covering to repel the blood. It and the axe can be seen today in the Smith Art Gallery and Museum in Stirling. These two gruesome relics are on display next to two small stone grave markers bearing each man's initials. A plaque on the wall of the Tolbooth in Broad Street in Stirling marks where they were put to death. Some time in 1820, a broadside reproduced two of Andrew Hardie's letters, one to his uncle and one to Margaret MacKeigh. The National Library of Scotland holds a copy of it.[27]

Thirty years after they were buried at Stirling, the bodies were exhumed and reinterred in Sighthill Cemetery in Glasgow, where a monument now commemorates the Scottish radicals of 1820.

When they hanged, Sheriff Ranald Macdonald was heard to remark, 'So there's an end to that.' He couldn't have been more wrong.

CHAPTER 26

Banish'd Far Across the Sea

October 1820

In 1975, Australian husband and wife team Margaret and Alastair Macfarlane published *The Scottish Radicals: Tried and Transported to Australia for Treason in 1820*. It's a slim volume but meticulously researched. It includes an excellent hand-drawn map of the site of the Battle of Bonnymuir showing the movements of Baird, Hardie and their comrades on that fateful day. It also packs in a lot of information on all nineteen of the radicals who were transported to Australia. One of them was Thomas Macfarlane, an ancestor of Alastair Macfarlane, co-author of the book.

Britain first started shipping convicts to Botany Bay in 1788. The United States' recently won independence meant there was no longer the option of sending them across the Atlantic as indentured servants to what had previously been British colonies. The practice of transportation continued until the middle of the 1800s and an estimated 50,000 people endured the arduous and months-long sea voyage to get there. Some did not survive the journey.[1]

Being transported was a lot better than being hanged but the prospect must have seemed like being condemned to a living death. Convicts were being sent quite literally to the other side of the world, as far away as it was possible to be from family, friends and native land. There is a folk memory of this in Maryhill in Glasgow, where a run of locks on the Forth and Clyde canal and the area around those are known as the Butney. By tradition, that's where prisoners from the west of Scotland were kept in barges before being sent to Botany Bay.

The introduction to *The Scottish Radicals* by the Macfarlanes was written by Dr Hazel King, who had been Senior Lecturer in History at the University of Sydney. She makes the interesting point that the Scottish radicals were an unusual group among the many convicts transported to Australia. They were political prisoners, not criminals. Other radicals were also transported. Five of the Cato Street conspirators and twelve of those who took part in the abortive Huddersfield radical rising of 1820 went to Tasmania, then known as Van Diemen's Land. Fourteen men involved in the radical rising at Pentrich in the Peak District in 1817 were sent to New South Wales in early 1818.[2]

Another Scottish radical who reached Australia before the Bonnymuir men was Gilbert McLeod, editor of radical newspaper the *Spirit of the Union*. Leaving Britain on 22 August 1820, he sailed on the *Asia*, a ship built by Hall's in Aberdeen. The journey took four months. When they arrived at Port Jackson in the natural harbour of Sydney on Boxing Day, they were inspected by the governor of New South Wales, Lachlan MacQuarrie. He came from the small Hebridean island of Ulva, near the larger isle of Mull.[3]

The Scottish radicals were skilled and educated men. They sent letters home, allowing us a glimpse of their lives and experiences. Alexander Hart wrote to his brother while he was still in prison in Edinburgh awaiting transportation. He asked John Hart to send him his toolkit. If possible, could he please put some sheet music in with it, as well as his violin?

Alexander contacted John again before the *Speke*, the convict ship he was on, left Sheerness in Essex for Australia. On 11 December 1820, he told John the clergyman aboard the ship had invited the Scottish prisoners to take Communion with him and his wife at Christmas. There were over 150 male convicts on the ship, including some boys. Alexander Hart described them, sympathetically, as 'wretches'.

Hart came from Old Kilpatrick, ten miles or so down the River Clyde from Glasgow. A cabinet maker to trade, he was twenty-six years old when he went with Andrew Hardie and John Baird to

Bonnymuir. He was badly injured there, with a sabre cut to the face, leaving him with a scar between his eyebrows for the rest of his days. He spent all of those in Australia, dying there at the age of eighty-two, more than half a century after he was wounded at Bonnymuir.

Like many transported to Australia, he married there. He and Irish convict Bridget O'Hara do not seem to have had children themselves but they had family around them. Alexander's niece, née Margaret Hart, went out from Scotland in the 1840s, married and had at least one child in Australia. Alexander Hart was living with Margaret and her family when he died.

Whether he yearned for home we cannot know, but he liked Australia very much. Keeping up a correspondence with his relatives in Scotland, he told them about living and working conditions and how much foodstuffs cost. In one letter, written after he had been in Australia for more than a quarter of a century, he wrote that 'we both like the country well and shall be satisfied to end our Journey here if such is the will of Providence'.[4] His burial record of 1876 includes the comment from the minister of the local Scots kirk that he was the last of the Bonnymuir radicals of 1820.[5]

Another transported radical who came to love his adopted country was John McMillan, known as Jock, a nailer and blacksmith from Camelon near Falkirk. He was arrested with several other nailers – Wright, Burt, Greene and McRory – and imprisoned in Stirling Castle. They were all accused of making pikes.[6] Although he was sentenced to transportation for life, by 1832 he was a free man and doing well as a blacksmith. He wrote to his wife Jane in Glasgow, asking her to sail out with their three daughters and join him in Sydney.

Transportation for life was not always the sentence for the men and women sent to Australia and Tasmania. Most were sentenced to either seven or fourteen years of servitude. Good behaviour was rewarded with a reduction in the number of years served. Those sentenced for life, like Thomas McCulloch, might hope to be granted a conditional pardon after ten or twelve years. Convicts could also apply for what was called a ticket of leave, which gave them a lot more freedom of action within the penal colony. Wives and children left behind in Britain could then apply to the government for passage out to Australia and Tasmania.

Jock McMillan's wife Jane must have been quite a woman, for she did so despite her husband's blood-curdling warnings. She was 'to take everyone for a rogue until you find them honest, trust no one out of sight, keep a closed mouth, never let anyone know your business, be as cunning as a fox & as wise as a serpent'. Nor was she to let anyone know what she had in the boxes she brought with her. He advised her to list every item in them.[7]

Jock couldn't resist a side-swipe at his sisters, asking his wife Jane to let them know how well he had prospered in Australia, which he called 'the land of full belly'. He was an employer now, with three free men and two convicts working for him. He had bought another house, which had cost him £100. Jane was to let those sisters who had thought him such a disgrace to the family in 1820 know she would have a servant, two if she wanted. She was also to tell them that 'I would not return to their storm-gutted country if they was [*sic*] to make me Sheriff of Stirling.'[8]

McMillan became a landowner. He bought twenty-five acres north of Sydney in 1839 which he developed as an orange grove: '. . . and within a very few years the young trees which he had planted brought him the means of an easy and comfortable livelihood. They had grown to a very large size, and his small, unpretending dwelling-house was nearly concealed in the midst of the thick green foliage, all dotted over with oranges, like spheres of gold.'[9] It sounds idyllic, and very different from storm-gutted Scotland.

Touchingly, he gave the name *Thrushgrove* to his plantation of oranges, after James Turner's estate in the north of Glasgow, where the huge reform meeting had taken place in 1816. McMillan pushed hard for absolute pardon documents to be drawn up for himself and the other Bonnymuir men, saying he could not leave Australia without a written pardon, although he seems not to have had any real desire to return to Scotland. He clearly felt keenly the injustice of the harsh sentence of transportation meted out to himself and his fellow radicals.

In his *Reminiscences of Glasgow and the West of Scotland*, journalist Peter Mackenzie wrote about how McMillan had sent him 'the actual irons which chained his legs from Stirling Castle to Botany Bay. [. . .] If any person doubts this, we are ready to show those identical irons, weighing nearly 20 lbs., with the letter of John McMillan transmitting them.'[10]

McMillan was bitter about a minister who visited him and his comrades when they were held prisoner in Stirling Castle. Hungry and shut away from the sunlight of the summer of 1820, Jock McMillan begged the man to bring him something to eat. The reverend returned the next day without food but gave him a Bible. As another minister, the Reverend John Morrison, author of *Australia As It Is*, wrote:

> The man never seemed to have been able to forget this; morning, evening and mid-day, it was the theme of his discourse, the clergyman being the subject of deep, bitter, vehement abuse and outcry. All the badness which this world could produce was in that man, and a favourite figure of speech of his was to make use of the clergyman's name when he wished to express horror or detestation of anything.[11]

Although Macmillan did keep the Bible. In his later years, he became a pillar of the Church, one of the trustees involved in building St Peter's Presbyterian Church in North Sydney. In their book, Margaret and Alastair Macfarlane paint a lovely little image of him in the 1870s, when he was in his early eighties.

> A passing glimpse of Jock McMillan was given by bus driver, Tom Watson, who drove the first coach from Milson's Point along the Lane Cove Road, now Pacific Highway, from about 1876. He recalls the old man wearing a tall hat and driving a white horse on his weekly visit to North Shore from his property, Comely Park, opposite Boundary Street, where he kept beehives and numerous cats.[12]

He died on 28 August 1877, the announcement appearing in the following day's *Sydney Morning Herald*.

Andrew White did return home to Scotland. He was the young bookbinder from Glasgow, barely fifteen years old when he fought at Bonnymuir. He died in Glasgow's Royal Infirmary in November 1872. He is buried in Sighthill Cemetery, not far from where the remains of Baird and Hardie lie.

Thomas Macfarlane came from Condorrat and had been very seriously wounded at Bonnymuir. He recovered, was tried and transported but returned to Scotland in 1839 after being pardoned three years earlier. In 1840 he was the guest of honour at an event put on by the Working Man's Association of Airdrie, which was a Chartist group. At that soirée, musical entertainment was provided by the singing of 'Dark Bonnymuir', written by Allan Murchie, another of the transported radicals.[13] The daughters of John Fraser of Johnstone also sang at the event.

Allan Murchie wrote 'Dark Bonnymuir' while in Stirling Castle. It was sung with great gusto by his fellow prisoners, using the same melody as 'Hey, Johnnie Cope'.

> Although our lives were ventured fair,
> To free our friends from toil and care,
> The British troops we dint to dare,
> And wish'd them a good mornin'.

> It's with three cheers we welcomed them,
> Upon the muir or bonnie plain,
> It was our rights for them to gain
> Caused us to fight that mornin'.

> With pikes and guns we did engage;
> With lion's courage did we rage –
> For liberty or slavery's badge
> Caus'd us to fight that mornin'.

> But some of us did not stand true,
> Which caus'd the troops them to pursue,
> And still it makes us here to rue
> That ere we fought that mornin'.

But happy we a' ha'e been
Since ever that we left the Green,
Although strong prisons we ha'e seen
Since we fought that mornin'.

We're a' condemned for to dee
And well ye ken that's no a lee,
Or banish'd far across the sea,
For fightin' on that mornin'.

If mercy to us shall be shown,
From Royal George's kingly crown,
We will receive't without a frown,
And sail the seas come mornin'.

Mercy to us has now been shown,
From Royal George's noble crown,
And we are prepared, without a frown,
To see South Wales some mornin'.[14]

Murchie, who was from Dunfermline, did well in Australia. His fiancée Elisabeth Marshall was given free passage to join him in New South Wales. They married there and had seven children. The Murchies prospered and for some time ran a general store in Sydney, selling cloth, sewing threads, toys, necklaces and strings for violins. Deploying his writing skills, he placed an advert in the *Sydney Herald* in December 1832. 'An Old Story, Once a Year Comes Christmas, Christmas Pudding Raisins by the box or pound.' Murchie's at 88 Kent Street in Sydney could sell you the ground spices too.

Thomas McCulloch was an Irishman from County Down, living in Glasgow in 1820. In a letter from Australia to his wife in Glasgow, dated 12 October 1821, he told her he saw Gilbert McLeod quite often and that McLeod was working as a schoolmaster. The editor of the *Spirit of the Union* had been joined by his wife and two children but unfortunately died young, aged thirty-seven, in 1828.[15]

Thomas McCulloch and Andrew Hardie did not know each other before the Battle of Bonnymuir but grew close while they were in prison. In a letter to his mother Marion dated 28 June 1820, Andrew Hardie asked her to call on McCulloch's wife in Cannon Street in Glasgow. She was to reassure Sarah Allan her husband was in good health and being well treated. Sarah was expecting a baby. She and her husband must have been able to communicate at some point or maybe she was allowed to visit him before he left Scotland. She gave birth to a son on 8 September 1820, the same day Baird and Hardie were hanged in Stirling. The boy was named Andrew Hardie McCulloch. He and his mother later joined Thomas McCulloch in Australia.

There were three men called Andrew Hardie McCulloch in the McCulloch family. Like many descendants of the Bonnymuir radicals, they distinguished themselves in various different fields: the law, politics, medicine, natural history and literature. Great-granddaughter of the first Andrew Hardie McCulloch, Eleanor Dark, was a novelist, who wrote of the early days of British-settled Australia in her trilogy *The Timeless Land*. She too was radical in her political views.[16]

One radical who went voluntarily to Australia was John Stevenson of Strathaven. The story goes that he ended up making a fortune in the Australian gold fields and became mayor of Melbourne. He had taken the flag of the Strathaven Pioneers with him, 'Scotland Free, or Scotland a Desart'. As he had requested, when he died it was used as his winding sheet and he was buried in it.[17]

The transported radicals of 1820 were all granted a free royal pardon in 1836, during the reign of William IV.

CHAPTER 27

Reform Is Won?

1832

Despite what Ranald Macdonald of Staffa said at the execution of John Baird and Andrew Hardie, the brutal punishment of the radicals of 1820 did not stifle the calls for political reform. People continued to meet and agitate for change. In South Wales in 1831, this boiled over into another rising at Merthyr Tydfil. Thousands of coal miners and iron workers took to the streets, protesting against the lowering of wages and growing unemployment. In their native Welsh, the protesters called out their demands: Cheese and Bread! Down with the King!

The protests spread across the area from May 1831 into June. More miners came out on strike and for a time the rebels were in control of Merthyr. The red flag was flown. This is thought to have been the first time it was used as a symbol of a workers' revolt, although Stevenson at Strathaven had mentioned it ten years before. The government in London sent in the military, a company of the Argyll and Sutherland Highlanders. The rebels resisted but were eventually defeated. Twenty-four of the strikers were shot dead by the troops and twenty-six people arrested.[1]

Two men were sentenced to death. Lewis Lewis, known in Welsh as *Lewsyn yr Heliwr*, had his sentence commuted to transportation to Australia. Richard Lewis, *Dic Penderyn* in the Welsh version of his name, was sentenced to death for stabbing one of the Argyll and Sutherland Highlanders in the leg. It is a crime many then and since don't believe he committed. Despite a petition asking for clemency, Penderyn was hanged at Cardiff Market in August 1831.

Meanwhile, moves were afoot to introduce a measure of political reform. Arthur Wellesley, the Duke of Wellington, was the hero of Waterloo. When he went into politics, his implacable opposition to reform led to his downfall. He might have escaped this if he had given way on the proposal to take MPs from two rotten boroughs (constituencies with a very small, sometimes even non-existent, electorate) in England, East Retford and Old Sarum, and give them instead to the fast-expanding cities of Manchester and Birmingham. This he refused to do. Old Sarum had two MPs but no electors at all. It was a hill in Wiltshire, the early site of the city of Salisbury, but totally uninhabited well before the early nineteenth century. These rotten boroughs were sometimes also referred to as pocket boroughs, because they were in the pocket of a local landowner.

Wellington and his Tory government were replaced by a Whig administration. The prime minister was now Earl Grey, formerly Mr Charles Grey. Back in 1793, he had championed the cause of reform in the House of Commons and expressed sympathy for the case of Thomas Muir and the other men transported to Australia.

Grey served under the new king, William IV, with a mandate to bring about 'Retrenchment, Economy and Reform'. The Great Reform Bill introduced in March 1831 did not extend the franchise to the working man. The right to vote was to be given to adult males of a certain financial status, essentially middle-class male householders. Despite this, the news that Glasgow was now to have two members of parliament to itself instead of sharing one with another constituency was received with wild enthusiasm by all classes of society. Peter Mackenzie described the city as being 'in a perfect glow of excitement'.[2]

Glasgow waited eagerly for news on the Great Reform Bill, brought in by the mail coach from London on the afternoon of Thursday, 3 March, a mild and pleasant evening. Peter Mackenzie made the interesting observation that the weather was much better than it had been in March of the previous year. 'The seasons, we think, are really changing from what they were wont to be in many ways.'[3] Nine hundred gentlemen gathered at the Royal Exchange in Queen Street. This was formerly the mansion of tobacco lord William Cunningham, then the Royal Bank of Scotland and subsequently Stirling's Library and is now the Gallery of Modern Art. A table had been set up to act as a hustings. David Bell was the secretary of the Royal Exchange. He climbed up onto the table and read out the highlights of the speech made by Lord John Russell at Westminster. The 900 gentlemen cheered loudly as Bell went along.

Lord Russell's speech was printed in a London newspaper called the *Sun*, a different animal from the twentieth- and twenty-first-century newspaper of the same name. It had been founded by a former British prime minister, William Pitt the Younger. Along at Glasgow Cross, in the Tontine coffee house, the same highlights of Lord Russell's speech were being read out by a man called Thomas Atkinson and Peter Mackenzie himself.

The bill was hotly debated for a week in the House of Commons, with the Tories dead set against it. They lost the argument. The cry was 'the bill, the whole bill, and nothing but the bill!' Glasgow sent petitions to both Houses of Parliament in support and one to King William IV, signed by Matthew Fleming, Acting Chief Magistrate of Glasgow.

Headed *To the King's Most Excellent Majesty*, to modern eyes the language used is very deferential. 'We, your Majesty's loyal and dutiful subjects, the merchants, bankers, manufacturers, trades, and inhabitants of Glasgow, approach your Majesty to express the attachment which this city, in common with every part of the empire, entertains for your Majesty's Royal Person and Family . . .'[4]

Yet it is rather cleverly worded too. The petitioners of Glasgow are convinced reform is a good thing, 'calculated to restore that part of our constitution which time and an oligarchical faction had well nigh destroyed, and that on the early and complete success of that measure, depend the stability of the Throne, the permanence of the aristocracy, and the constitutional liberty, the prosperity, and the happiness of the people . . .'[5]

That reference to the desirability of 'the permanence of the aristocracy' was the opposite of Thomas Muir's description of the Houses of Paliament as being occupied by 'a vile junta of aristocrats'. You can imagine many reformers rolling their eyes heavenwards and muttering an exasperated curse or two under their breaths.

The brief petition ended by asking the king to do everything in his power to secure reform 'and we pray that your Majesty may long and happily reign over a free, loyal, and happy nation'. Nearly 30,000 people in Glasgow signed and endorsed the petition, which was then sent to the Lord Advocate to be passed on to the king. The former was now Francis Jeffrey, the lawyer who had defended Baird and Hardie in court back in 1820.

Peter Mackenzie was cock-a-hoop when Francis Jeffrey reported back that William IV had been surprised by how many signatures were on the petition. The king had read the whole thing through and given it his seal of approval. Mischievously, Mackenzie wrote that the petition allowed him 'to assume the name and character of *Loyal* Reformer!'

Mackenzie went on to found a newspaper called the *Loyal Reformers' Gazette*, although the authorities weren't quite ready for free speech. Not just yet. Mackenzie and some of those working with him ended up in prison for two weeks. He wrote letters of protest to Earl Grey, Lord Advocate Francis Jeffrey and others, and they were released.

Made law in 1832, the Great Reform Act stopped very far short of universal suffrage. However, it paved the way for further reforms. The concept of reform had been accepted. This was a major victory. Led by Earl Grey, the Whig or Liberal government also introduced some restrictions on the use of child labour and oversaw the abolition of slavery in the British Empire in 1833. Grey also gave his name to the famous tea. It is thought he had received some as a gift and asked tea blenders in Britain to re-create it. He retired from politics in 1834 to spend more time with his family in Northumberland. He was known to be close to them, and this was a genuine wish, not the coded euphemism it has now become.

For Andrew Hardie's mother Marion, the passing of the Great Reform Act was bittersweet. She had lost her beloved son in the most brutal way imaginable. There's no way she could ever have got over that. She put a placard up in the window of her house in Castle Street in Glasgow:

> Britons, rejoice, Reform is won,
> But 'twas the Cause that lost me my son.[6]

When the news reached Glasgow that the Great Reform Act had been passed, the city went wild. At eight o'clock on the designated evening, all the church bells pealed out, swiftly followed by people putting lights in their windows in celebration. Some individuals and institutions went farther, utilising one of the wonders of the age: gas lighting.[7]

Lord Provost Dalglish used it to the full at his house in St Vincent Place. He had 3,000 'gas jettees' in front of the building spelling out the city's motto: 'Let Glasgow Flourish'. The same words were picked out on garlands of gold and silver behind the illuminations. 'Surmounting the whole were the splendid figures of Trade, Commerce, and Manufacture, hailing Reform . . .' Everyone agreed the lord provost's lights were far and away the best in the city that evening.

The Royal Exchange was lit up at its entrance with the figures of Britannia and Glasgow's coat of arms with the word *Reform* in the middle of those. With his tongue firmly in his cheek, Peter Mackenzie wrote that in 1832 the equestrian statue of the Duke of Wellington had not yet been erected in front of the Royal Exchange, which was probably just as well.[8]

On this same night, an effigy of the Iron Duke, implacable enemy of political reform, was set alight in the streets of Glasgow. Another effigy of him was arrested at Glasgow Cross and taken to the police station. There was much hilarity over this. Sadly, Peter Mackenzie decided not to repeat the 'ludicrous and offensive statements' made at the time. Perhaps we might suggest that the Glasgow tradition of placing a traffic cone on the head of the statue of the Duke of Wellington is a time-honoured continuation of robust political comment.

According to Kilmarnock's nineteenth-century historian Archibald McKay, people there were disappointed that the right to vote had not been extended to the majority. 'Yet they hailed the passing of it as the dawn of a happier era, and the bill itself as a measure that would ultimately bring peace and prosperity to the people at large.'[9]

As in Glasgow and elsewhere, the people of Kilmarnock came together in a celebration of the Great Reform Act. Numerous flags fluttered, more than a hundred of them at one meeting alone. Their slogans were varied and neatly illustrate the contemporary intertwining of Scottishness and Britishness: Arise, people of Britain, and be as one man; United to support, not to injure; Richt wrangs naebody; We seek reform, not from power, but principle; Scots! do your duty; Timely reform prevents revolution; The spirit that animated our fathers at Bannockburn remains with their children.[10] That last one must have been a big flag.

There was still a long way to go along the muddy and rough road to democracy. The 1840s saw the agitation of the Chartist movement. They made the same demands as the radicals of twenty years previously: universal suffrage, annual parliaments and secret ballots. They deployed the same tactics, holding huge public meetings. The *Caledonian Mercury* reported on one held at Glasgow Green on Monday, 21 May 1838. Whilst allowing that estimates of how many people are at a big protest may depend on whether supporters or opponents are doing the counting, it put the numbers attending this meeting at almost 150,000 people.

The newspaper offers evidence of the scale of the meeting. There's a slightly patronising comment that the meeting was all the more impressive from having been organised by working men without help from Glasgow's middle-class reformers. The *Caledonian Mercury* was certainly impressed. 'The men walked from four to six deep, in close order, and at a quick pace, and the whole procession took upwards of an hour and a half to pass any given point. The music was abundant and excellent, and the banners were numerous.'[11] One was the old Strathaven Covenanting banner, being given another airing in the cause of radicalism.

In November 1839, 10,000 Chartists marched in Newport in Monmouthshire, South Wales. They were calling for the same changes to government as the radicals of 1820. They wanted universal suffrage and voting to be done by secret ballot. They also wanted a salary for MPs, so men who weren't well off could afford to stand for election. Led by John Frost, the Chartists marched on the Westgate Hotel in Newport. They believed some of their number

were being held there. As at Merthyr Tydfil, many of the marchers were coal miners. Troops fired into the crowd and twenty-two
people were killed. John Frost, William Jones and Zephaniah
Williams were tried and found guilty of high treason. They were
sentenced to be hanged, drawn and quartered, the last time this
sentence was handed down in a British court. It was commuted to
transportation. The three men were transported to Van Diemen's
Land.

Forty years later, Liberal Prime Minister William Ewart Glad-
stone argued the case for home rule for Ireland. In a pamphlet he
published in 1886, he argued for home rule for Scotland and Wales
too, home rule all round. He thought the United Kingdom should
be replaced by a federal Britain. In the same year, the Scottish Home
Rule Association was formed. The Independent Labour Party was
founded a few years later, in 1893. From the beginning, the two
movements were closely interlinked. Keir Hardie, who sat for
fifteen years as a Labour MP for Merthyr Tydfil, was a whole-
hearted supporter. Home rule for Scotland was now most definitely
on the political agenda.

Universal adult suffrage was not achieved until 1918, when all
men over twenty-one and women over thirty (with a certain amount
of property) were given the vote. In 1928, this unfairness was cor-
rected, so that all adults over the age of twenty-one – regardless of
whether they owned any property – had the right to vote for their
representatives in parliament.

CHAPTER 28

The Scottish Radicals of
1820 Remembered

Memorials across central Scotland remember the radicals of 1820. The first, to John Baird and Andrew Hardie, was erected on Mr Turner's estate at Thrushgrove, north of Glasgow Cathedral and off what is now Springburn Road. The monument was raised in 1832, the year in which the Great Reform Act was passed.

Peter Mackenzie split his earnings from his *Exposure of the Spy System Pursued in Glasgow* between Andrew Hardie's widowed mother and the cost of building the memorial to her son and his comrade in arms. He pledged the money would support Marion Hardie 'so long as she lived'.[1]

Mackenzie and other supporters of a memorial initially met opposition to the idea. They had planned to site it in the grave-yard of the Church of the Holy Rude in Stirling, where Baird and Hardie were buried after their execution. Although the minister and kirk session agreed to the proposal, the provost and magistrates of Stirling refused permission. Mackenzie appealed to James Turner in Glasgow, who sent him a letter in response.

> Thrushgrove, 29th October, 1832.
> DEAR SIR,—I so much approve of your exertions to get up the Monument to Hardie and Baird, whereby a triumph will be obtained over the tyrannical conduct of the infamous system pursued by the Government of Sidmouth and Castlereagh in 1820; and learning

that you have met with opposition and difficulty in procuring ground on which to erect the monument, I hereby offer to you sufficient space on my lands of Thrushgrove, where, as you are aware, the great meeting of the inhabitants of Glasgow was held this very day sixteen years ago, and you may therefore proceed with the erection as soon as you please.

I am, dear sir,

Yours sincerely,

JAMES TURNER.

To Mr. Mackenzie.

The monument at Thrushgrove was in the classical style. It had a solid low stone plinth and was surmounted by a fluted stone column with a vase and draped cloth at the very top. The sculptor must have already finished it when Mackenzie and Turner exchanged letters. It was installed and unveiled only a fortnight after Turner offered a place for it at Thrushgrove, on 10 November 1832. A drawing made at the time shows thistles growing at its foot. The head of one of them is dipped, as though in mourning. The inscription reads:

Sacred to the Memory of

ANDREW HARDIE, Aged 28; and JOHN BAIRD, Aged 32;

WHO WERE

BETRAYED BY INFAMOUS SPIES AND INFORMERS,

AND

SUFFERED DEATH AT STIRLING, on the 8th Day of September, 1820,

FOR THE CAUSE OF REFORM NOW TRIUMPHANT.

———

1832

Mackenzie and his friends repaired that evening for a grand public dinner at the Argyle Hotel in Glasgow. This stood on the corner of Argyle Street and Buchanan Street. What Peter Mackenzie described as 'one of the most gorgeous buildings of its kind in the city' later became what he called the 'great emporium of Messrs. Stewart & McDonald'.[2] Later still it became Fraser's, another great emporium. Dugald Sinclair was the proprietor of the hotel. Admiringly, Mackenzie noted the hotelier charged only one shilling and sixpence (about £4.50 in today's money) per head for such public dinners.

Over 120 'respectable reformers' enjoyed the dinner. They came from Glasgow, Paisley, Greenock and elsewhere. Andrew McKinlay was the guest of honour. He was the weaver whom Alexander Richmond had entrapped into taking an illegal oath. Peter Mackenzie was incensed that the unveiling of the memorial and the dinner went unreported in Glasgow's newspapers. He was convinced he knew why. They feared his 'tales of the spy system would choke some of their best patrons and customers'.

Fifteen years after that fine dinner, Mackenzie witnessed the exhumation and reburial of Baird and Hardie's remains at Sighthill Cemetery, across the road and up a little way from Thrushgrove. By this time, James Turner had long since given up his estate at Thrushgrove. Industrial development and the growth of the railway network were increasingly encroaching on the place where thrushes once sang in green fields. A group of working men in and around the area now known as St Rollox took up a collection to raise money for a new memorial. The fund reached £150. Peter Mackenzie, James Turner and other gentlemen helped them approach Stirling Council for permission to exhume the bodies of Baird and Hardie.

This was initially refused, on the basis that when the two men were sentenced to death, it had been specified their remains were to be 'disposed of where our Lord the King shall think fit'. This callous reply moved the men's relatives and other supporters of the idea to send a petition to the Lord Advocate for Scotland, who by this time was Andrew Rutherford. He replied that as long as the kirk session in Stirling had no objection, he could see none, referring to Hardie and Baird as 'these unfortunate men'. There was one condition. The exhumation and reinternment had to be carried out quietly, without publicity and 'in the presence of a few friends only'.

A party of three arrived in Stirling on the evening of Monday, 19 July 1847. They were Mr Cullen, Mr Walker and Peter Mackenzie. Relatives of Baird and Hardie met them there, pointing out the grave. The two men had been buried one on top of the other. A question was asked as to how they were to identify each man. John Baird's brother Robert had the answer. 'You will easily know my brother from the manner the headsman cut and mutilated his chin.' Robert Baird withdrew, leaving the cemetery. He could not bear to see what was left of his brother's body.

The exhumation started around 4 a.m. Three hours later, they had the remains of the two men in one new coffin. They carried this on their shoulders to the 'mourning coach' they had brought with them. Despite the stipulation there was to be no fuss made, they then travelled in procession through Stirling and on to Glasgow.

The news of what they were doing spread very quickly. A horse-drawn mourning coach rumbling down the hill from the Church of the Holy Rude was probably a bit of a giveaway. People all along the route were eager to pay their respects. 'At every village and country town we came to, we were met by young and old, rich and poor, who brought us flowers of all kinds, begging that we would plant them on the graves of the martyrs.'[3]

They reached Glasgow at Provanmill, where a hundred 'well dressed persons' were waiting to greet them. That these mourners were well dressed was the old reminder that reformers were respectable people. The coffin was transferred from the mourning coach to a hearse, horse-drawn of course. When they had gone to their executions they were dragged on a hurdle, a mark of humiliation. On this journey, their bodies were given every mark of respect.

By the time they reached Sighthill, perhaps a thousand people were following 'slowly and seriously'. Baird and Hardie's relatives lowered the coffin down into the grave which had been prepared for it. The flowers collected along the way were strewn over the grave.

Peter Mackenzie waxed lyrical over the significance and solemnity of the occasion, describing it as 'A nation's worthy tribute to the patriotic dead.' Who, he asked sternly, would plant a rose or a lily on the graves of Castlereagh or King George IV? Nobody.

'But over the graves of their victims, a nation will mourn, and the stranger, when visiting them, will recall to mind the deeds of the past, and say, "Patriots, rest, your dust is sacred, the memories of your persecutors we remember with reproach."'[4]

A new memorial was erected over the grave. It has been restored several times over the century and a half since. It stands on lush green grass in front of an abundant rowan tree, high up on Sighthill, overlooking Glasgow. The stone bears many inscriptions, remembering not only Baird and Hardie but also James Wilson of Strathaven and the Bonnymuir men transported to Australia for their part in the radical rising. It includes the full text of the Lord Advocate's letter giving permission for the exhumation and reburial of Baird and Hardie. There is also a poem, as there had to be. The name of the poet is not known.

> Here lie the slain and mutilated forms
> Of those who fell, and fell like martyrs true,
> Faithful to freedom through a time of storms,
> They met their fate as patriots always do.
>
> Calmly they view'd Death's dread and dank array,
> Serene in hope, they triumphed o'er dismay;
> Their country's wrongs alone drew forth their sighs,
> And those to them endeared by Nature's holiest ties.
>
> But truth and right have better times brought round,
> Now no more traitors scorn by passing breath,
> For weeping Scotland hails this spot of ground
> And shrines, with all who fell for Freedom's faith,
> Those sons of her's now fam'd made glorious by their death.

A monument to James Wilson was erected in his home town in 1846. A slender and beautiful obelisk, it stands on the site of his old home, where Strathaven's Castle Street becomes North Street. His grave is in the cemetery behind it. Devastated by her loss, Helen Wilson went on many evenings to her husband's grave.[5] Thanks to

the good offices of the 1820 Society, his last resting place now has
a gravestone. The inscription reads:

THIS
IS THE BURIAL PLACE
OF JAMES 'PURLIE' WILSON
HANGED
30TH AUGUST 1820
GLASGOW
MARTYRED IN THE CAUSE OF
FREEDOM
AND EMANCIPATION OF
WORKING PEOPLE

The obelisk was erected in 1846, designed by James Park, a local
man. This was the same year in which the Corn Laws were repealed.
The monument was unveiled by James Wilson's niece in August 1846,
with bands playing music to mark the occasion. John Stevenson
also spoke, firstly about the Covenanting battles of Drumclog and
Bothwell Brig before saying: 'But, gentlemen, we stand on historic
ground. Another rising for civil and religious liberty took place at
Avondale in 1820.' The wording on the obelisk reads:

ERECTED BY PUBLIC
SUBSCRIPTION
IN AFFECTIONATE MEMORY
OF
JAMES WILSON
A PATRIOTIC SCOTSMAN
WHO SUFFERED DEATH AT
GLASGOW
30TH AUGUST 1820
FOR ENUNCIATING THOSE
PRINCIPLES
OF PROGRESS AND REFORM

BY THE ADOPTION OF WHICH
GREAT BRITAIN
HAS SECURED DOMESTIC PEACE
AND CONSOLIDATED HER POWER
AMONG THE NATIONS
BORN AT STRATHAVEN
3RD SEPTEMBER 1760

Interesting that he is lauded as a patriotic Scotsman while Great Britain is also praised. On one face of the plinth are two small stone thistles. One bows its head, echoing the Scottish symbolism of the drawing of the original monument to Baird and Hardie at Thrushgrove.

Although none of the Paisley radicals died as martyrs or suffered transportation for the cause of reform, feelings ran high there. Many in the town had been committed radicals, several had been imprisoned, four tried for high treason. A monument to commemorate Baird, Hardie and Wilson was erected in Woodside Cemetery in 1867. The belief that all three men had been entrapped into direct action was now the dominant strand of the story, as the speech by Provost Macfarlane at the unveiling ceremony demonstrated. He also said the monument did not glorify the use of violence to achieve political aims but honoured the memory of men devoted to the cause of reform, which was now successful.[6]

The Paisley memorial is another tall and slender obelisk. The sculptor was William Robin, working to a design by the famous Glasgow architect Alexander (Greek) Thomson. It is decorated with the characteristic palm leaf motif typical of Greek Thomson's work. The monument can be reached by car or on foot by heading up the main path, taking the left fork, the first path on the right and then the first path on the left.[7]

Again there is poetry. This is Paisley, after all. The inscriptions are somewhat weathered but a book available from the cemetery office gives them in full. Robert Allan of Kilbarchan penned two of the lines:

The martyr's grave will rise
Above the warrior's cairn.

There are three more poems on the monument. Attributed only
to 'a Paisley working man', one longer verse tells the story of what
happened to Baird, Hardie and Wilson.

Our heath-clad hills and lonely mountain caves
Are marked by battlefields and Martyrs' graves.
This stone accords the last embattled stroke
Which Scotchmen [*sic*] struck at vile oppression's yoke.
At Bonnymuir they trod their native heath.
And sought a Warrior's or a Martyr's death.
Sad choice! for there they found their enterprise
To claim or force Reform by arm'd surprise.
Was circumvented and betrayed by spies
And thus ensnared in Treason's feudal laws.
Their personal honour in the people's cause
Compelled the fight which claims our pity and applause.
Freedom's battle once begun
Bequeathed by bleeding sire to son
Though baffled oft is ever won.

For two men who were at the unveiling of the Paisley monument
it was very personal. Teacher James Chalmers had been a young
man in 1820. By coincidence he had been in Glasgow on 30 August
1820 and had seen James Wilson hang. He told a story he thought
he alone knew. On the night before Baird and Hardie's execution, a
'number of godly men', some of whom Chalmers had known, had
met in Glasgow to hold a prayer vigil for the condemned men.[8]

On the evening the Woodside memorial was unveiled, a dinner
was held in Paisley to celebrate. Chalmers again spoke briefly, com-
menting on how different life and politics were in 1867 as compared
to 1820. John Fraser of Johnstone also spoke. He was the schoolmaster who was falsely imprisoned for four months after the rising.
After a toast had been made 'in solemn silence' to the memory

of Hardie, Wilson and Baird, Fraser told his own story. When these three men were executed, he had been in prison in Paisley, sharing that cramped cell with John Neil, Alexander Thomson and James Speirs.[9] Although it was only Speirs who was tried for high treason, all four men had feared they too might hang.

Reflecting that his old radical comrades were all now dead, John Fraser spoke about how he had felt on reading the newspaper reports of the deaths of Baird, Hardie and Wilson. 'You cannot conceive the intensity of distress and horror I experienced in reading the bloody events, heightened and deepened by the thought, that in a very few days the same fate might be my own.'

Deeply moved, Fraser welcomed the newly unveiled monument in Woodside Cemetery. He told his fellow diners that when they had all passed on, the monument would endure, telling the stories to generations yet to come:

> ... it will preach and proclaim to the unborn that the genuine love of liberty, hatred of oppression, undying sympathy with the noble martyrs, characterised the sentiments and conduct of the thorough-going reformers of Paisley. It is, then, a monument to yourselves as well as to the martyrs. It will stand here in your beautiful cemetery a little volume of Scotch [*sic*] political history; kindling the love of liberty in their hearts, and making them rejoice that there were Scotsmen in those days, who fearlessly dared to do and to die for glorious freedom, as there were Scotsmen to do and to die for religious freedom.[10]

Fraser also quoted a poem by Ebenezer Elliott, known as the Corn-Law Rhymer. This very poignantly sums up the attitudes of many in the middle and upper classes towards the poor during the years of deprivation and struggle for reform.

> I saw a nation sunk in grief –
> I heard a nation's wail;
> And their deep-toned misery was caught
> By every passing gale.

Want guarded every peasant's door,
Swept each mechanic's board,
Yet the earth had teamed – *but only teamed*
To swell the rich man's hoard.

I saw the nobles of that land
In pride and pomp roll by;
And I read contempt for the poor man's lot
In every haughty eye.[11]

John Fraser himself died in 1879 at the age of eighty-four, still devoted to the cause of universal suffrage. In the 1840s, he was an active Chartist, always advocating peaceful reform. He set up and became editor of a newspaper called the *True Scotsman*, which put the Chartist point of view. Music remained a passion and a means of earning a living. Known professionally as the Fraser Family, he and his children toured Scotland and beyond, giving concerts.

Memorials to the radicals of 1820 have been created in our own times. As well as James Wilson's gravestone at Strathaven, the 1820 Society also marked the site of the Battle of Bonnymuir. Surrounded by a wooden fence, a solid piece of granite sits at the foot of the hill on which the skirmish took place. It reads:

ON 5TH APRIL, 1820, A BAND OF SCOTS
WORKING CLASS RADICALS FOUGHT
HERE FOR THEIR DEMOCRATIC RIGHTS
AGAINST A TROOP OF HORSE
FROM THE BRITISH ARMY.

At Bonnybridge, two plaques mark the Radical Pend, the tunnel under the Forth and Clyde canal through which the wounded and captured from the battle were taken to Stirling Castle. On Saturday, 4 April 1981, local councillor Billy Buchanan organised an historical pageant to commemorate the battle. Winnie Ewing unveiled the modern plaque. At its foot are the words *Bonnybridge History Lives On.*

At the site of the massacre of the people who rescued the radical prisoners from gaol at Greenock, there is a multi-faceted remembrance. Sculpted by Angela Hunter, the Radical War Memorial is a pink stone plinth surmounted by a circle in which two people reach out to clasp each other's hands. On a wall opposite the site of the old prison or bridewell in Bank Street, a plaque placed there by the Riverview Players lists the eight victims of the massacre by the Port Glasgow militia.

Set into the wall, individual blocks bear the names of all those who died. One sums up the event:

REMEMBER THE 8th OF APRIL THAT BLOODY DAY
WHEN MANY WERE WOUNDED & CARRIED AWAY

Not far from Greenock is Kilbarchan, where the dogs didn't bark. The Weaver's Cottage, a property of the National Trust for Scotland, is a time machine, vividly evoking the lives of handloom weavers and their families. So too are the Sma' Shot Cottages in Paisley.

In Condorrat at Cumbernauld, the house where John Baird stayed with his brother and sister-in-law is still there. It has long had a wooden plaque attached to the front wall.

JOHN BAIRD
LEADER FOR
REFORM AND FREEDOM
IN SCOTLAND AS
COMMANDANT,
CONDORRAT RADICAL

___

MARTYR TO THE CAUSE OF LIBERTY
AND SOCIAL JUSTICE

___

HANGED AND BEHEADED
AT STIRLING AS A 'TRAITOR'
SEPTEMBER 8, 1820

On the other side of the roundabout, between the Baird house and the public library, a triptych of stones remembers three groups of people: local members of the armed forces who lost their lives in wars, forty-seven coal miners who died in a fire at the pit at Auchengleich in 1959 and Condorrat's radical weavers, 'who fought for democracy for all in 1820'. The motto at the base of this stone reads, Weave the Truth. Nearby is a bench where foot-sore historians can sit and reflect. The brass plaque fastened to it is labelled, Weavers Rest/1820.

Not too far away from Condorrat, Bishopbriggs Library has a fine permanent display on the life and times of Thomas Muir of Huntershill. It includes Alexander Stoddart's striking bust of Muir, the father of Scottish democracy. Its duplicate sits in the Museum of Australian Democracy.

In Glasgow's People's Palace, as well as the paintings by Ken Currie on the history of the city's working people, there is a banner dating from the time of the Spanish Civil War. Commissioned by the Camlachie branch of the Independent Labour party in 1938, it makes common cause between Scotland's radical martyrs and the Spanish people. 'Thomas Muir, Baird and Hardie died that you should be free to choose your government. Workers in Spain are dying because they dared to choose their own government. Unite for the Struggle!' Or as a modern pamphlet on Thomas Muir says: 'Your vote has history'.

Popular song also remembers these turbulent times. 'Tom Paine's Bones' by Dick Gaughan has been recorded by him and others. The Shee do a marvellous version of it. 'The Parting Glass', attributed to Alexander Boswell of Auchinleck, sworn enemy of the radicals, has also been recorded by various artists. Remembering how many hand-loom weavers there once were in Scotland, 'The Wark [or Work] o' the Weavers' has been sung by many folk groups and can be found online. 'Dark Bonnymuir', the haunting elegy written by Allan Murchie for Baird and Hardie's gallant little army, is sung by mod-ern troubadour Alan Dickson.

In 2015, the Strathaven Choral Society premiered a spe-cially commissioned piece of music composed by Mark Carroll. Honouring the memory of James Wilson, it's entitled *Shame, Shame, He Dies for His Country*.

Kept safely away from the light, some relics of the radical rising remain. The pikes carried by the Bonnymuir men picked up off the field and taken to Stirling Castle are now in the care of Historic Environment Scotland. They are a tangible and evocative connection to John Baird, Andrew Hardie and the men and boys who marched with them to Bonnymuir. They recall those heady days when men and women called for democracy, social change and fairness. They recall the men who fought and died for the rights of old Scotland and democracy for all.

List of Men Executed, Transported and Imprisoned for their Radical Activities

Event	Tried	Date
Pentrich, Derbyshire		**9 June 1817**
Brandreth, Jeremiah Ludlam, Isaac Turner, William	County Hall, Derby	Hanged then beheaded, 7 Nov. 1817, Friar Gate Gaol, Derby
14 transported to New South Wales, 6 gaoled, 12 released		
Cato Street, London		**23 February 1820**
Brunt, John Davidson, William Ings, James Thistlewood, Arthur Tidd, Richard	Sessions House, Old Bailey, London	Hanged then beheaded, 1 May 1820, Newgate Prison, London
5 transported to Van Diemen's Land, 1 gaoled		
Bonnymuir, Stirlingshire		**5 April 1820**
Baird, John Hardie, Andrew	Court House, Stirling	Hanged then beheaded, 8 September 1820, Broad Street, Stirling
Strathaven, Lanarkshire		**5 April 1820**
Wilson, James	Glasgow High Court	Hanged then beheaded, 30 August 1820, Glasgow Green
In Scotland a total of 98 were accused, 52 'not in custody', 19 transported to New South Wales, the rest released. In addition, Gilbert McLeod, editor of the *Spirit of the Union* newspaper was transported to New South Wales, 3 September 1820.		

Huddersfield, Barnsley and Sheffield, Yorkshire		1 to 12 April 1820
12 transported to Van Diemen's Land, 12 gaoled		
Merthyr Tydfil, Glamorgan		**1 to 7 June 1831**
Lewis, Richard aka Dic Penderyn.	Glamorgan Assizes, Cardiff	Hanged, 13 August 1831, Cardiff Market
5 transported to New South Wales, 20 gaoled		
Newport, Monmouthshire		**4 November 1839**
3 transported to Van Diemen's Land, 18 gaoled		

Author's Note

I've wanted to write this book for more than thirty years. The spark was struck during a visit to Paisley Museum and Art Gallery back in the late 1980s. I had gone there to look at their shawl collection and find out more about the world-famous Paisley pattern which makes these so beautiful. Training to become a Blue Badge Scottish Tourist Guide, I had chosen Paisley shawls for a course project, to be submitted to our principal tutor at what was then known as the Extra Mural Department of Glasgow University.

I came away from the museum with my head full of images of the jewel-bright shawls in the classic Paisley tear-drop pattern, a handful of postcards to illustrate my project and lots of information about the people who made the shawls. I already knew something about the Paisley weavers. My great-great-grandfather on the Craig side was one of them. It's a cherished family tradition that Robert Tannahill, the foremost of the weaver-poets of Paisley, sits somewhere in the branches of our family tree. He seems to have bequeathed to many of us who came after him the inclination to write and an inclination also towards the radical side of politics.

I learned some Scottish history at school and much more at home. I'd heard of Thomas Muir but I had never heard of the Radical Rising of 1820. I wasn't alone in that. I learned about Thomas Muir and the Friends of the People from our inspirational History teacher, Donald Asher. I have the feeling he believed we should know not only about the French Revolution on a global scale but also how it influenced people in our own backyard in Scotland. Thomas Muir, the radical from Bishopbriggs, had lived not so very many miles away from where Mr Asher was teaching us at Bearsden Academy.

In this bicentenary year of the Scottish Radical Rising of 1820, I hope I have brought something fresh to the table. My goal has been to tell the story in as straightforward and honest a way as possible. I have tried to coax as many of the men and women involved as possible to step forward out of the shadows and into the light.

They lived through all this: those who took direct action and those who opposed them; those who helped, hid and consoled the radicals who suffered for their words and actions. So many lives were devastated and changed forever by the events of April 1820. So many wives, parents, brothers, sisters, sons, daughters and friends were left to grieve, great gaping holes torn in the fabric of their lives.

My main sources have been the published accounts of the state trials, letters, reports, memoirs written by people who were there and contemporary newspaper accounts, always bearing in mind the latter can be biased one way or the other. Whenever possible, I have gone looking for corroboration of what one person or newspaper account said.

The memorial to the Condorrat radicals of 1820 which stands outside the local library bears the words 'Weave the Truth'. I've done my level best.

Select Bibliography

Anon., *The Pioneers: A Tale of the Radical Rising at Strathaven in 1820*, Strathaven: J.M. Bryson, *c.* 1846.

Anon. (attributed to 'An Odd Fellow'), *Gotham in Alarm*, Glasgow: J. Napier, 1816.

Bewley, Christina, *Muir of Huntershill*, Oxford: Oxford University Press, 1981.

Brooke, Alan and Kipling, Lesley, *Liberty or Death: Radicals, Republicans and Luddites 1793–1823*, Huddersfield: Huddersfield Local History Society, 2013.

Cameron, John, *The Parish of Campsie*, Kirkintilloch: MacLeod, 1892.

Cannon, Richard, *History of the 10th Royal Hussars*, London: J.W. Parker, 1843.

Carruthers, Gerard and Martin, Don, *Thomas Muir of Huntershill: Essays for the Twenty First Century*, Edinburgh: Humming Earth, 2016.

Cartwright, F.D. (ed.), *The Life and Correspondence of Major Cartwright*, London: Henry Colburn, 1826.

Casely, Claire (ed.), *Lines Written on a Summer Evening: The Works of Alexander Wilson*, Amazon CreateSpace, 2016.

Clark, Anna, *The Struggle for the Breeches: Gender and the Making of the British Working Class*, Berkeley: University of California Press, 1995.

Clark, Sylvia, *Paisley: A History*, Edinburgh: Mainstream Publishing, 1988.

Donnelly, Michael, *Thomas Muir of Huntershill*, Bishopbriggs: Bishopbriggs Town Council, 1975 & 2016.

Downie, William Fleming, *A History of Strathaven and Avondale*, Glasgow: Eric Moore & Company, 1979.

Drysdale, William, *Old Faces, Old Places, and Old Stories of Stirling*, Stirling: Eneas Mackay, 1898.

Ellis, P. Berresford & Seumas Mac A' Ghobhainn, *The Radical Rising: The Scottish Insurrection of 1820*, London: Gollancz, 1970.

Ewan, Elizabeth, Rose Pipes, Jane Rendall and Siân Reynolds (eds), *The New Biographical Dictionary of Scottish Women*, Edinburgh: Edinburgh University Press, 2018.

Fletcher, Eliza, *Autobiography of Mrs Fletcher*, Edinburgh: Edmonston and Douglas, 1875.

Gauldie, Enid, *Spinning and Weaving in Scotland*, Edinburgh: NMS Publishing, 2004.

'Gilbert McLeod & *The Spirit of The Union*', University of the Third Age website, https://u3asites.org.uk/files/g/glasgow-west-end/docs/gilbertmcleodandthespiritoftheunion.pdf.

Gillespie, Robert, *Round About Falkirk*, Glasgow: James MacLehose, 1868.

Green, C.J., *Trials for High Treason in Scotland, under a special commission, held at Stirling, Glasgow, Dumbarton, Paisley, and Ayr, in the year 1820*. In three volumes, Edinburgh: Manners and Miller, 1825.

Hamilton, Janet, *Poems, Essays, and Sketches*, Glasgow: James MacLehose, 1880.

Hutchison, James, *Canal Boats & Miners Rows: Kilsyth 1750–1970*, Kilsyth: Scotia Books, n.d.

Inverclyde Tourist Group, *Greenock Historic Quarter* (booklet), n.d.

Johnston, Thomas, *A History of the Working Classes in Scotland*, Glasgow: Forward, 1922.

Kay, John, *A Series of Original Portraits and Caricature Etchings*, Edinburgh: West Port Books, 1999.

Keenan, Michael, *Garngad*, self-published, n.d. Available for consultation at Royston Library, Glasgow.

Lyon, Margaret, *Camelon and the Nailers* (pamphlet), 2005.

Macfarlane, Margaret and Alastair, *The Scottish Radicals: Tried and Transported to Australia for Treason in 1820*, Stevenage: Spa Books, 1981.

Mackenzie, Peter, *An Exposure of the Spy System Pursued in Glasgow, During the Years 1816–17–18–19 and 20, With Copies of the Original Letters of Andrew Hardie*, Glasgow: Muir, Gowans & Co., 1833.

Mackenzie, Peter, *Reminiscences of Glasgow and the West of Scotland*, vols I and II, Glasgow: John Tweed, 1865.

McKay, Archibald, *The History of Kilmarnock*, Kilmarnock: Archibald McKay, 1858.

Paine, Thomas, *Rights of Man, Common Sense and Other Political Writings*, Oxford: Oxford World's Classics, 2008.

Parkhill, John, *The Life and Opinions of Arthur Sneddon*, Paisley: James Cook, 1860.

Paterson, James, *Autobiographical Reminiscences*, Glasgow: Maurice Ogle, 1871.

Pentland, Gordon, 'Radical Returns in an Age of Revolution', *Études écossaises* 13, 2010, pp. 91–102. Available online at https://journals.openedition.org/etudesecossaises/222.

Pentland, Gordon, *The Spirit of the Union: Popular Politics in Scotland, 1815–1820*, London: Pickering & Chatto, 2011.

Prebble, John, *The King's Jaunt: George IV in Scotland, 1822*, London: Collins, 1988.

Prentice, George, *The Stories Behind Some Paisley Memorials*, Paisley: Loganmuir, 2015.

Reilly, Valerie, *The Paisley Pattern*, Glasgow: Richard Drew Publishing Limited, 1987.

Riding, Jacqueline, *Peterloo: The Story of the Manchester Massacre*, London: Head of Zeus/Apollo, 2018.

Roach, W.M., 'Radical Reform Movements in Scotland from 1815 to 1822 with Particular Reference to Events in the West of Scotland', Glasgow University, unpublished PhD dissertation, 1970.

Rodger, Alexander, *Poems and Songs, Humorous, Serious, and Satirical*, Paisley: Alexander Gardner, 1897, reprinted by Hard Press Publishing, Miami, n.d.

Smith, Henry, *Autobiography of Lieutenant-General Sir Harry Smith*, London: John Murray, 1903.

Stevenson, John, *A True Narrative of the Radical Rising in Strathaven*, Glasgow: W. & W. Miller, 1835.

Tennant, Charles, *The Radical Laird: A Biography of George Kinloch, 1775–1833*, Kineton: The Roundwood Press, 1970.

Thompson, E.P., *The Making of the English Working Class*, London: Penguin Classics, 2013.

Whatley, Christopher, *Scottish Society 1707–1830*, Manchester: Manchester University Press, 2000.

Wilkes, Sue, *Regency Spies: Secret Histories of Britain's Rebels & Revolutionaries*, Barnsley: Pen & Sword, 2015.

Williams, Gwynn, *The Merthyr Rising*, Cardiff: University of Cardiff Press, 2013.

Young, John, *Pictures in Prose and Verse; Or, Personal Recollections of the Late Janet Hamilton, Langloan*, Victoria (Australia): Leopold Classic Library, n.d.

Notes

Dates and places of births and death all come from, or have been confirmed by, the images of original parish registers on the *Scotland's People* website.

Unless otherwise stated, contemporary newspaper reports have been accessed via the *British Newspaper Archive* website.

All websites accessed in October 2019 unless otherwise noted.

Abbreviations

DRO Devon Record Office
NA National Archives (London)
HO Home Office Papers
NLS National Library of Scotland

Foreword

1. Riding, J., *Peterloo: The Story of the Manchester Massacre* (hereafter: Riding), pp.14–15.
2. Wilkes, S., *Regency Spies: Secret Histories of Britain's Rebels & Revolutionaries* (hereafter: Wilkes), pp. 164–7.
3. Roach, W.M., 'Radical Reform Movements in Scotland from 1815 to 1822 with Particular Reference to Events in the West of Scotland', unpublished PhD dissertation, Glasgow University, 1970 (hereafter: Roach), p. 218.
4. Pentland, G., *The Spirit of the Union* (hereafter: Pentland), p. 99.
5. Anon., *The Pioneers: A Tale of the Radical Rising at Strathaven in 1820* (hereafter: Pioneers), p. 52.
6. NA HO 102/32 (Home Office Papers).
7. Green, C.J., *Trials for High Treason in Scotland* (hereafter: Green), vol. III, pp. 491–2.

PART I
THE ROOTS OF SCOTTISH RADICALISM

1
The Strike of the Calton Weavers

1. Moss, M., 'Industrial Revolution: 1770s to 1830s', Mitchell Library, *Glasgow Story* online. https://www.theglasgowstory.com/story/?id=TGSC0.
2. NLS Maps online at https://maps.nls.uk/joins/2767.html.
3. *Saunders's News-letter, and Daily Advertiser*, 19 October 1787. https://www.britishnewspaperarchive.co.uk/search/results/1773-01-01/1787-12-31?newspapertitle=Saunders%27s%20News-Letter.
4. *Caledonian Mercury*, 11 October 1787. https://www.british-newspaperarchive.co.uk/search/results/1739-01-01/1756-12-31?newspapertitle=Caledonian%20Mercury.
5. Glasgow Caledonian University, Radical Glasgow website: www.gcal.ac.uk/radicalglasgow/chapters/weavers/html.

2
Thomas Muir of Huntershill and
the Friends of the People

1. Logue, K.J., *Popular Disturbances in Scotland, 1780–1815* (Edinburgh: John Donald, 1979), p. 10.
2. *Bygone Dundee* website: http://bygone.dundeecity.gov.uk/bygone-news/december-1909/index.html.
3. *The Nine Trades of Dundee* website: http://ninetradesofdundee.co.uk/download/city_history/city_history_documents_and_pictures/tree_of_liberty/1793%20History.pdf.
4. Cartwright, F.D. (ed.), *Life and Correspondence of Major Cartwright* (hereafter: Cartwright), p. 113.
5. Johnston, T., *A History of the Working Classes in Scotland* (hereafter: Johnston), p. 219.
6. Mackenzie, P., *Reminiscences of Glasgow and the West of Scotland* (hereafter: *Mackenzie's Reminiscences*), vol. I, p. 196.
7. Johnston, p. 219.
8. Bewley, C., *Muir of Huntershill* (hereafter: Bewley), p. 43.
9. Ibid., p. 47.

10. Ibid., p. 36.
11. Fletcher, E., *Autobiography of Mrs Fletcher*, p. 70.
12. Ibid.
13. Johnston, p. 219.
14. Ibid., p. 222.
15. *Australian Dictionary of Biography*, vol. 1, Melbourne University Press, 1967.
16. Johnston, p. 220.
17. Ibid., p. 221.
18. Robert Southey, quoted in www.romantic-circles.org.
19. Bewley, p. 91.
20. Ibid.
21. *Australian Dictionary of Biography*, vol. 1, 1967.

3
The People Are in Great Distress

1. Renfrewshire Council, Local Studies Library, via the SCRAN website: https://www.scran.ac.uk/database/record.php?usi=000-000-497-430-C&scache=4i51a8oh4y&searchdb=scran.
2. Roach, p. 28.
3. Parkhill, J., *The Life and Opinions of Arthur Sneddon* (hereafter: Parkhill), p. 31.
4. Rodger, A., *Poems and Songs* (hereafter: Rodger), p. 116.
5. Parkhill, p. 21.
6. Gauldie, E., *Spinning and Weaving in Scotland*, p. 35.
7. Scottish Mining website: http://www.scottishmining.co.uk/2.html.
8. NA HO 33/2.
9. Ellis & MacA' Ghobhainn, *The Radical Rising: The Scottish Insurrection of 1820* (hereafter: Ellis & Mac A' Ghobhainn), p. 136.
10. DRO 152M/1820/OH62.
11. Ibid.
12. Balfron Heritage website: https://balfronheritage.org.uk.
13. Roach, p. 155.

4
Met in the Open Fields: The Thrushgrove Meeting

1. Pentland, p. 15.

2. Smith, J., *Recollections of James Turner, Esq., of Thrushgrove*, Glasgow: The Examiner Office, 1854 (hereafter: Smith), p. 22.
3. Ibid.
4. Ibid.
5. *Belfast Commercial Chronicle*, 4 November 1816.
6. *Morning Chronicle*, 5 November 1816.
7. Ellis & Mac A' Ghobhainn, p. 102.
8. Smith, p. 29.
9. Cartwright, p. 112.
10. *Liverpool Mercury*, 8 November 1816.

5
Lay the Axe to the Tree of Corruption

1. McKay, A., *The History of Kilmarnock* (hereafter: McKay), p.185.
2. Ibid., p. 186.
3. Ibid.
4. Ibid., p. 188.
5. Paterson, J., *Autobiographical Reminiscences* (hereafter: Paterson), p. 71.
6. Ibid.
7. Ibid., pp. 71–2.
8. Ibid.
9. *Spirit of the Union*, 30 October 1819.
10. Ibid.
11. Ibid.
12. Wilkes, pp. 141–4.
13. State Library of Queensland, www.convictrecords.com.au.

6
Pestilential Publications and Twopenny Trash

1. Pentland, p. 67.
2. Ibid.
3. Roach, p. 231.
4. *Spirit of the Union*, 30 October 1819.
5. Roach, p. 183.
6. *Glasgow Herald*, 1 September 1820.
7. Roach, p. 231.

8. Paterson, p. 66.

9. Ibid., pp. 66–9.

10. *Dictionary of the Scots Language* online; writer Sheila Grant, in an email to the author.

11. Paterson, p. 67.

12. Ibid., pp. 67–9.

13. *Mackenzie's Reminiscences*, p. 103.

14. Paterson, p. 69.

15. *Westmorland Advertiser and Kendal Chronicle*, 20 November 1819.

16. NA HO, Sidmouth Papers.

17. Hamilton, J., *Poems, Essays, and Sketches* (hereafter: Hamilton), p. 362.

18. Spartacus Educational website: https://spartacus-educational.com/Black_Dwarf.htm.

19. Riding, p. 135.

20. *Manchester Observer*, 10 July 1819 (via *Peterloo 1819 News*, @Live1819).

7

The *Spirit of the Union*

1. 'Gilbert McLeod & *The Spirit of The Union*', University of the Third Age (hereafter: 'Gilbert McLeod'). https://u3asites.org.uk/files/g/glasgow-west-end/docs/gilbertmcleodandthespiritoftheunion.pdf.

2. *Spirit of the Union*, 30 October 1819.

3. Ibid., 6 November 1819.

4. Ibid.

5. Ibid.

6. Ibid.

7. *Spirit of the Union*, 4 December 1819.

8. Ibid.

9. Ibid.

10. *Spirit of the Union*, 30 October 1819.

11. Ibid.

12. Ibid., 6 November 1819.

13. Ibid. (Colloquially, the terms 'provost' and 'Lord Provost' are interchangeable.)

14. Rodger, p. 148.

8
Keep Your Eye on Paisley

1.   Casely, C. (ed.), *Lines Written on a Summer Evening*, p. 11.
2.   *Paisley on the Web*, https://www.paisley.org.uk/famous-people/alexander-wilson/.
3.   Riding, pp. 223–83.
4.   *Morning Chronicle*, 18 September 1819.
5.   Pentland, p. 72.
6.   Ibid.
7.   *Westmorland Advertiser and Kendal Chronicle*, 25 September 1819.
8.   Ibid.
9.   Ibid.
10. *Morning Chronicle*, 18 September 1819.
11. Ibid.

9
'We're All Radicals Here!'

1.   Clark, S., *Paisley: A History*, p. 57.
2.   Parkhill, p. 74.
3.   Ewan et al, *The New Biographical Dictionary of Scottish Women*, p. 186.
4.   Hamilton, preface, p. viii.
5.   Ibid., p. ix.
6.   Ibid., p. 362.
7.   Ibid.
8.   Parkhill, p. 76.
9.   NA HO 40/9–08, p. 2.
10. Thompson, E.P., *The Making of the English Working Class*, pp. 723–4.
11. Parkhill, p. 77.

10
Heroines and a Hero of Liberty:
The Clayknowes and Dundee Meetings

1.   *Spirit of the Union*, 6 November 1819.
2.   Ibid.

3.   Ibid.
4.   *Morning Chronicle*, 5 November 1819.
5.   *Glasgow Herald*, 5 November 1819.
6.   *Morning Chronicle*, 5 November 1819.
7.   *Spirit of the Union*, 6 November 1819.
8.   Ibid.
9.   Tennant, C., *The Radical Laird*, pp. 131–43.
10. Ibid., facing p. 129.
11. Ibid., p. 135.
12. Ibid., p. 160.
13. Ibid., p. 246.

11
Web of Deceit

1.   Mackenzie, P., *An Exposure of the Spy System* (hereafter: *Spy System*). The allegation is made throughout and the frontispiece of the book shows the original monument to Baird and Hardie at Thrushgrove, with these words carved into it, '. . . betrayed by infamous spies and informers'.
2.   *Spirit of the Union*, 4 November 1819.
3.   Wilkes, p. 157.
4.   Riding, pp. 120–5.
5.   *Liverpool Mercury*, 5 October 1838.
6.   Roach, p. 248.
7.   DRO 152M/1820/OH/62
8.   *London Courier and Evening Gazette*, 23 December 1834.
9.   Ibid.
10. *Spy System*, p. 14.
11. *Mackenzie's Reminiscences*, vol. II, p. 369.
12. Ibid.
13. Wilkes, pp. 154–6.
14. *London Courier and Evening Gazette*, 23 December 1834.
15. Ibid.
16. DRO 152M/1820/OH/62.
17. DRO 152M/1819/OH/39.
18. Ibid.
19. Parkhill, p. 25.
20. DRO 152M/1819/OH/39.
21. Parkhill, p. 79.

22. Parkhill, p. 136.
23. Smith, H., *Autobiography of Lieutenant-General Sir Harry Smith*, p. 326.
24. Parkhill, p. 139.
25. Wilkes, pp. 164–7.
26. Pentland, p. 93.

PART II
ONE WEEK IN APRIL

12
Liberty or Death

1. NA 102/32 f. 296.
2. Roach, p. 87.
3. *Ayr Advertiser*, n.d., reprinted in the *Public Ledger and Daily Advertiser*, 20 April 1820.
4. *Morning Post*, 7 April 1820.
5. As quoted from the Scottish Claim of Right in documents on the Scottish Courts and Tribunals website, for example:https://www.scotcourts.gov.uk/docs/default-source/cos-general-docs/pdf-docs-for-opinions/2019csih49.pdf?sfvrsn=0.
6. *Liverpool Mercury*, 8 November 1816.
7. *Morning Post*, 7 April 1820.
8. *Spy System*, p. 8.
9. Ibid., p. 87.
10. Paterson, p. 73.
11. Ibid., pp. 73–4.
12. Parkhill, p. 77.
13. Roach, p. 243.
14. Parkhill, p. 74.
15. NA HO 40/12–1, ff. 56–7.
16. Parkhill, p. 74.
17. Ibid., p. 87.
18. Hamilton, p. 364.

13
'Stop the Work!' – The General Strike

1. Green, vol. I, p. 130.

2. NA HO 40/10, ff. 184–5.
3. Green, vol. III, p. 85.
4. Ibid., p. 249.
5. Ibid., pp. 441–2.
6. Ibid., pp. 34–6.
7. Ibid.
8. Parkhill, p. 90.
9. Ibid., p. 89.
10. Ibid., p. 91.
11. Ibid.

14
That Fearful Night

1. Hamilton, p. 366.
2. Ibid., p. 369.
3. Ibid.
4. *Manchester Observer*, 22 April 1820.
5. Hamilton, p. 369.
6. Ibid.

15
'I Will Shoot All Glasgow to Please You!'

1. Pentland, p. 99.
2. *Spy System*, p. 76.
3. Roach, pp. 221–2.
4. *Spy System*, p. 105.
5. Roach, pp. 221–2.
6. Smith, pp. 91–112.
7. *Mackenzie's Reminiscences*, p. 221–32.
8. Ibid., pp. 222–3.
9. Ibid., p. 195.
10. *Spirit of the Union*, 4 December 1819.
11. Ibid.
12. *Spy System*, p. 234.
13. *Autobiography of Lieutenant-General Harry Smith*, pp. 324–8.

16
The March to Carron

1. *Spy System*, p. 91.
2. *Spirit of the Union*, 4 December 1819.
3. Hardie's account in his letters listed in Mackenzie's *Spy System*, pp. 199–223, and in an appendix to Ellis & Mac A' Ghobhainn, pp. 308–34.
4. *Spy System*, p. 210.
5. Ibid., p. 211.
6. Ibid.
7. Ibid.

17
The Battle of Bonnymuir

1. Green, vol. I, p. 213.
2. Mileham, P., 'The Stirlingshire Yeomanry Cavalry and the Scottish Radical Disturbances of April 1820', *Journal of the Society for Army Historical Research*, vol. 63, no. 254, Summer 1985 (hereafter: Mileham), p. 105.
3. Green, vol. I, p. 327.
4. *Spy System*, p. 117.
5. Green, vol. I, pp. 326–7.
6. *Spy System*, p. 212.
7. Mileham, p. 106.
8. Macfarlane, M. and A., *The Scottish Radicals* (hereafter: Macfarlane), p. 31.
9. Gillespie, R., *Round About Falkirk*, pp. 68–73.
10. *Spy System*, p. 117.
11. *Mackenzie's Reminiscences*, p. 399.
12. Cannon, R., *History of the 10th Royal Hussars*, p. 75.
13. Green, vol. I, p. 199.

18
Tae Fecht for the Rights o' Auld Scotland

1. *Pioneers*, p. 25. Unless otherwise stated, all quotes in this chapter come from this booklet.

2. Ibid., p. 26.
3. Ibid., p. 29.
4. Ibid., p. 25.
5. Green, vol. II, p. 41.
6. Ibid., p. 52.
7. *Glasgow Herald*, 1 September 1820. In a biographical sketch he is described as a free-thinker.
8. Green, vol. II, p. 50.
9. Stevenson, J., *A True Narrative of the Radical Rising in Strathaven* (hereafter Stevenson), p. 11.
10. Green, vol. II, pp. 50–1.
11. Stevenson, p. 12.
12. Ibid., p. 13.
13. *York Herald*, 15 April 1820.
14. DRO M/1820/OH/53.

19
Radicals Arrested at Milngavie

1. Parkhill, p. 92.
2. *Newcastle Courant*, 15 April 1820.
3. *Caledonian Mercury*, 10 April 1820.
4. Ibid.
5. Ibid.
6. Ibid.
7. Smith, pp. 51–2.
8. Ibid.
9. Ibid.
10. Ibid., p. 55.
11. Ibid., p. 56.
12. Rodger, p. 141.
13. Smith, pp. 69–71.
14. Ibid.

20
'Remember Manchester!' – The Greenock Massacre

1. Paterson, p. 77.
2. Ibid., p. 78.

3. NA HO 102/32. Unless otherwise stated, all other eyewitness accounts in this chapter come from this collection of documents.
4. *Carlisle Patriot*, 15 April 1820.
5. *Scots Magazine*, April 1820, p. 378.
6. Ibid.
7. *Glasgow Herald*, 10 April 1820.
8. *Glasgow Courier*, 12 April 1820.

PART III
AFTERMATH

21
Levying War Against the King

1. *Glasgow Herald*, 10 April 1820.
2. Ibid.
3. *Morning Post*, 18 April 1820.
4. *Spy System*, p. 213.
5. Ibid. Hardie never states the man's name but comments that he did not get his promised reward.
6. Ibid.
7. Ellis & Mac A' Ghobhainn, pp. 139–40.
8. Pentland, pp. 4–5.
9. Green, all three vols. The *Address to the Inhabitants of Great Britain & Ireland* was read out at all the trials.
10. Green, vol. I, p. 125.
11. Ibid., p. 130.
12. Ibid., p. 136.
13. Ibid., p. 65.
14. Drysdale, W., *Old Faces, Old Places, and Old Stories of Stirling* (hereafter: Drysdale), pp. 193–4.
15. Green, vol. I, p. 542.
16. Ibid.

22
The Trial of James Wilson

1. Roach, p. 301.
2. Green, vol. II, p. 17.
3. Ibid., p. 108.

4. Ibid., pp. 108–9.
5. Ibid.
6. *Mackenzie's Reminiscences*, vol. II, p. 406.
7. Green, vol. II, p. 26.
8. Ibid., pp. 375–6.
9. *Glasgow Herald*, 1 September 1820.
10. *Pioneers*, pp. 63–4.
11. Ibid., pp. 65–6
12. Smith, p. 19.
13. Ibid.
14. *Mackenzie's Reminiscences*, vol. II, p. 406.
15. NA HO 104/5.
16. NA HO 102/33.

23
'We Apprehend You on a Charge of High Treason!'

1. *Paisley and Renfrewshire Gazette*, 5 April 1879. Unless otherwise stated, quotes and information referring to John Fraser come from the same newspaper article.
2. *Aberdeen Press and Journal*, 8 March 1879. (Fraser's obituary.)
3. Wilkes, p. 82.
4. *Manchester Observer*, 22 April 1820; NA HO 40 12.5 ff. 42.
5. *Paisley and Renfrewshire Gazette*, 5 April 1879.
6. Wilkes, p. 170.
7. Smith, p. 49.
8. *Paisley and Renfrewshire Gazette*, 29 March 1879. This article was part of a series written by Fraser's son, based on his father's diaries, published after Fraser's death.
9. Ibid.
10. Ibid.
11. Ibid.
12. Green, vol. III, p. 489.
13. Ibid.
14. Balfron Heritage website: https://balfronheritage.org.uk/.
15. *Greenock Telegraph and Clyde Shipping Gazette*, 27 December 1893.

24
'Did Ye Ever See Sic a Crowd, Tammas?'

1. *Glasgow Herald*, 1 September 1820.
2. Ellis & Mac A' Ghobhainn, pp. 337–8 .
3. Stevenson, pp. 13–14.
4. Smith, p. 20.
5. *Glasgow Herald*, 1 September 1820.
6. Ibid.
7. Downie, W.F., *A History of Strathaven and Avondale* (hereafter: Downie), p. 241.
8. *Glasgow Herald*, 1 September 1820.
9. Ibid.
10. Stirling Archives, SB1/15/188.
11. Prebble, J., *The King's Jaunt: George IV in Scotland, 1822*, p. 5.
12. *Glasgow Herald*, 1 September 1820.
13. Ibid.
14. Ibid.
15. Ibid.

25
'I Die a Martyr in the Cause of Truth and Justice'

1. *Spy System*, pp. 209–14.
2. Ibid., p. 213.
3. Drysdale, pp. 218–19.
4. *Spy System*, p. 126.
5. *Mackenzie's Reminiscences*, pp. 128–9.
6. Ibid.
7. Ibid.
8. *Spy System*, p. 214.
9. Ibid., p. 119.
10. The Dr Lucas diaries: https://thedrlucasdiaries.wordpress.com/other-years/1820-.
11. *Spy System*, p. 223.
12. Ibid., pp. 221–2.
13. 'Employment of the Steamship in the Scottish East Coast Trades to 1850', http://hdl.handle.net/10023/6418 and Dr Lucas's diary, as note 10.

14. Pentland, p. 85.
15. *Spy System*, p. 131.
16. Drysdale, pp. 190–1.
17. *Spy System*, p. 226.
18. Drysdale, p. 187.
19. *Spy System*, p. 227.
20. Drysdale, p. 188.
21. Ibid., p. 189.
22. Ibid.
23. Ibid.
24. Ibid.
25. Stirling Archives, SB1/15/188 (Lucas diaries).
26. Stirling Archives, SB1/15/186 and SB1/15/188 (Lucas diaries).
27. National Library of Scotland: https://digital.nls.uk/broadsides/view/?id=15292.

26
Banish'd Far Across the Sea

1. National Library of Australia online: https://www.nla.gov.au/research-guides/convicts.
2. State Library of Queensland: www.convictrecords.com.au.
3. 'Gilbert McLeod'.
4. Macfarlane, p. 45.
5. Ibid., pp. 40–1.
6. Ibid., p. 43.
7. *Caledonian Mercury*, 10 April 1820.
8. Macfarlane, p. 41.
9. Ibid., p. 46.
10. *Mackenzie's Reminiscences*, vol. II, pp. 385–6.
11. Macfarlane, p. 45.
12. Ibid., p. 43.
13. Pentland, 'Radical Returns in an Age of Revolution'.
14. Macfarlane, p. 50.
15. 'Gilbert McLeod'.
16. Ibid.
17. Cameron, J., *The Parish of Campsie*, p. 119.

27
Reform is Won?

1. Williams, G., *The Merthyr Rising*.
2. *Mackenzie's Reminiscences*, vol. II, p. 229.
3. Ibid.
4. Ibid., p. 234.
5. Ibid.
6. Ibid., p. 333.
7. Ibid., pp. 248–50.
8. Ibid., p. 249.
9. McKay, p. 192.
10. Ibid.
11. *Caledonian Mercury*, 28 May 1838.

28
The Scottish Radicals of 1820 Remembered

1. *Mackenzie's Reminiscences*, vol. II, pp. 394–5 and p. 496.
2. Ibid., p. 395.
3. *Northern Star*, 21 August 1847.
4. Ibid.
5. Downie, p. 241.
6. *Paisley Herald and Renfrewshire Advertiser*, 27 July 1867.
7. Prentice, G., *The Stories Behind Some Paisley Memorials*, p. 75.
8. *Paisley Herald and Renfrewshire Advertiser*, 27 July 1867.
9. *Greenock Telegraph and Clyde Shipping Gazette*, 4 March 1879.
10. *Paisley Herald and Renfrewshire Advertiser*, 27 July 1867.
11. Ibid.

Index

Address to the Inhabitants of Great Britain & Ireland 83, 87–88, 110–12, 115, 120, 136, 153, 166, 242n
agents provocateurs 70–72, 75, 78, 85–86, 89, 134
Airdrie 62, 99, 100, 199
Anderston 5, 39, 66, 72, 130, 159
Australia, transportation to xviii, 18–19, 34, 41, 55, 71, 158, 194–203, 213
Ayrshire Advertiser 84
Ayrshire xiii, xv, 25, 35–36, 83, 90, 94, 103, 109, 166–67, 174

Baird, John (of Kilmarnock) 36
Baird, John xvi, 71, 97, 110–15, 117–18, 152–57, 169, 184, 186–95, 199, 201–202, 205, 209–13, 215–21, 223, 237n
Baird, Robert 2, 188, 212
Balfron xvi, 26, 47, 62, 83, 94–95, 157, 175, 233n, 243n
Bannockburn, Battle of 18, 121, 175, 207
Barr, Margaret 161

Bill of Rights 85–86, 91
Black Douglas 101
Black Dwarf 44, 48–9, 235n
Black, James, Lord Provost of Glasgow 27
Bonnymuir, Battle of xvii, 114–19, 182, 194, 201, 218
Boswell, Alexander of Auchinleck 25, 90, 128, 220
Bradford, Sir Thomas 76, 118
Braxfield, Lord (Robert MacQueen) 17
Brayshaw, Joseph 42–44, 136
Brooksbank, Mary 46
Brown, Captain xv, 47, 76–77
Bruce, Robert the 31, 85, 127, 152
Buchanan, George 31–32
Burns, Robert 15, 18, 62

Caledonian Mercury 130, 207, 232n, 241n, 245n, 246n
Calgacus 121
Calton Burial Ground 3, 8
Calton Weavers' Strike xviii, 3–9, 10, 21, 84

Calton, The 74, 130

Camelon xvi, 97, 111–12, 157, 175, 196

Campbell, John 75

cap of liberty 12, 38, 40, 45, 63, 66

Carlisle 57, 76, 90, 110, 167, 242

Carron Iron Works, march to xvi, 15, 97, 109–13, 182

Cartwright, Major John 11, 33, 49, 67, 232n

Castle Street, Glasgow 31, 87, 181, 205, 213

Cathkin Braes xvii, 105, 122, 125–28

Cato Street Conspiracy xv, 78, 152, 154, 195, 223

Church of the Holy Rude, Stirling 192, 209, 212

Claim of Right 86, 238n

Clayknowes meeting 64, 65–67

Condorrat xvi, 94, 97, 110–13, 188, 199, 219–20, 226

Condy, Isabella 186

Cook, Thomas 112, 115, 155

Corn Laws xiii, 27, 38, 90, 127, 214

Covenanters 32, 40, 85, 92, 109, 207, 214

'Dead March' from *Saul* (Handel) 39

Dale, David 23

Dark Bonnymuir (song) 199–200

Declaration of Arbroath 85

Denniston, Baillie John of Greenock 141, 143–45

dog tax 32

Drumclog, Battle of 40, 130, 214

Drumpellier Woods 99

Drygate Bridge 5–8, 22

Duke Street Prison 31, 78

Dumbarton xvii, 78, 130, 152, 166

Duncan, Granny 183, 187, 191

Dundee 11, 33, 65–69

Duntocher xvi, 83, 95, 129, 131, 166

East Lothian Yeomanry 99

eclipse of the sun 1820 186, 192

Edinburgh Castle 183, 187–88

Edinburgh Convention 13–16, 43

Edinburgh Yeomanry 139

Eglinton Toll, Glasgow 31

Ewing, James 161, 164

Falkirk xvi, 111, 113, 118

flags and banners 37–40, 53, 57–59, 66, 68, 100, 207

Fletcher, Andrew of Saltoun 32

Fletcher, Eliza 14

Forth and Clyde Canal xvi, 111–13, 194, 218

Fraser, John 166–73, 199, 216–18

Fraser, Marjory 170

French Revolution 10–14, 78, 186, 225

Galston 38, 94, 173

Garscube 130

general strike xv, 64, 78, 89, 94–98, 160, 167

George IV *see also* the Prince Regent 105

George Square, Glasgow 12, 103

Gilfillan, Moses 175

Glasgow Cathedral xiv, 5–6, 22, 28, 110, 181, 184, 209

Glasgow Chronicle 44, 52, 58, 75

Glasgow Courier 145, 242n

Glasgow Green 5, 8, 27, 103–04, 176, 207

Glasgow Herald xvi, 44, 51, 54, 60, 66, 104, 143, 149, 162, 176, 178, 180–81

Glasgow High Court xi, 8, 16, 31, 37, 103, 159, 176, 180, 223

Glasgow Royal Infirmary 28, 199

Glasgow secret radical committee 43

Glasgow Sharpshooters xvi, 51, 71, 103–07

Gorbals, The 5, 39

Gotham in Alarm (play) 103

Gray, Benjamin 29–31

Great Reform Act (1832) xviii, 69, 138, 203–09

Greenock xvii, 47–8, 102, 129, 139–45, 172, 211, 219

Hamilton, Janet 48, 62, 95, 99

Hamilton, Jean 160

Hardie, Andrew xvi, 71, 87–89, 94, 109–18, 150–57, 169, 182–95, 199, 201–05, 209–21

Hardie, James (magistrate) 86–87, 155

Hardie, Marion (mother of Andrew) 87, 201, 205, 209

Hart, Alexander 115–16, 195–96

High Street, Glasgow 5, 13, 28, 31, 104, 132, 136

Hodgson, Lieutenant Ellis 112, 114–18, 190

House of Commons 16, 49, 52–53, 137, 203–04

Howat, William 123, 126, 128

Hullock, Serjeant 154, 157–60

Hunt, Henry (Orator Hunt) 50, 57, 70

Hunter, Samuel xvi, 51, 104–05

7th Hussars 107

10th Hussars xvi, 112, 114, 116, 240n

Jeffrey, Francis, advocate 152–53, 157, 205

Johnston, Alexander 116

Johnstone, Renfrewshire xv, 47, 83, 94–96, 166–68, 173, 199, 216

Kearsley, Alice 52

Kellet, Colonel 6–7

Kennedy, John 36–37

Kilbarchan xvi, 13, 92–98, 215, 219
Kilmarnock 13, 35–40, 44–48, 76, 89, 139, 207
Kilsyth xvi, 62, 94, 112, 114–18, 157
King, John 111, 117
Kinloch of Kinloch, the Radical Laird 67–69, 109
Kirkman Finlay, Lord Provost of Glasgow 72, 75, 103, 164
Kirkwood, Davie 151
Knox, John 30, 31

Lady of the Lake, The (steamship) 188
Lang, John 166, 169, 173
Langloan 48, 62, 92, 95, 99–101
Liberty Tree 11, 39
Lightbody, Will 92–93, 100–01
Liverpool Mercury 34, 72
Lucas, Dr Thomas, 186, 192
Ludlam, Isaac 41, 223

MacDonald, Jacques, Marshall of France 109
Macdonald, Ranald, of Staffa and Iona 157, 191, 193, 202
MacKeigh, Margaret 184, 193
Mackenzie, Peter 36, 71, 89, 106, 109, 155, 164, 177, 197, 203–06, 209–12
Maclaren, Alexander 35, 37
Magna Carta (also *Magna Charta*) 58, 85–86, 91

Manchester xiv, xv, 34, 39–40, 52–53, 57–9, 61, 67–68, 71, 75, 85, 91, 107, 143, 167, 203
Manchester Observer, 44, 49–50
Matty, Strathaven spaewife 123–26
Mauchline 173–74
McArthur, John 131
McCulloch, Thomas 196, 200–01
McIntyre, William 125, 159
McKay, Archibald 206
McKay, Thomas 173–75
McKinlay, Andrew 73–75, 211
McLeod, Gilbert 51–55, 59, 65, 106, 195, 200, 223
McNaught, Bailie John of Greenock 172
Meikleriggs Moor, Paisley xiv, 38, 57–60, 76
Merthyr Tydfil 202, 208, 223
Milngavie xv, 62, 94–95, 129–38
Mitchell, Captain xv, 132
Monteith, Lord Provost of Glasgow xv, 53–54, 91, 103, 184
Morning Chronicle 29, 66
Morning Post 84, 86
Motherwell, William 129
Muir, Thomas of Huntershill 10–20, 37, 87, 203, 220, 225
Murchie, Allan 199–200, 220

Napoleonic Wars xiv, 21, 36, 45, 63, 135

Neil, John 63, 91–92, 109, 166, 170, 217
Neilston Band 58–59
New Lanark 232–34, 33, 49, 73
Newport Rising 207, 224
Nottingham xv, 41, 57, 63, 90–91

Oliver, William (aka Richards) 40–41, 71
Owen, Robert 24, 33, 72–3

Paine, Thomas 10–13, 16, 170
Paisley 13–14, 24, 47, 56–60, 61–64, 77–78, 91, 130
Parkhill, John 22, 61–63, 75–78, 90–2, 97–98, 129–30, 167
Paterson, James 37–38, 40, 44–48, 89
Peddie, Major 118, 189
Penderyn, Dic (aka Lewis, Richard) 202–03, 224
Pentrich Rising 40–41, 63, 71, 195, 223
Peterloo xiv, xv, 34, 39, 50–53, 57–58, 69, 71, 76, 107, 143
pikes xvi, xvii, 41, 61, 92, 95, 97, 114–15, 118, 122, 126, 129–30, 156, 160, 166–67, 196, 199, 221
Pioneers, The xvii, 124–25, 162–63
Pitt, William the Younger, Prime Minister 23, 204

Political Martyrs' Monument, Edinburgh 20
Port Glasgow Militia xvii, 140–45, 219
Powlet, Major 7
Prince Regent, *see also* George IV xiv, 23, 27, 30–31, 33, 35, 37, 42, 54, 65, 67, 79, 118

Radical Dyke 117
Radical Pend 117, 218
Rae, William, Lord Advocate 76–77, 107, 131
Ranald Macdonald of Staffa and Iona 157, 191, 193, 202
reading rooms 47
39th Regiment of Foot 6, 7
42nd Regiment of Foot 27, 31
56th Regiment of Foot 7

Richmond, Alexander 72–75, 211
Rights of Man 10, 12, 15, 39, 121
Rights of Woman 15
Riot Act 53, 59–60
Roach, William 72
Rodger, Alexander (Sandy) 22, 54, 135
'Rule Britannia' 33, 39–40
Russell, Jamie 123
Rutherglen xvii, 39, 43, 66

Scotland Free or Scotland a Desart [sic] xvii, 121, 122, 125, 152, 161, 201

Scott, Sir Walter 67, 188

Scots Wha Hae 15, 18, 38–39, 59, 152, 171

Semple, Willie 44

Shields, James (messenger from Glasgow Radical Committee) 122, 125–28

Sibbald, Captain 150–51

Sidmouth, Lord xv, 25, 33, 47, 54, 68–70, 72, 75–77, 128, 151, 164–65, 184, 209

Sighthill Monument, Glasgow 193, 199, 211–13

Smith, Lieutenant-General Henry (Harry) 78, 107–08

Speirs, John 168–69, 171–72

Speke (convict ship) 195

Spirit of the Union 51–55, 59, 65, 106, 135, 195, 200

steamships 144, 183, 186–7

Stevenson, John 120–21, 126, 152, 177, 201–02, 214

Stewarton 90, 173–4

Stirling xvii, 33, 149–58, 183, 186–88, 192–93, 201, 209–12, 219, 223

Stirling Castle xvii, 117–18, 150–51, 182–86, 189–90, 192, 196, 198–99, 218, 221

Stirlingshire Yeomanry xvi, 114, 116–17, 156

Strathaven xvii, 13–14, 43–44, 50, 76, 83, 94, 120, 122, 124–28, 133, 152, 159–61, 177, 181, 201–02, 207, 213, 215, 218, 220

Tacitus 121

Tamson, Geordie 46–47

tartan 67

Thistlewood, Arthur 78–79, 152, 154, 223

Thomson, Jamie 33, 92, 101

Three Stanes Farm, Strathaven 120

Thrushgrove xv, 27–34, 61, 74, 86–87, 103–04, 132, 137–38, 197, 209–11, 215

trials xvii, 152–53, 162, 164, 170, 173, 226

Turner, Duncan 109, 117

Turner, James 28, 33, 43, 104, 131–38, 150, 163, 209–11

Turner, William 41

Union of the Parliaments 32, 85–86

Union Societies 42–43, 47, 49–50, 65, 76

Wallace, William 31–32, 43, 58, 85, 113, 127, 152, 182

Waterloo, Battle of xiv, 104, 115, 203

Weavers' Burial Ground, Calton, Glasgow 3, 8

Weavers' Strike of 1812 21, 72

Wellington, Duke of 45, 122, 203, 206

'Western Campaign, The' (song) 139–40

Westminster Parliament xiii, xiv, 4, 40, 53, 136, 151–52, 204

Westmorland Advertiser and Kendal Chronicle 58

Wilson, James, xvii, 14, 43, 122–28, 133, 152, 159–65, 176–81, 213–20, 223

Woodside Cemetery, Paisley 215–17

Wooler, Thomas 49

Yorkshire rising 167–68, 195, 224

Young, Thomas (headsman) 179–80, 193